The Online Investor

Levelling the Information Playing Field

The Online Investor

Levelling the Information Playing Field

Peter Temple

John Wiley & Sons

CHICHESTER • NEW YORK • WEINHEIM • BRISBANE • SINGAPORE • TORONTO

Copyright © 1997 by John Wiley & Sons Ltd,
Baffins Lane, Chichester,
West Sussex PO19 1UD, England

National   01243 779777
International   (+44) 1243 779777
e-mail (for orders and customer service enquiries): cs-books@wiley.co.uk
Visit our Home Page on http://www.wiley.co.uk
or http://www.wiley.com

Reprinted September 1997

Other Wiley Editorial Offices

John Wiley & Sons, Inc., 605 Third Avenue,
New York, NY 10158-0012, USA

VCH Verlagsgesellschaft mbH, Pappelallee 3,
D-69469 Weinheim, Germany

Jacaranda Wiley Ltd, 33 Park Road, Milton,
Queensland 4064, Australia

John Wiley & Sons (Asia) Pte Ltd, 2 Clementi Loop #02-01,
Jin Xing Distripark, Singapore 129809

John Wiley & Sons (Canada) Ltd, 22 Worcester Road,
Rexdale, Ontario M9W 1L1, Canada

Library of Congress Cataloging-in-Publication Data

Temple, Peter.
    The online investor : levelling the information playing field /
Peter Temple.
        p.   cm.
    Includes bibliographical references and index.
    ISBN 0-471-96910-9
    1. Investments—Computer network resources.   2. Internet (Computer
network)   3. World Wide Web (Information retrieval system)
I. Title.
HG4515.95.T46   1997
025.06'3326—dc21   96–40880
                                                        CIP

British Library Cataloguing in Publication Data

A catalogue record for this book is available from the British Library

ISBN 0-471-96910-9

Typeset in 11/13 Palatino from the author's disks by Dorwyn Ltd, Rowlands Castle, Hants
Printed and bound in Great Britain by Bookcraft (Bath) Ltd, Midsomer Norton, Somerset
This book is printed on acid-free paper responsibly manufactured from sustainable forestation, for
which at least two trees are planted for each one used for paper production.

Contents

Levelling the Information Playing Field

One of the reasons for writing this book was born from my own experience of working for many years in the UK stock market, then leaving it and becoming an ordinary private investor. This meant a move from a world where information is on tap to one where it isn't. Professional investors, brokers and market-makers have instant availability of prices and news via Reuters or ICV screens. They also have access to information about companies that is denied to other investors.

The private investor gets a raw deal by contrast. Only by spending thousands of pounds a year can the average investor get comprehensive 'live' share prices and news. In practice, there is no opportunity for duplicating the information 'edge' that professionals have. The playing field is tilted very steeply against the private investor.

The Internet and World Wide Web offer the opportunity to level it. For around £10 a month for online connection, you can have access to, among many other things: the electronic editions of quality newspapers at home and abroad; online reference publications such as the *Hambro Company Guide*; data from stock exchanges around the world; company Web sites; the possibility of debating investment issues and exchanging information with other online investors; online personal finance data; and the ability to download and use (either free or at low cost) a variety of useful investment software. This book will show you how to take advantage of this profusion of information.

But there was a second reason for writing this book. Personal computer (PC) users in the UK outnumber active private investors several times over. They may already have begun the process of organising their finances by using a personal financial management program. But to take the next step to becoming more active investors, they need information that can be accessed privately, without pressure from brokers or cold calls from salespeople. This book will help them do this by explaining World Wide Web sites and other resources, to the point of dealing in shares by computer.

In writing this book I have had to assume that readers have some knowledge of the basics of both computers and share investment. (For those that do not have the latter, my book *Getting Started in Shares*, also published by John Wiley, provides the essential background.) I have, however, tried to keep the language both simple and jargon-free.

I need to insert a caveat. Web sites are prone to changing quickly, often undergoing radical redesign. This is not conducive to the publication schedule required in producing a book. Most of the Web sites surveyed in this book were researched in the summer of 1996, and revisited in the autumn. In all cases the remarks made about Web sites relate to my own view of their usefulness or otherwise to a UK-based online investor at the time of research.

Lastly, a few thanks. To Nick Wallwork, my publisher at John Wiley, who has been unfailingly enthusiastic about this project from the moment I proposed the idea of the book to him. Thanks are also due to Sally Vince, who edited my original manuscript and improved it considerably. I must also thank Gillian O'Connor, personal finance editor of the *Financial Times*, for the opportunity to test out in print ahead of publication some of the ideas presented. And to my wife Lynn, for putting up with my absences during the long evening and weekends spent researching and writing, and 'surfing' the Net in search of interesting material.

Peter Temple

Acknowledgements

This book was written on a Macintosh Powerbook in Microsoft Word, with tables produced using Microsoft Excel.

Web page and software images used as illustrations throughout the book were accessed on an IBM-compatible PC through an Internet connection from CIX and used a Netscape Navigator Web browser and Nildram Software's Screen Thief for Windows software.

Illustrations are reproduced by kind permission of the owners/ operators of the following Web pages and software products:

CIX; Commodity & Futures Trading Commission; DejaNews; Durlacher; E*Trade Securities; Electronic Share Information; Hemmington Scott Publishing; IBM infoMarket; Informatik Inc.; Infotrade; Investor-WEB; LIFFE; Liszt; MetaCrawler; Michigan State University; Moneyweb; MoneyWorld; Léon Moon; NetWorth; Qualcomm Software; Qualisteam; Securities & Exchange Commission; Shareware.com; TrustNet; UK-Com; University of Strathclyde; Wall Street Directory Inc.; and Yahoo!

CHAPTER 1

Investing Online

In the definitive history of the twentieth century the invention of the microprocessor and the advent of affordable computing power will rank alongside jet air travel and splitting the atom as the most revolutionary events of the era.

Computers are everywhere. We use them unconsciously—in cars, TVs, electronic calculators, personal organisers and CD players. Desktop computing power and sophisticated software is prevalent in offices and increasingly so in ordinary homes.

A secondary aspect of the computer revolution, and what this book is largely about, relates to the invention of the modem and the ability it brings to transmit information between computers. For the uninitiated, a modem (short for MOdulator/DEModulator) sends data from one computer to another by turning it into a form that can be sent down a telephone line to be received by another modem, which decodes it ready for access by the user of the receiving computer.

Acres of newsprint have been devoted to the online revolution, and especially to the burgeoning interest in the Internet and World Wide Web. Remarkably little, however, has been said or written about this revolution's potential significance for investors. This book focuses on how accessing information from online sources—mainly the Internet, but also via other media—can be used by ordinary investors to level the investment 'playing field'.

Computers enable personal investors to make decisions on the basis of information that approaches the same quality and timeliness as that used by the professionals.

I try, wherever possible, to avoid the use of computer jargon in this book. The descriptions of what can be done, the information sources and services available and how to reach them, are in as simple terms as possible. The glossary towards the back of the book gives brief definitions of those terms it has been unavoidable to use, and the inevitable abbreviations are explained as they are met and are listed, together with their definitions, at the back of the book. Further information can be found in the books listed in the Bibliography.

Why Investors Need Online Information

There is a very real advantage to the online revolution, which all of those with the interests of ordinary investors at heart should welcome. In the UK the roots of it go back to the election of the Thatcher administration in 1979, and policies of privatisation that were initiated by that government a few years later. Partly through self-interest—the need to create a demand for shares in the steady flow of large-scale privatisations—the government then espoused the cause of wider share ownership.

The flow of privatisations has now dried up. But its effect has been to leave many individuals with small parcels of stock tucked away in the bottom drawer, and a relatively warm feeling about the idea of owning shares. With a few notable exceptions, profits on privatisation shares held over the long term have been significant. Yet there have been few incentives for these embryo investors to find out more about the general investment scene or about the possibility of investing in other companies.

The popular and partly correct view is that City professionals always have the upper hand, not only in terms of their financial fire-power, but also in their access to information. The result is that the average individual tends to feel that his or her nest egg is better off invested by a professional through the medium of a unit trust or some such other collective vehicle, rather than through a do-it-yourself approach to investing.

This feeling is scarcely discouraged by the powers-that-be in the City. A change in the rules at the beginning of 1996 cut out private investors from the smaller new issue scene, for rather spurious reasons. This was done by abandoning a previous long-standing rule that, for issues of a certain size, a proportion of the shares would always be retained for distribution to the public.

The committee set up to defuse the row that followed was chaired by a well-known advocate of collective investment rather than individual share ownership. This committee produced an anodyne report.

Those one-time investors left high and dry in the wake of the privatisation era and the new regime on new issues may not have thought of using their PC as a means of accessing information on shares and putting those languishing share certificates to work.

Equally, there are many long-standing investors who remain to be converted to the merits of using computers to further their investment habit.

It is to these two categories that this book is primarily addressed. In other words, it seeks to revive the interest of the normal computer-literate person in the process of investment through using a PC to access online information and services. And it seeks to explain to already serious and experienced private investors how using a computer and online services can improve their investment performance.

There may be a third category of reader. The young computer-literate person, already tuned in to the online world, who may be tempted to view the investment process as simply akin to another video game, all the more interesting because it is played with real money. To those readers I must stress that there is more to the investment process than this, and it is essential to take time to read up on investment techniques before embarking on investment decisions with real money. Familiarise yourself with the subject by reading my book *Getting Started in Shares*.

Online Investing Defined

Before going any further, let's define precisely what we mean by online investing. This is not, for example, a book about using computers to chart share prices and make decisions using the various types of investment-oriented software available. Nor is it a book solely about using the Internet and World Wide Web for accessing investment information.

To qualify for inclusion in the book, an information source or service has to be available online. That is, it has to be accessible by modem, or by some other electronic or broadcast means. Access could be via the Internet and World Wide Web, through a private network, or through satellite, TV or pager technology.

This text is written primarily for the UK reader. In the USA, using electronic means to access data on shares and to trade them is much further advanced. At the moment, Internet and World Wide Web content is still heavily oriented towards US investors, although information from non-US sources is growing quickly. This book includes examples of the ways in which online information is available from US sources, as well as ones that are more important to international and UK-based investors. One result of the availability of the vast amount of information available on the Internet is the globalisation of investment by private investors. It is, for example, already relatively easy for investors based in the UK to get online the information needed to make investment decisions on US companies.

Private investors will, I think, welcome this process. They should, however, stick to developed markets such as the USA and continental Europe, and deal with a broker that can offer a dealing service in these markets and the ancillary facilities to go with it. Beware, though, that the currency factor produces an added dimension to international investing. Stock market profits (and losses) can be eroded by a depreciating currency or enhanced by one that is increasing in value.

The Advantages of Online Investing

Investing online will give you distinct advantages over investing in the traditional way. And all you need to be able to do it is the necessary equipment, which you may well already have—a suitable computer, a modem and a telephone line—and an average degree of computer literacy.

Later, we will look at exactly what capturing these advantages costs, but for the moment we'll focus on the benefits. Terms that are unfamiliar will be fully explained in later chapters.

The advantages of online investing can be grouped into five broad areas: speed, comprehensiveness, cost, convenience, and enlarged investment horizons.

Speed

When they first buy a modem, few users are really prepared for the sheer speed with which data can be transferred from or to a remote computer. Downloading data giving the daily high, low, opening, closing prices and trading volume for 400 shares, converting it and storing it in an orderly fashion takes only a couple of minutes on the two-year-old (and, therefore, relatively elderly) computer I use.

Depending on the capacity of the modem used, downloading a basic software program might take five or ten minutes. The main point to re-member is that it is the capacity of the modem that governs the speed of the data download, rather than the speed of the receiving computer's processor or the size of its memory. So buy the fastest modem you can afford.

The advantages of using on-line information sources are already ob-vious. If we take the capturing of share price data as an example, compare my two-minute download by modem to the time it would take manually to enter 400 closing share prices into separate datafiles in your PC, not to mention the boredom of doing so day after day.

Similarly, acquiring a software program through conventional means might involve scanning through several different catalogues, choosing a suitable program, sending for a demo disk, installing it in your PC, decid-ing whether or not to buy the full version, and then going to the shop to buy it or waiting for it to arrive in the post. The online investor is able to view details of a program on screen, download a demo version in the time it takes to have a short coffee break, install it, check out how it works, and order the full working version online and download that.

Comprehensiveness

It is no exaggeration to say that online information and services, par-ticularly World Wide Web sites, are expanding at an exponential rate. A recent survey counted five million host computers linked to the Internet, any one of which could be home to hundreds of files and dozens of Web sites.

Consider what this means. At one particular Web site devoted to soft-ware there are links to and information on more than 300 organisations offering downloadable demonstration versions of investment software. A popular shareware Web site (by no means the only one or the largest) contains 160,000 different pieces of free software. No more hit and miss program buying on the basis of vague newspaper advertisements.

Look at another example. The London International Financial Futures Exchange (LIFFE) Web site offers closing price and volatility data on every single equity and index option series traded on the exchange. (See Figure 1.1 for an overview of what's on offer at the LIFFE web site.) The Alternative Investment Market has a site with information on its listed stocks. Many companies now have Web sites containing information such as annual reports and archived press releases. Assembling and storing this information in the conventional paper-based form is a huge task. The alternative, twenty-first century solution is available online now—no paper involved, and no time-consuming filing.

These are simple examples that serve to demonstrate the resources available to investors. The two sites mentioned came on stream within a

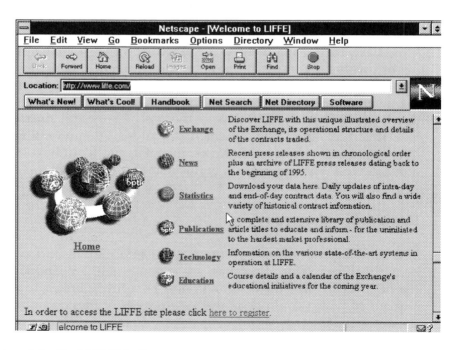

Figure 1.1   The LIFFE Web site

few weeks of each other in late 1995, and the period between then and the publication of this book has seen dozens more appear that could equally have been mentioned.

Cost

Online investing is a low-cost activity. The Internet and World Wide Web offer huge information resources at little or no cost. An online connection with an average amount of use may cost in the region of £10–15 per month, plus telephone charges for the length of time you are online at local call rates. And although there are services on the Web that require subscriptions to be paid, very often a restricted (though still useful) version is available free of charge. In any case, charges made for online services tend to be low and the services offered are ones that would otherwise normally be out of reach of the average UK private investor.

The best examples of free information are online newspapers and magazines. Most successful investors are avid readers, studying several newspapers each day, and several investment magazines and newsletters. Many of these are now available online and free of charge. For instance, the UK online investor can read the City pages of *The Times*, the *Daily Telegraph*, the *Financial Times* and the *Evening Standard* for free. If you have broader horizons you can browse the *LA Times* or the *San José Mercury*, *Le Monde* or *Die Welt*.

Many US magazines, such as *Barrons* and *Business Week*, keep archives of past articles. These are available free, even though getting an up-to-date online copy of the publication may necessitate a subscription. But online newspapers are—for the moment at least—predominantly funded by advertising, so you can avoid an excessive paper bill and yet still be well-informed.

Convenience

It should be obvious by now that one of the really compelling aspects of online investing is that data, news, software programs, and other information can be gathered electronically without the need for much physical effort. The information is stored online and can be called up when necessary. The updating is done for you.

Information downloaded from the Internet and other online sources can also quickly be incorporated into existing software with the minimum of effort and technical knowledge. If you wish to spend more time research-ing stocks and less time tramping the streets to the paper shop, the library, or your local software supplier, this is a compelling advantage.

On a personal level, I have worked from home for over nine years. As I have become more familiar with the online world, the time I have saved in visits of this nature has been astonishing. I have also been able to gain access to information sources I might never have thought of before. My productivity both as a writer and as a practising private investor has been improved as a result of getting connected to the online world.

Broader Horizons

As well as enabling you to obtain information about the domestic stock market, it is an inevitable part of using online sources that you will also gain access to information on other markets, different types of securities, new investment ideas and techniques that might otherwise have gone unnoticed.

This can be at the simple level of being exposed to information about (say) US companies, or the ability to access information about software, investment books, newsletters, and other publications on a much wider scale than that simply encompassed by national boundaries. National boundaries mean little in the online world and, as the habit of online invest-ing spreads, this is likely to spill over into the stocks that private investors deal in, the brokers they deal with, what their software and data costs, the nature and price of the information they use, and in many other ways.

This should not be source of concern provided that you follow sound investment disciplines.

Private versus Professional Investment

It is no exaggeration to say that the private investor has had a raw deal from the City and the corporate sector over many years.

The exception is the advent of cheap execution-only dealing, which has genuinely cut costs for small investors. This aside, the City has often been a pretty unfriendly and unhelpful place to private investors, particularly those with comparatively modest sums to invest.

On the one hand, the small investor has been seen as a convenient target for the flood of privatisation issues and other large-scale flotations emanating from the Square Mile. On the other, despite official lip-service being paid to wider share ownership, in many other respects the private investor has remained at a significant disadvantage to the professional. This is especially true in terms of access to the technology to help value shares. Prompt access to the flow of news and information that move share prices day by day is out of the reach of many small investors.

The advent of online investing presents an opportunity to private investors—at relatively low cost—to remove some of these disadvantages. The online revolution still has some way to go. And it arguably needs the co-operation of the corporate sector to benefit the private investor fully. Some organisations and companies—for example, the Treasury, Tesco, Cable & Wireless, Severn-Trent and others are showing the way, but a lot more remains be done. As usual, US companies lead the way in providing information online to private shareholders.

To illustrate this point, let's look briefly at how the facilities and information open to private investors differs from those available to the professionals, and how the online revolution can help to level the playing field for the small investor.

The differences can be categorised as: software, share prices, fundamental data, economic and company news, dealing, and relationships with companies.

Software

The *professional investor* has access to the latest versions of highly sophisticated technical analysis software and vast computing power to help analyse share prices and make investment decisions.

The *private investor* has the choice of a limited number of packages. Few of these are available through high street retailers and comparative information about them is difficult to obtain. The investor has to make a purchasing decision on the basis of imperfect information, and may well end up with a package that is unsuitable for his or her needs.

As an *online investor*, with software packages available on the Internet and World Wide Web, you have easy access to a wide range of programs, and you can download demo versions at will. You can tap into software that previously may only have been sold to US investors, although you must take care to ensure that such software can use data downloaded from non-US sources. Subject to that proviso, the availability of online software makes it more likely that, as an online investor, you will be able to choose a package closer to that used by the professional, or at the very least one that is precisely tailored to your needs at an affordable price.

Share Prices

The *professional investor* has the advantage of price display systems that relay price changes as they happen. These real-time services are often integrated with sophisticated technical analysis packages. The ability to view share price changes as they happen is something of a two-edged sword. While this facility is essential for 'day-trading', for longer-term investors it can be a distraction. Professionals and private investors alike have to try and ignore the short-term volatility of the market and focus on underlying trends and values.

Real-time price feeds are expensive, too—so much so that they are beyond the reach of all but a few private investors. In the past this has given the professional an information advantage in the market, particularly when shares react to price-sensitive information.

The *private investor* faces two problems. One is getting hold of up-to-date daily price information on which to make trading decisions and gauge the underlying state of the market. The second is obtaining cheap price data that can be fed into whichever technical analysis package is being used.

The wish to keep in touch with prices during the day can be solved in part by simply using the normal teletext services, which all have their roster of share prices updated several times daily. These can be supplemented if necessary by the telephone services—such as FT Cityline—which give up-to-date share price quotes.

Investment decisions made by individual investors are in any case rarely improved by having access to real-time prices. It is difficult enough for the average investor to act in a way that is contrary to the 'crowd'—as is often necessary—if he or she is bombarded by a stream of prices suggesting that doing the opposite may be best.

So the major problem the private investor faces is obtaining comprehensive share price and trading volume data to download at a price that is cost-effective. Downloading prices from teletext is both free and more reliable than it once was, but its absence of volume data makes it less than satisfactory for many investors. At the other end of the scale are expensive subscription services that deliver comprehensive data by disk or modem, but at a hefty cost.

The *online investor* has some extra options available. Electronic Share Information (ESI)—a Cambridge-based organisation, which was the first to offer online dealing over the Internet—is a case in point (see Figure 1.2 for ESI's home page). It offers data for a large list of stocks that includes daily opening, closing, high and low prices, plus daily trading volume (known as OHLCV data). This costs £160 per annum for existing customers of its cheapest subscription service. Prestel's Citifeed offers full market OHLCV data downloadable by modem after 6.30 p.m. for £125 (plus VAT) a year.

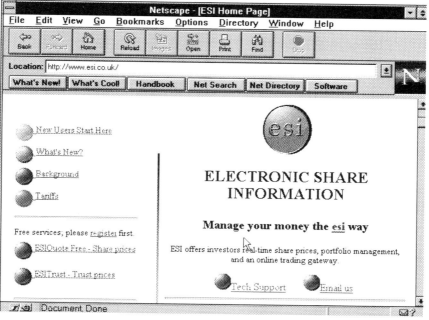

Figure 1.2 ESI's home page

Online investors in the USA have long had the benefit of cheap data to feed into technical analysis packages, and exchanges there have been rewarded by increased trading by private investors as a result. This lesson has yet to be learnt fully in the UK, but electronic dissemination of share price data is beginning to make its presence felt as a cost-effective solution for the ordinary private investor.

Fundamental Data

The *professional investor* has a variety of means available by which to obtain and analyse fundamental information, especially company accounts. These include large online databases of accounts information and share price data maintained by organisations such as Reuters and DataStream, electronic Extel Cards analysing company accounts data, electronic access to reports from brokers' analysts, and a variety of other sources.

The *private investor* traditionally has had to rely on newspapers and magazines to get hold of fundamental information, supplemented by tips from friends or a stockbroker. Few private investors even go so far as buying reference publications, or telephoning a company to obtain copies of the annual report.

The *on-line investor* can make this process relatively painless and more systematic. Reference publications such as the *Hambro Company Guide* are increasingly being published in an online form and, for those interested in investment trusts and unit trusts, there are online sites now operating that enable large databases of fund performance data to be searched free of charge for those precisely matching particular requirements.

One possibility for the future is that the UK will be able to follow the lead of the USA in making the data contained in statutory company filings available online free of charge. The EDGAR database of the US Securities & Exchange Commission (SEC) is an online equivalent of the UK's Companies House (see Figure 1.3). US listed companies now have to file their accounts information and other statutory documents electronically. EDGAR is a searchable electronic resource that enables an online investor anywhere in the world to access up-to-date information on any listed company in the USA.

Will the UK's Companies House follow suit and simplify and cheapen the means by which ordinary investors can access company information,

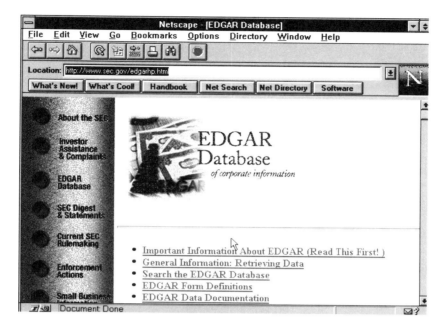

Figure 1.3 SEC's EDGAR database

at least for listed companies and their subsidiaries, without a physical visit to its City Road premises? Time will tell.

Economic and Company News

The *professional investor* has access to instantaneous company news on-screen from services such as Reuters, Bloomberg and Bridge, as well as the regulatory service relating to company announcements emanating from the Stock Exchange. This gives professional investors a significant edge. The cost of services of this type in the form in which they are used by the professionals is prohibitive for the average private investor.

The *private investor* has traditionally relied on daily newspapers, supplemented during the day by teletext and TV news bulletins, to obtain information of this type. However, these services are somewhat selective in their coverage, and slower to distribute time-sensitive information. ICV's Market Eye and similar services provide rapid and accurate coverage of economic and company news, but they are expensive and out of reach of many private investors.

The *online investor* can meet this problem half-way. Internet editions of various quality newspapers enable the rival City pages to be scanned for titbits of news each day, while several online services provide free access to major news stories relating to business and finance and of interest to investors. These services are evolving rapidly as time goes by. One particularly interesting development is an electronic mailing list operated by the Treasury that provides instantaneous availability of press releases relating to economic and financial news.

Dealing

The *professional investor* has the advantage of direct lines to brokers and market makers offering the ability to transact orders instantaneously, often electronically.

The *private investor* has traditionally had a telephone-based service from a broker. This relies on the broker providing accurate market prices on which to base dealing decisions, as well as producing valuations and other services.

The *online investor* still has to deal through a broker but those for whom such a service appeals can do this via a PC without need for human contact with a dealer. These services currently take two main forms. One is Internet-based, like the service offered by the ESI and ShareLink partnership, whereby the investor is able to access live quotes on shares prior to dealing, can enter an order (suitably password protected), and have the trade executed and confirmed electronically.

Other services, such as the one offered by the execution-only broker Fidelity, are more radical. The Fidelity offering is based on a private network, but enables the client to enter the broker's own trading system, view details of the account, access price information on a range of stocks, and execute an order electronically with no intervention from a trader. Systems of this type operating in the USA have proved increasingly popular to the extent that major 'retail' brokers now execute a substantial proportion of their business in this way.

It is possible that eventually the cost savings that such systems should produce will be passed on to the client in the form of lower commission charges.

Relationships with Companies

The *professional investor* has traditionally had many advantages in dealing with companies. One big one takes the form of privileged access to management, at one time via one-on-one meetings but now increasingly through large-scale briefings for brokers and institutional investors. Here price-sensitive information may be disclosed, but it is considered to be disseminated sufficiently widely not to result in charges of insider dealing. On a more mundane level, press releases on company results and other announcements are distributed rapidly to City institutions.

The *private investor* has never been part of this process, except in the sense of being able to attend the company's annual shareholder meeting. The private investor does not normally receive corporate press releases and is left to receive a printed copy of the appropriate announcement some time later, or to read the news in the City pages.

The *online investor* could soon see some improvement over this unsatisfactory state of affairs. Some companies, although all too few in the UK at present, have Internet sites at which shareholders and other interested parties can view or download press releases and other company news and documents.

A system like this, together with automatic email lists, would go a long way towards rectifying the problem keenly felt by many private investors: that the information 'playing field' is tilted too steeply in favour of the professional.

It may be possible perhaps even in the near future, for online investors to log on easily to a video or audio version of the meetings that companies traditionally hold with analysts. This will enable a much wider audience to hear management's response to the probing questions that are typically posed at these meetings. Such links are already technically feasible.

What is required to make these things happen is the goodwill of the corporate sector, or some form of compulsion by the Stock Exchange or legislation to make it obligatory for companies to facilitate a broader electronic dissemination of shareholder information.

The Purpose of this Book

You should by now have some idea as to how an online investor can gain cheap access to more information than a private investor operating in a more traditional way.

The following chapters cover how to get connected to the online world and what doing so will cost. They look in more detail at the banks of information the online investor has at his or her fingertips. In most cases accessing the Internet and the online sources of information it offers is not expensive. Online sources can save time and substitute for more expensive 'hard-copy' forms of information.

The technicalities that need to be mastered are not too forbidding and will be covered in the next two chapters. Thereafter we examine in turn the various facets of online information and the investment process. We look in detail at the online sites available, the information they contain, and how useful they are at helping an investor gain access to up-to-date information and services.

Throughout this book there are illustrations of pages from World Wide Web sites. There are also tables that attempt to give an objective comparison of several similar sites in order to provide an overview of the information each contains in a standardised form. Greater detail on each site is given in the text along with the Internet address (or URL—uniform resource locator) of where you can find it.

The aim is to help private investors to gain access to cheap tools that can help improve their investment performance through better information and, in so doing, perhaps even beat the professionals at their own game.

This is an objective that accords with the laudable goal of widening and deepening share ownership. It is a concept to which many City worthies have paid homage over the years but which, by their action (or inaction), they have done little to advance. The online revolution has the power to take the process out of their hands and so make private investors in the UK and Europe the force they are in markets such as the USA.

It is a revolution which is long overdue.

CHAPTER 2

The Internet—What it is and How it Works

For those not connected to the Internet, perceptions of it range from universal panacea to overhyped waste of time. It is variously viewed as indispensable, an expensive luxury, or a Pandora's box that will open up your PC to a flood of scams, viruses and other ills that are best avoided.

As usual, perceptions and reality are some way apart. What is certain is that sooner or later most PC users will come face to face with it. Computers are increasingly being sold in an Internet-ready form, with built-in modems, pre-loaded Internet access software, and a ready-made service provider to log into. The issue is not whether you use the Internet and World Wide Web, but how soon.

To get the best out of the Internet we need to understand a little of its history, exactly how it works, what precisely is the difference between the Internet and the World Wide Web, and some of Net's central concepts. Also important is the Internet's geography and demographics—its users, where they are, and how they use it.

The following is an outline of how the Internet works in basic conceptual terms, rather than in high-tech jargon. Experienced Net users will be familiar with much of the contents of this chapter.

Any description of the structure of the Internet in statistical terms—for example the number of users, the number of individual World Wide Web sites—is likely very quickly to become out of date. Internet use is growing at double digit percentages each month. It is quite conceivable, for instance, for usage to have doubled simply between the time the typescript for this book was submitted to the publisher and when it was published.

We'll start by going back 30 years to some very ancient Internet history.

The Internet's Origins

The basic idea behind the Internet is a simple one. It is that connecting two computers, whether via a normal commercial telephone line or some other form of electronic linkage, enables information on them to be shared and transferred from one to the other.

You may be familiar with this concept through having participated in a local area network (or LAN), having your desktop PC at work connected to those of colleagues. LANs enable memos to be sent electronically, and word processed documents and spreadsheets to be shared, as well as information from outside service providers to be distributed to everyone on the network.

Take this idea one stage further and imagine that two LANs, each with 50 computers connected to them, are linked together. What this now means is that not only can the participants in each LAN connect with others in that LAN, but that any one of them can connect to any computer in the other network, assuming suitable access arrangements have been built into the system.

Now assume that hundreds of LANs are connected together in what is known as a wide area network (WAN). Each user in each LAN can contact another user in their own LAN and also any other user in any other network connected to the larger network.

Multiply this idea several hundred times over and add in millions of individual users connected through their home computers, and you get some idea of the scale of the Internet. Paul Gilster's book, *The New Internet Navigator*, suggests that the Internet now penetrates 100 countries, and involves more than 50,000 separate networks. These are typically at corporations, educational institutions, or governments. The Internet, says Gilster, contains more than five million host computers and has more than 30 million active users.

How the networks link together is illustrated in Figure 2.1. The various components shown in this diagram are explained later in this chapter.

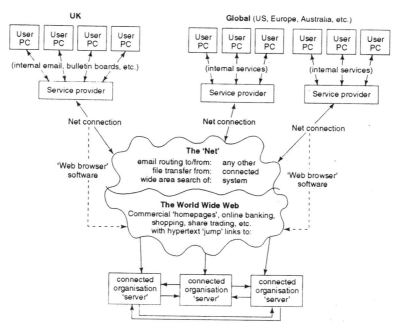

Figure 2.1 How the Internet works

The number of connected networks has grown from the original in 1969 to around 100 in 1985, through 500 in 1989, to perhaps 4,000 by mid 1991 and well over ten times that number now. The sheer volume of information available is mind-boggling. Let's assume, for simplicity, that each network has 200 computers connected to it and that each computer's hard drive contains 100 separate accessible files. Say that there are 50,000 networks connected to the Net. The implication is that any user could have access to any single one of a billion files.

Any file could, in theory, be downloaded by any user anywhere in the world in a matter of a few minutes or less. A message could be sent from any computer anywhere on the network to any other computer. Files in any format could be sent attached to messages.

It is only comparatively recently that what was more or less a closed network used for the benefit of government, military and academic institutions was opened up to normal home PC users. These new users, estimated at a potential 150 million in number, can now dial in at will—

using a modem and a normal telephone line—via an Internet service provider who has the wired-in connection to the Net.

It happened like this. The Internet started life as the ARPANET in the late 1960s. The idea was to let academic researchers share information and communicate with each other. The network was at that time funded by the US Advanced Research Projects Agency (ARPA). One objective in designing it was to create a web-like structure so that if any one computer or a series of computers was knocked out (say by an earthquake or a nuclear war), the network could still continue to function. Initially there were four sites, based at US universities; many other institutions connected to it during the 1970s, once the concept of what the network could accomplish really began to take hold.

In the 1980s ARPANET continued to function, with a military-oriented network hived off from it. In the mid 1980s the US National Science Foundation created a souped-up version of ARPANET using supercomputers and high-speed access. The management of this network was turned over to a group of universities and eventually it absorbed ARPANET. By 1990 the almost exclusive academic nature of the network was beginning to be lost. The enacting of the US High Performance Computing Act in 1991 also meant that commercial organisations were brought into the loop for the first time. Other networks were also being created during this period, including ones in countries other than the USA.

The ability of these networks to connect with each other stemmed from the US Defence Communications Agency's insistence, back in 1983, that a standard set of computer instructions be used for all communications through ARPANET. This allowed each network that might connect to it to function autonomously, yet it also permitted messages and instructions to be passed through 'gateways' into the wider network.

An upgrading of the structure of the network was undertaken between 1990 and 1992, in what amounted to a joint venture between America's National Science Foundation and commercial organisations, for example MCI and IBM. When the new Internet 'backbone' began operating in late 1992, it resulted in a 700-fold increase in the traffic capacity of the network.

The result of this was to free up capacity on the network, hitherto the preserve of the military, government and educational establishment, to enable commercial and private users to get connected.

Why has the Internet caught the imagination of so many users? One particularly interesting aspect is that no one owns or controls it. Because the networks that comprise it are made up of many different organisations, no single body can truly influence or censor the Internet's content. Governments and commercial organisations may club together to upgrade basic communications infrastructure, but each network linked to it is autonomous. A side-effect of this is that the Net can be used for purposes for which it was not originally intended.

There has been considerable focus in the press on the use of the Internet as a channel for pornography, for example. There are concerns about its use as a possible conduit for leaking sensitive information, and there are some moves from governments to attempt to censor or control information passed over the Internet. But because of its deliberately flexible web-like nature, attempts like this prove difficult to administer, and defining the bounds of good taste and legality may have to be left to Internet service providers to administer as best they can.

But amid all the criticism of the Internet there is little acknowledgement of its role as a force for promoting democratic ideals and free speech, and in opening up hitherto closed societies to outside influences and uncensored news. It is significant, for example, that Internet access is unavailable in countries such as Iraq, North Korea, Mongolia and Burma.

The Internet's Size

Charting the Internet is like hitting a moving target. Gilster estimated that in 1994 40,000 networks were connected to it. At the time this book was written in late 1996, the figure for connected networks has almost certainly increased substantially. And of the networks joining the Internet, by far the fastest growing segment is represented by those located outside the USA. A couple of years ago the US alone probably represented slightly more than a 50 per cent share of the total. This is almost certainly no longer the case.

Looked at from another direction, from the standpoint of exactly who is using the Net, the figures are equally hard to pin down. Current worldwide user numbers are put at around 33 million, of which just under two-thirds are academic-based (mainly students with free access) and around 20 per cent are employees of large companies. Small businesses and individuals make up the remainder. Much of this usage is confined to email and other basic services.

But just as the make-up of the number of connected networks is changing, so also is that of Net users. Individual users are growing in number by leaps and bounds. A breakdown by Durlacher Multimedia at the end of 1995 showed around 13.6 million US subscribers to online bulletin board services (BBS). These are an electronic half-way house that allow use of Internet facilities, for example electronic mail (email), and have their own exclusive content.

At the end of 1995, those with full Internet access through a dedicated Internet service provider numbered about 1.7 million (of which around a million were in the USA). Full access of this type guarantees access to graphics-based World Wide Web pages. In the UK, non-academic users represent some 500,000, of which around one-fifth have full access. There are around a million UK academic users, mainly students.

A recent survey provides a more understandable measure. According to a report from the Belgian-based International Research Institute, around 8 per cent of the US population have Internet access at home and 9 per cent have it at work. In the UK the figures are currently 2 per cent with home access and 6 per cent with access at work. Home access exceeds 4 per cent in Scandinavia, while work-based access there is up around the 11–12 per cent mark.

All the signs are that by the end of 1997 the UK numbers could have tripled from this late 1995 level. European use is patchy, although the UK, Germany, Holland, Switzerland, Finland and Sweden are the most developed in terms of Internet usage. Some seven million private users are expected in Europe by the end of 1997.

Some sources suggest taking a different view of the way the Internet is structured. This envisages a 'core' Internet group comprising people and computers who offer interactive services, whether they are sites on the World Wide Web, files available for transfer, or other facilities. On the other side is the consumer Internet. This consists of those who have the ability to connect to the World Wide Web, download files and make other use of the services provided by the 'core'.

The remainder represents an outer core that lacks a true interactive connection, but who have the ability to send and receive email and access basic Internet services through it.

In geographic terms, full Internet conductivity is available across North America and much of South America and across Europe and Asia, including China and the former Soviet Union, in Australia, India, Saudi Arabia,

South Africa, Egypt and Indonesia. Much of Africa has either no Internet connection, or connectivity only by email. These exceptions apart, the Internet stretches from Alaska to Antarctica, and from Vancouver eastwards to Sakhalin and down to Tasmania, and from Tierra Del Fuego to Greenland and across to Siberia.

A simple point, and one we will return to later, is that the Internet's content, and that of the World Wide Web (the Net's commercial information bank) broadly reflects its user base. Much of the information of interest to online investors currently has a US bias. But, in line with the rapid growth of non-US users, this is changing fast.

How it all Works

There are a number of concepts that are fundamental to understanding how the Internet works. The main ones to be grasped are those of data packets, packet switching and computer communications protocols.

The Internet is sometimes called the information superhighway. The metaphor is a good one, and can be used to explain things more clearly.

Information sent over the Net is broken down into small packets of information. Data packets are in effect the vehicles that travel along the Internet road, packet switches are junctions that allow them to take different routes to their destination, and the communications protocols involved are the highway codes that allow each to get to the right destination safely.

The use of this metaphor has been taken to an even higher degree, describing Internet service providers as the toll roads that offer access to the Internet, a PC and modem as a car, and a PC with a dedicated line as a truck.

The 'highway code' protocols that allow the Internet to work as it does are known as TCP/IP, which stands for transmission control protocol/ Internet protocol. In effect, because the Internet was deliberately designed to function without a central controller, each computer connecting to the Net must be able to establish contact with any other. Protocols establish a common language by which different computers can communicate, whether they are IBM/Windows based, Apple Mac-based or UNIX-based. These simple logical rules were first written in the 1970s and have stood the test of time.

They specify how the network is to move messages and handle errors. IP is responsible for network addressing, while TCP is designed to ensure that messages are delivered to the right destination. Other networks that form part of the Internet may use different protocols to talk to each other, but once messages pass through to the Internet, the TCP/IP standard kicks in. So a good definition of the Internet is that it is a global link-up of those networks that are capable of running the TCP/IP protocols.

For the ordinary Internet user, however, the switching between networks and protocols is done automatically, without any human intervention needed.

The diffuse nature of the Internet relies on fibre-optic backbones to transmit high volumes of data around the network—and particularly in and out of the USA, where most users are currently concentrated. It is supplemented by routers, special computers that decide how the information being transmitted is to reach its destination. The route taken is via a series of hubs, rather like the motorway network, and the information then transfers to smaller local roads to reach its destination.

Imagine I am travelling from my home in NE London to visit my mother in Blackpool. I travel from my driveway via several side roads to the A12, from there to the M11, from the M11 either via the A14 or the M25 to the A1 or the M1, continuing the journey either on the M6 or the M62, then the M55, and then on local roads until I reach my destination. There are several different ways in which I can vary the journey. If one road is blocked, or clogged with traffic, I can take a detour in order to save time, perhaps travelling slightly further but arriving sooner.

This is a good way of imagining how data, say the electronic mail message I send from London to a friend in Southern California, might reach its destination. I am not really interested in whether the message is routed via Miami, Minnesota, Los Angeles or Tokyo, as long as it reaches my friend in the quickest possible time.

There is another element to be considered. In an electronic message, anything other than a very brief piece of data is unwieldy. This is why technique has been developed whereby the inherently unwieldy message you send is broken up into small sections, or packets, each with a code attached that determines its eventual destination.

These packets, each with only about 200 bytes of data in them, are then sent on their way, perhaps travelling via different routes to their destination. In the course of their journey they may split further or be combined with other packets. Eventually, though, thanks to the logic in the TCP protocol, they are reassembled in the correct order to be read by the recipient.

There are several advantages to this method. One is that this transmission system automatically adjusts for the different running speed of sender and recipient computer, acting as a buffer between them. A second advantage is that if a packet is lost or destroyed, the system will pass back an instruction for it to be re-sent, persisting until the complete message is assembled. Another positive aspect is that packets from many different sources can share the same telecommunications line, which means that the available capacity (known as bandwidth) can be used with a high degree of efficiency. Bandwidth is a scarce resource, and every effort needs to be made to conserve it.

The drawback to the present packet switching regime is that packets travel through the Net on a first-come, first-served basis. If usage is heavy at a particular time of day, delays may be the result. Many UK Internet users may notice, for example, that their connections are more sluggish than usual in the evening, when US demand is at its peak. It's the equivalent of an electronic traffic jam.

That's the TCP. The IP protocol is, in effect, a system of uniquely numbered addresses. Over and above this group of numbers, a user may also be identified by an address in normal characters, rather than numbers. CompuServe—a leading BBS and Internet service provider—is an exception to this, in that the Internet addresses of its users are usually a hybrid of letters and numbers.

The IP system has another use besides making sure messages get to the correct address. When sending and receiving electronic mail and participating in newsgroups it is possible to tell something about the other party by examining their email address.

This can best be illustrated by some examples. Most UK Internet users, certainly private individuals, will probably have an email address that ends .uk. Mine is peter@ptemple.compulink.co.uk. This also indicates, for instance that my Internet service provider is Compulink Information Exchange (CIX for short), that it is a company (.co), and that it is based in the UK. The word to the right of the @ sign is a shortened version of my company name, Peter Temple Associates, and the word to the left of the @ sign is my first name. My wife's email address, as easy to set up in the email program as getting a separate filing basket for the post that arrives for her via Royal Mail each day, would be lynn@ptemple.compulink.co.uk. My son's would be david@ptemple.compulink.co.uk. And so on.

Country names generally provide the end of Internet addresses, with the exception of the USA. Hence .fr is France, .de is Germany (Deutsche-land), .es is Spain (Espana), .ca is Canada, and so on.

Commercial organisations may have the suffix .com (if they are of US or international origin), or .co (if they are in the UK). There are a variety of other suffixes that describe the function of the user—such as .gov (government), .ac (academic institution), .org (other organisation) and so on.

The Internet and the World Wide Web

Before they sign up, would-be Internet users are sometimes confused by references to the World Wide Web. The distinction between the Web and the Internet is sometimes not entirely clear.

The best way to explain it is that the Web is a giant interactive library that occupies part of the Internet. Internet tools such as electronic mail and file transfer function independently of the Web. In fact, an Internet user can perfectly easily never visit the Web. You might never go to your local library, but that doesn't stop you finding reading matter.

The Web has exploded in size in the past few years because of its value as a shop window for commercial organisations wishing to tap into the large number of users the Internet brings with it. Internet users are typically viewed as being in socioeconomic groups attractive to commercial organisations, or (in the case of student users) likely to be so in the future.

But the Web is not only about commercial self-promotion. Governments, universities, and a whole host of other organisations also have a presence there.

So online investors may find themselves not only using the classic functions of the Internet—electronic mail, newsgroups and bulletin boards (which are really an extension of electronic mail), and file transfer—but also visiting World Wide Web sites to access the information there.

The Web can be accessed in both a monochrome text-based form and via full colour text and graphics-based pages. Either way, the concept behind it is that certain highlighted parts of the text (or images) at Web sites contain embedded links to other pages of information, either within a particular site, or in a Web page on a related subject operated by someone else. By a simple keystroke or mouse click, the link can be activated and the data transferred to enable the contents of the new link to be viewed.

Similarly, the new site may contain links back to the original one, but will also contain links to others, totally different to those at the first site visited, and so on. The concept of links that activate the downloading of new data is known as hypertext.

Web sites operate through computers known as servers, which automatically respond to site visitors and route them through the site as they wish. Web sites vary in the functions they perform. They can be a library or reading room, an encyclopaedia or reference book, an amusement arcade, or a shop.

The Web servers act as librarians or cashiers depending on the nature of the site. The Web is developing fast as a means of transacting business, whether buying information, trading shares, or purchasing some other form of goods and services.

Basic Internet Tools and Concepts

In the next chapter we will look in some detail at how to get connected to the Internet and what benefits your connection might bring. At the risk of putting the cart before the horse, this section looks at some of the basic features of the Internet and how they can help you function efficiently as an online investor.

Don't worry if you don't understand the concepts alluded to in this section, as we will go into them in more detail later.

Electronic Mail

Electronic mail—email—is arguably the single most important aspect of the Internet for most of its users. It was originally included in the forerunner to the Internet as something of an afterthought. But email subsequently became an indispensable part of the Net, as users discovered it was an easy way to exchange ideas quickly with colleagues, friends and collaborators.

With email you can:

❒ Send a message to one or more addresses anywhere in the world at negligible cost, provided you know the exact email address.

❑ Receive messages.
❑ Send (and receive) text files attached to email messages.
❑ Retrieve information through automated electronic mailing lists.
❑ Mail Web pages to yourself for later perusal offline.
❑ Participate in electronic bulletin boards (these are simply emails collected together at a central point and viewed by all members of the group).

These features alone are worth the expense of signing up for an online account. Sending text files by email is considerably cheaper than using a fax or the conventional postal system (known derisively as 'snail mail' by Net users). Sending conventional letters by email is cheaper than snail mail, even for those going short distances. Above all it offers convenience and, because of the ease with which messages can be composed and sent, it encourages both speedy responses and brevity. An example of an email message ready to send is shown in Figure 2.2.

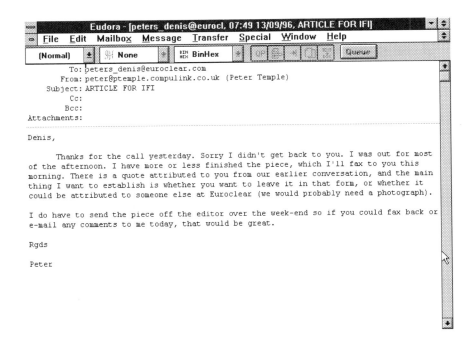

Figure 2.2   An email message ready to send

Email is the most common form of access to the Internet, and many of the Internet's features can be accessed, albeit by a somewhat circuitous route, through email alone. There are specialised programmes that enable an email user to access directories and file lists by return automatic email. Then, via sending simple messages, it is possible to download the files they contain in text or binary format. The process is laborious, but it can be done.

For the rest of this book, however, I'm assuming that you will have a connection that enables full use of the Internet's resources without resorting to these subterfuges.

File Transfer

One of the outstanding properties of the Internet is the opportunity it offers to download to your computer a variety of publicly available files at various remote computers on the network. The system by which this works is known as file transfer protocol (FTP).

An online investor might use this to download a particular piece of investment software (which might otherwise currently only be available in the shops in America). Demo programs, shareware, and a variety of other programs can be acquired comparatively simply by this method at little or no cost.

Sometimes software programs are restricted in some way, either with their functions severely hampered or with a time limit to their use. Only when the full cost of the program is paid can the authorised version be downloaded. None the less, even in this case much of the software is exceptionally good value by UK standards, and the ability to get hold of a demo version without undue fuss is valuable in itself. This topic, and the types of programs available, is discussed in more detail in Chapter 8.

The procedure for downloading varies depending on where the 'target' file resides. If it is in a normal commercial Web site, merely clicking on the indicated link will automatically set up a download to a specified directory on your own computer's hard drive. It is a good idea to have an empty directory available to take the download.

This is not the end of the story, however. Many downloadable files come in zipped form, i.e. with their contents compressed to limit the amount of time taken to download them. Once downloaded they must be 'unzipped' by using PKZIP or a similar utility. This small program or its equivalent can be downloaded from several FTP sites.

Once unzipped, a variety of files will be released into the directory. One of these should have a *.exe* or *.ini* suffix. Clicking on this will load the program or initiate its set-up sequence.

If the file you require is not contained at a Web site, the process is a little more complex. The basic procedure is to go to the appropriate FTP site, log in as a guest user, interrogate the remote computer using a bespoke software package or standard commands, find the file, and download it.

The ease with which this can be accomplished depends on the type of Internet connection you have. As already explained, these connections come in two main forms, an indirect connection or a direct SLIP/PPP connection. The indirect connection still enables a user to connect to the Web, but only with a text-based browser. In effect the user is logging in via the service provider's Internet connection. Any files downloaded are sent first to the service provider's computer to a special IP file dedicated to that particular user, but must then be downloaded again from the service provider to their final destination.

The direct connection enables a graphics-based browser such as Netscape to be used, and any files can be downloaded directly from the Net to the user's computer. Direct Internet connections typically have inbuilt programs that work rather like a Windows file manager. These simplify the process of choosing files to download.

If you have an indirect connection, you may have to learn a few basic UNIX commands in order to get what you require. Although this sounds complex and convoluted, in practice it isn't.

Using UNIX

It may be cheating slightly to include UNIX in this section on Internet tools, since it is much more than that. It has been described as the *lingua franca* of the Internet and you may find you need a smattering of it to get by. This applies even if you happen to be using software programs that automate procedures such as FTP, because it may be necessary at some point to interrogate the remote computer.

It is probably a good idea to read a general Internet guide (see the Bibliography) to get a good understanding of UNIX commands, but a few basics can be illustrated with an example of file transfer using what is known as 'anonymous login'.

Why anonymous login? Because you are not a normal user of the remote computer you will not have the password access to many parts of the computer's hard drive. Those parts that are, as it were, open to the public must still be accessed using a password. The normal procedure is to type in the word *anonymous* as your user name, with the password being your full email address.

If you are connecting from an indirect site, the first thing to do is follow the instructions in your user manual to get to an IP prompt. This may well look as follows:

IP >

To activate the file transfer protocol, type the following:

IP >ftp sunsite.doc.ic.ac.uk

This is the address of the FTP site for documents and files at Imperial (.ic), an academic institution (.ac) in the UK (.uk).

You will then be asked to login to the system. Type in *anonymous*, *guest*, or simply *ftp* and you will be asked for a password. Enter your full email address.

If this is successful—and sometimes it isn't—you should be presented with a small amount of dialogue explaining a little about the site, and a prompt. UNIX prompts are, by convention, normally either a colon (:), a percentage sign (%) or a dollar sign ($).

Now we come to more basic UNIX work. To download a file, you need to know roughly what it might be called, have some idea of the directory in which it is located, and perhaps (as a foolproof way of identifying it) know roughly what size it is in bytes.

From the basic UNIX prompt typing *ls* [*enter*] will list the files and directories in the top directory in the structure. The list will contain some random characters at the left of the screen, numbers representing the size of the files in the centre, and the file or directory names to the right. Directories can be recognised by the letter 'd' being the first letter in the left-hand string.

Let's assume that the file we require is in the directory called *public*. We now need to change to that directory and list the files contained in it to find the one we require.

Typing *cd* or *cwd* followed by a space and then the directory name logs on to that directory. Once that is done typing *ls* will list the files in that directory. Note that once in a directory part way down the tree, just typing *cd* will return to the home directory.

So typing *cd public* [*enter*] followed by *ls* [*enter*] will again provide us with a list of files and subdirectories in the *public* area. Let's assume that the file we require is called *xnetsc22.zip* and is roughly 3 Mb in size. We locate the file.

Downloading the file is accomplished by typing the command *get* followed by a space and then by the filename. Thus typing *get xnetsc22.zip* [*enter*] will begin the download process and transfer the file (assuming you have an indirect Internet connection) into your IP file at your service provider. From there it can be downloaded to your own computer at leisure, normally via an automatic script provided for the purpose.

Once the download has been completed, typing *logout*, *bye*, or *quit* will exit the remote computer and return to an IP prompt. Typing *bye* again will disconnect the modem.

As with DOS, with which many computer users will be familiar, UNIX has many other commands, but few of them will be required. A useful one is *pwd*, which shows the name of the current directory, *cat* (for catalogue) followed by the filename displays the file on screen in a scrolling form, while *help* is a universal command. The command *more* followed by a filename displays the file one page at a time, so that it can be read before it disappears off the top of the screen. Hitting the spacebar scrolls to the next page.

Provided you have a reasonable idea of what the file is called, what directory it is in, and how big it is, the commands mentioned here will probably be all the UNIX you'll ever need to know.

And since we've put the cart slightly before the horse by discussing this before even explaining how to get connected, we'll recap on UNIX commands when we come to discuss downloading software from the Net in Chapter 8.

Other Internet Tools

The objective of this chapter is to provide an initial insight into what can be done using the whole of the Internet, and not just the World Wide Web. So we'll conclude by examining some tools that are readily available, but which are receiving less attention now because of the explosive growth of the Web.

Telnet   Telnet involves logging into a distant computer network and then, once access has been gained, moving around it as though one's keyboard were actually attached to a computer on that remote network.

The login procedure is much the same as for 'anonymous' file transfer or FTP, but it helps to know in advance that the specific site you are accessing has the type of information you require. More important, it must accept anonymous guest logins. If it does not, or if you happen to enter an incorrect password, the remote computer will quickly disconnect you, making Telnetting (in my experience) a rather frustrating activity.

Having said that, there are those who swear by Telnetting as a way of retrieving data. My experience suggests, however, that many of the resources available are related to the academic world (university libraries and other institutions) and are therefore of only limited interest to the average online investor.

Internet purists who have used this technique successfully for many years will doubtless pour scorn on this suggestion. But for most investors the objective of using the Internet and its resources is quick and easy access to information relevant to their particular interest.

But let's not dismiss Telnet out of hand. One big exception to its drawbacks is that it can be used to get to Archie.

Archie   Archie is a way of conducting a thorough search of a database of Internet resources assembled at a large computer (server) specifically dedicated to that purpose. The purpose of conducting an Archie search is to identify a file that can subsequently be downloaded by the normal FTP method described earlier.

There are Archie servers in most countries that have an active Internet population. But, though it is theoretically possible to Telnet to any one of them, for language and other reasons it makes sense generally to use the one nearest to you.

The addresses of the main Archie servers for the UK are:

archie.doc.ic.ac.uk

and

archie.hensa.ac.uk

These are sites operated, respectively, by Imperial College and the University of Kent at Canterbury.

The method of logging into an Archie server is deceptively simple. Telnet to the server site and login anonymously using your email address as a password. Again, rudiments of UNIX are necessary to get the best out of the site. To access their services simply type (from an IP prompt):

```
IP > telnet archie.doc.ic.ac.uk
```

and log in as a guest user in the normal way. Assuming traffic through the server is not particularly heavy, in which case you may be invited to try later and be disconnected, you will be presented with a prompt and some simple instructions.

All Archie servers work in much the same way. The UNIX command *find* followed by a space and then the search-term will activate a search.In the course of researching this chapter, for example, I performed a search on the Imperial College archie using the word 'derivative'.

The search took less than a minute and returned a page and a half of sites at which files containing the word 'derivative' were located.

There are very brief descriptions available on screen, which give some clues as to what the file or document may contain. Mostly, though, the user will be left to resort to some detective work. This could, for instance, involve using the domain name of the site concerned, the name of the directory, and the suffix to the filename—for example, *.doc* (a document), *.xls* (an Excel spreadsheet), *.exe* (an executable program file)—and so on, to gauge whether to pursue the enquiry further.

The description of search results also includes the host computer name, the directory and subdirectories in which the relevant file is located, the filename, its size, and when it was last updated.

The real value of Archie may in fact simply be to highlight sites (rather than files) that look as though they may contain relevant information. Visiting the site using FTP and having a root around to see what else it contains of interest may be a good next step in this process.

I have skated over some of the refinements of Archie searching in the interests of brevity, but it is possible to search using criteria that are both more flexible and more precise. This is done by using the command *set search* followed by a specific search type command such as *exact* or *sub*, which respectively will record a 'hit' only if the exact filename that corresponds to the search term is found, or if the search term forms part of a filename.

You can see from this that Archie is a pretty powerful tool if used in the right way. The important point for investors is that it may track down files and information that never find their way on to World Wide Web sites.

While for most investors the Web may well be the first port of call, spending a few minutes conducting an Archie search is a useful additional technique to try. Burrowing out hard-to-find information can clearly be rewarding in investment terms.

Gopher   The last basic tool is known as Gopher. Gopher sites are accessed in one of two ways. Either by typing *gopher* from a normal *IP* > prompt, which should connect automatically with the local Gopher site. Or by typing in the location of a specific gopher site, many of which are contained in the normal directories of Internet resources. Most Gopher sites also contain links to other such sites.

But what exactly is Gopher? A simple explanation is that the Gopher network is similar to the World Wide Web, in that each of the sites contains a series of menu choices and links, including connections to other sites. The beauty of Gopher resources is that there are no complicated commands to master. Moving through Gopher sites can be done easily just by using the cursor keys on the keyboard—↑ to go up a menu item, ↓ to go down a menu item, → (or [*enter*]) to follow a link, ← to go back a step, '?' for help, 'q' to quit and so on.

As an illustration, typing *gopher* at my *IP* > prompt connects me to the main Internet Gopher at Michigan State University. The opening menu is shown in Figure 2.3. Following menu option 9 gives us the menu shown in Figure 2.4. From this we can easily access other menu items.

This is a flexible resource that, compared to the average graphics-based World Wide Web connection, is fast and flexible. The time taken to download each menu option is a fraction of that taken for links to popular Web sites. Many of the same resources are available, as well as some that aren't on the Web.

Is the Internet Right for You?

We have so far only scratched the surface of what can be accomplished using the Internet as both a communications medium and a source of

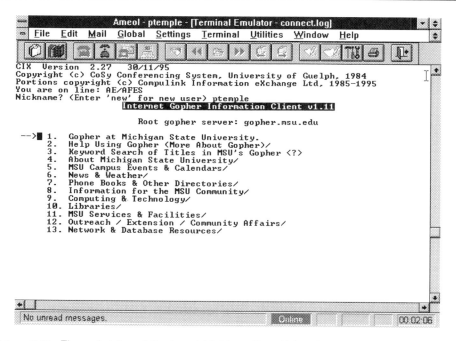

Figure 2.3 The main Internet Gopher at Michigan State University

online information. Later chapters will show how the online world can work for you as an investor.

But the contents of this chapter probably covers 90 per cent of techniques the average user will need to learn to get the full benefit from the resources the online world has to offer. I have dwelt at some length on the mysteries of using UNIX commands (which are difficult to avoid if you are to use the system's assets to the full). With a little practice these are not difficult for the average computer user to grasp.

In my experience, persisting for a couple of hours at a time every second or third day for a week or so will get the average user up to a proficient standard. As with most aspects of computing, all you need to learn are enough of the necessary techniques to get by.

I have not dealt here with the software that is normally supplied when a user first connects to the system, since each Internet service provider uses a different set of programs.

But there is, for instance, no need to use UNIX commands to send email messages, although you could do so if you wish. A ready-made email

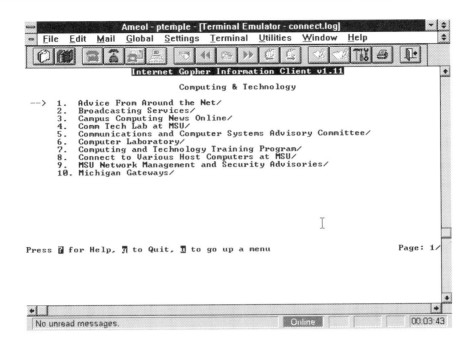

Figure 2.4 Gopher's menu 9 option

program is normally provided. The same is true of many other Internet functions, where software is provided to make telnetting and organising FTP sessions relatively simple.

What I hope this chapter has done is whet the appetite to get connected and explore the Internet's investment-related resources further.

CHAPTER 3

Getting Connected

For most ordinary users, getting computers to do what's needed involves a good deal of heartache and frustration. Getting connected to the Internet is no exception.

Its saving grace—take it from me—is that the effort is very definitely worthwhile, and that for the most part Internet users are a co-operative and friendly bunch. This includes the support staff of many service providers, especially the smaller ones, who respond quickly to queries and manage just the right amount of hand-holding for newcomers.

This chapter is organised in sections covering:

❑ what you need to get started as an Internet user
❑ how to get connected—including an assessment of the relative merits of individual service providers and their charges
❑ what you get for your money—including a section on using Web browsers
❑ some current issues relating to Internet service providers
❑ the profile (according to recent research) of a typical net user and their service preferences
❑ some do's and don'ts related to the Internet and how to use it.

What You Need

The very basic answer to the question of what equipment the online investor needs is simple:

❐ a computer
❐ a modem
❐ a telephone line
❐ an Internet service provider (ISP).

We'll deal with ISPs later; first we'll look at the basic hardware.

Computer

Computers come in all shape and sizes. So we need to be specific about precisely what is required. One or other service provider can normally offer software compatible with either the Windows or Macintosh operating systems. But whether you are using an IBM-compatible computer or an Apple machine, there are some other essentials.

The first is system memory. A minimum of 4 Mb of system memory (or RAM) is probably necessary to get the best out of the Internet and its offerings, and arguably 8 Mb is better.

The speed of the computer's processor matters rather less. The Internet and World Wide Web work on the basis of downloading information over a phone line. It is the capacity of the device that does this, the modem, that is the potential bottleneck in the process, rather than the speed with which the information is processed once it has been received.

Having said that, a 486 or Pentium processor is likely to be used, but extra high 'clock' speeds (usually measured in MHz) make little difference to the way the information is handled. I have run my own Internet connection without any problems for the last couple of years on a standard IBM-compatible 486 machine with 8 Mb of RAM and a 66 MHz clock speed.

There are some other essentials, though. One is that your system should have a hard drive, and that there should be plenty of surplus storage space on it. The reason for this is that some of the activities an online investor is likely to participate in (newsgroups and downloading software are examples) can use up significant quantities of hard drive capacity and it is as well not to have to worry too much about space. A 500 Mb hard drive should be ample, depending on the other software you are running on the system.

Lastly, it is worth stressing that a full-size colour monitor is also an essential. Although it is perfectly possible to connect to the Internet and download email from a remote location via a laptop computer, for every-day use a full-size screen makes everything much easier to view.

In short, the answer to most of the questions about basic hardware is that a reasonably up-to-date machine in either Mac or Windows format will do the job perfectly adequately.

Which Modem?

More attention needs to be given to the type of modem. The modem is the device by which the computer communicates with the outside world down a telephone line. Many computers are now being supplied with built-in modems, but equally common are modems that are internal or external add-ons to an existing PC.

The modem's function is to translate the information generated by a computer into a signal that can pass down a telephone line to be decoded (or demodulated) by the modem at the other end into the appropriate instructions or information.

Most modems also enable faxes to be received by the computer and transmitted from it, without the need for a stand-alone fax machine. They also usually come supplied with the simple communications and fax software required to perform these functions.

The most important aspect of all to take account of is the speed of the modem. Internet users will inevitably experience frustration at the comparatively slow speed at which some Web pages download, irrespective of their modem's speed. This is partly due to the level of Internet traffic. None the less, it is very definitely worth investing the modest extra amount to get the fastest modem possible.

The modem's speed is measured in bits per second (or baud). The fastest generally available mass market modems currently run at 28,800 bps and are priced around the £180 mark. Although this price is perhaps 50 per cent more than the price of the slower 14,400 bps modems, it is worth paying. Even faster (and more expensive) modems are now being marketed. The slower the modem speed the longer the time needed to stay online to download a specific piece of information, and therefore the higher the telephone charges incurred. Buying a slow modem is false economy if you are planning to use it to access the World Wide Web.

How long does it take to download data? In my own case, with a 28,800 bps modem I can reckon on file downloading taking in the region of a minute per 100,000 bytes. In other words, a 1 Mb file might take around 10 minutes to download. In theory the time taken should be rather shorter than this, but transmission times are affected by the quality of the telephone line and by the speed at which the two computers—yours and the one to which you are connected—agree between themselves to exchange it.

Modems are also a generic product and although there are some well-known brand names, a product from any well-known supplier is probably as good as any other. Well-known ones from US manufacturers are US Robotics, Pace, Psion Dacom, and Hayes. You need to specify the operating system when you buy the modem: modems are available for both Windows and Mac operating systems, but they are not interchangeable.

Do You Need a Separate Telephone Line?

It is a moot point whether a modem and a normal household phone should share the same line. It is perfectly feasible to do this. Provided you do not expect to receive faxes at all hours of the day and night (in which case the computer must be turned on and the fax software set to automatic for a fax to be received if the machine is unattended) each can co-exist without much disturbance to the other, or to the user.

Internet sessions are initiated by the user—unlike faxes which may come in from outside at an unexpected time—so in this respect, too, sharing a line makes little difference. However, if your normal phone line is used for your Internet connection, when you are online your phone will be out of action for any other purpose.

My own preference is to have a separate telephone line dedicated to fax and Internet use. That also enables a realistic check to be kept on telephone costs related to the telecommunications aspect. A phone handset can also be attached and used if need be for outgoing calls, or reserved for business use.

You can reduce costs by using a line that offers the cheapest costs for the times that you usually make your calls and the average time you are online. Compare Mercury and others with BT. Don't forget, also, that you can use the various companies' schemes for reducing costs, such as BT's Friends and Family. At the time of writing this gives a 10 per cent discount on ten designated numbers—put your ISP down as one of them.

Alternatively you could connect to an ISDN (integrated services digital network), although this is a more expensive option. You will need an ISDN card for your PC, which costs about £300, instead of a modem. An ISDN line provides two channels, which means you can hold an ordinary telephone conversation on one while at the same time sending or receiving data down the other. The cost of calls is the same as with an ordinary (analogue) line, but the line rental is higher (at the time of writing, £133.75 a quarter compared to the £21.06 a line for analogue—plus VAT, of course) and it costs in the region of £200 to have a line installed. The two great advantages with ISDN, though, is the bandwidth of the link (you can send digital and voice information at speeds of 128 Kb—four to five times the speed of a normal modem) and the speed at which connections can be made and ended. It takes only milliseconds to establish a digital connection, compared to the tens of seconds it takes to set up a call with a modem and analogue line.

Indirect or Direct Connection?

With computer and modem up and working, you now need a connection to the Internet via an ISP before you can take trips into cyberspace.

It is at this point that the next big decision needs to be made. The problem is essentially one of choice. At the last count there were well over 100 ISPs in the UK. These ranged from established suppliers with national coverage to those serving specific geographical areas.

The choice of service provider really depends on what you feel you will require from the service, and what the different providers offer.

The choice boils down to making two basic decisions. First, whether you want your Internet connection supplied with lots of other services and facilities provided by an established bulletin board operator such as CompuServe, or whether you want a simple no-frills service that simply gets you on to the Net with the minimum of fuss. Secondly, whether you want a direct or indirect Internet connection.

An indirect connection, sometimes called a 'shell' connection, essentially means that, while you get an email address and access to other Internet services, the software that runs those services is located in the service provider's 'host' computer.

Service providers operating these indirect accounts normally supply a front-end program, often called an offline reader (OLR). This allows the user, for example, to compose email and messages to newsgroups while offline. A connection can then be initiated, and the software acts as an auto pilot, accessing the appropriate software in the host computer, performing all the necessary tasks as efficiently and quickly as possible (for instance, downloading incoming email and unread newsgroup messages) and then disconnecting. It allows mail and other messages to be read offline, saving on connection charges.

Using the same software, FTP sessions can be set up either using 'scripts' (pre-set routines that make the process of connecting to the FTP site a little easier) or directly via an Internet protocol (IP) prompt. I mentioned some ways in which this could be used to access files and conduct searches in Chapter 2.

World Wide Web sites are also accessible via indirect Internet connections. But the big drawback of this is that they can only be viewed in text form. A text-based browser, normally Lynx, is accessed at the host computer for this purpose. For some this text-based approach is perfectly adequate, but in my view it will become increasingly frustrating as Web sites increase in sophistication and have more graphics.

Already some Web pages seem to have been deliberately designed to frustrate a visitor using a text-based browser, although the more enlightened have special text-friendly versions.

Another drawback of an indirect connection of this type is that any file downloading has to be done twice. Once from the Internet into the service provider's host computer and a second, separate, time from the host computer to the user's machine.

A direct network connection, on the other hand, allows the user to run the appropriate 'client' software from his or her own computer rather than at one step removed, and is therefore more flexible.

These direct connections are known as SLIP (serial line Internet protocol) or PPP (point to point protocol, which is now superseding SLIP) and allow the user to have the basic Internet communications software, known as a TCP/IP stack, on a personal computer. In turn this supports a variety of Internet-related programs, including graphics-based Web browsers such as Netscape Navigator, email programs, and FTP file selection and transfer programs.

There is now little difference in cost between having an indirect or direct connection—and a direct one is much to be preferred. Some operators offering shell accounts have bundled in PPP/SLIP connections into their service provision so that existing users can operate the two side by side at little additional cost.

The main advantage of having a shell account is that an offline reader is arguably better than browsing through newsgroups while online. But online investors should at least aim for a service provider that offers a direct connection as part of the package.

Bulletin Board System or No-frills Operator

The evolution of the Internet has resulted in the gradual emergence of three distinct strands of online connection:

❏ The basic UNIX system that has been used by academics for years to communicate with each other, share files and collaborate on research.
❏ Direct connection to the Net and the World Wide Web but little else.
❏ Online bulletin board services (BBSs). These originally functioned as closed systems, albeit in some instances quite large ones, which allowed subscribers to communicate with each other and to tap into centralised databases of information, but not to communicate with the outside world. Now bulletin board members can log into their host system and tap into resident databases. These systems also have Internet gateways to enable users to send and receive Internet email, conduct FTP and Gopher sessions, and have access to the World Wide Web.

From the standpoint of the online investor, there is a choice between signing up either with a 'no-frills' service provider, or with a BBS that will offer a Net connection with other services and information as well. Leaving aside for a moment the question of cost, does it matter which you choose?

In a way it doesn't matter much at all. A no-frills SLIP/PPP connection may be all you need. On the other hand, UK-based BBSs can be something of an antidote to the heavily US-oriented parts of the Internet that crop up elsewhere.

For example, my own Internet service provider is CIX (Compulink Information Exchange). In addition to offering both direct and indirect connections, CIX, because of its origins as an electronic bulletin board for computer buffs, also offers a large number of its own newsgroups that are specifically oriented towards computing, current affairs and to investment, personal finance and investment technology topics.

As the number of non-US users increases at CompuServe—a global BBS—the same is becoming true there too, and many other ISPs that originally started up as BBS systems can probably claim the same.

The following section addresses in more detail the issue of who to choose, what it all costs, and what you get for your money.

UK ISPs

UK Internet service providers fall into two categories: those who operate primary Internet capacity via fixed links to the US Internet 'backbone', and secondary providers who lease capacity from them.

In practice, for the average online investor there is little to choose between the two. Primary providers include organisations such as BT, Sprint, Demon and PIPEX; these large providers typically provide corporate access as well as accounts for individual subscribers. Opting for a secondary supplier does not, however, affect the ability of that supplier to offer SLIP/PPP connections.

As of the end of 1995, Demon was the largest provider of normal non-bulletin board type dial-up services, with around 60 per cent of the market, but when BBS suppliers were brought into the equation, the company came second after CompuServe, which had three times as many UK subscribers. CompuServe and Demon together (as of late 1995) had around 200,000 subscribers. Other suppliers such as CIX, UUNet Pipex, Delphi and others were all much smaller. More recent figures quoted in the *Financial Times* in December 1996 put CompuServe in the lead with 200,000 plus subscribers, AOL with 90,000, MSN with 85,000, Demon with 70,000 and Pipex with 50,000 or so.

Where BBS services do differ from the no-frills providers is that their operating costs are higher and their charges tend to be usage related. This makes a BBS connection expensive if you intend to make a lot of use of the Internet on a regular basis.

It is hard to generalise, but while a typical no-frills supplier such as PIPEX or Demon might charge a flat, say, £10 a month for unlimited access, CompuServe would have a lower minimum threshold, but charge correspondingly more if the user logged, say, 25 hours a month 'surfing the Net'. If a user expected to be surfing three hours a day, day in day out, then a BBS cost could be several times the flat charge asked by other providers.

In practice few users would make such demands. If they did, the obvious solution would be to have two separate accounts, one to access the chosen BBS databases in their own right, and a separate account with a no-frills ISP for straight Internet and World Wide Web use. Using a BBS as a way of accessing the Net can be an expensive proposition for a heavy user.

Individual online investors reconcile this dilemma in different ways. In my time as an Internet user I have found my average monthly bill for using the CIX BBS to be in the region of £20, with lows in high double figures and a high, during a period when I was downloading software and files on a fairly intensive basis, around the £70 mark, excluding telephone charges.

So it is worthwhile investigating the cost aspect of the equation fully before committing yourself. Although there is no reason why you should not change from one service provider to another, remember that a move will mean changing your email address. This may be inconvenient if it has become the one with which friends and business contacts are familiar. The various monthly magazines devoted to the Internet, such as *Internet*, *.net* and *Internet Today*, all provide guides to ISPs, including their monthly costs. The guide also gives the telephone number for each provider, together with its email address and Web page URL. Charging structures do change from time to time, however, and it is worth keeping a check on the up-to-date position.

Other points to check are: whether or not the service provider offers software compatible for your operating system; whether all the requisite Internet facilities (FTP, Telnet, and so on) are available; whether the ISP supplies the latest version of Web browser. The latter point is less important than you might think, since up-to-date browser software can be downloaded easily from software company Web sites.

The response and reliability of help desks operated by the main providers is also worth checking. Try calling them to see how quickly they respond, or whether the numbers are permanently engaged (see Table 3.1 for telephone numbers of the better-known UK ISPs). The popular Internet magazines regularly test ISPs and compare them for quality and speed.

Another important consideration is ease of access to the system, which essentially boils down to having a low ratio of subscribers to modem points at the host computer. Traffic tends to be heavy in the evening, for instance, and it is frustrating if your attempts to connect are likely to meet with an engaged tone at the other end.

Lastly, it is vital that the supplier you choose has a local point of presence (POP); in other words, that your connection is made at local call rates. The larger providers have nationwide coverage, which can simplify logging on to collect email while on the road. Otherwise the process can be an expensive one. A small local provider may be OK if you are not planning to 'surf' while on the move. But checking on telephone call charges and access points is always worthwhile before you subscribe.

With all this in mind the following is a brief profile of some widely used UK ISPs.

CompuServe

CompuServe is arguably the original and most comprehensive BBS, although in terms of straight subscriber numbers it has been recently overtaken by America On Line (AOL). Late 1995 figures show CompuServe with around four million users worldwide. Around 500,000 of those are in Europe and 200,000 in the UK.

As with any BBS, using CompuServe just to access the Internet is an expensive option relative to the charges of no-frills suppliers. According to some reports, access also tends to be slower than would be the norm with purer ISPs. According to a survey from Durlacher Multimedia published in 1996, fewer than 40 per cent of CompuServe's subscribers actually use its Internet service, many having separate accounts with cheap ISPs. CompuServe has been moving to address this point with more flexible pricing structures.

The longer-term issue for CompuServe is the extent to which its content provision (unique when the Internet and World Wide Web were in their infancy) will be superseded as more people gravitate to using the Net.

One final point about CompuServe is that for historical reasons its email addresses are number-based. A typical CompuServe email address, for example, might be 123678.111@compuserve.com. Other providers use mixtures of letters, normally based around the user's name, and are consequently rather more memorable.

CIX

CIX was one of the original UK service providers, growing out of a bulletin board conferencing system for computer buffs and computer journalists. The company has a wide offering of internal 'conferences', several thousand in all, of which perhaps around half are still computer-related. Encouragingly for the online investor, there are several active discussion groups with UK-related investment content. The company started a dial-up Internet service in Autumn 1995. Charges for this part of the service can be bundled in with normal BBS charges.

BT

BT has the potential to become a major supplier but to date has achieved only minimal penetration, with Internet users and potential users preferring the perceived advantages of dealing with smaller, supposedly more helpful, suppliers. None the less, and regulators permitting, it clearly has the potential and resources to be a significant supplier in the no-frills dial-up market.

UUNet Pipex

Formerly Unipalm-PIPEX before its takeover by UUNet, this operator is primarily oriented towards corporate connections over leased lines. It had approaching 1,000 corporate subscribers at the last count, although its dial-up service has also attracted around 50,000 individual subscribers.

Demon

From a standing start in July 1992, Demon has grown to be the largest pure ISP in the UK, with in excess of 60,000 subscribers. The service is low cost and no-frills, but the company also operates Cityscape, a more expensive service. This offers individuals the opportunity to create their own Web sites. It is moving to enter the market for corporate Internet subscriptions.

Delphi

Delphi is another well-known name. It is a BBS service originating in the USA and now owned by News International. Independent reports suggest that its impact on the UK has so far been comparatively low. It is believed to have around 15,000 subscribers. Its service includes a full range of discussion groups including a number of interest to online investors.

Others

There are a large number of other suppliers of Internet dial-up and BBS services. These include the BBC Networking Club, Atlas, EasyNet, Abel, Poptel, and Direct Connection. Some of these are predominantly regional suppliers. Abel, for instance, is centred around Birmingham, and Poptel in London, Manchester and West Yorkshire. Demon, CIX, UUNet Pipex and EasyNet all offer local call access for the majority of the country.

Table 3.1 gives a summary of these and other Internet service providers together with telephone numbers, email addresses and a summary of charges.

To reiterate, I strongly recommend that you investigate the issue of charges and the level of service provision before signing up. The broad general rule is that pure ISPs will charge a signing-on fee and then a flat charge of £10–15 per month irrespective of usage. Remember that the cost of telephone calls is not included in this, and consequently that the availability of local call access is very important. BBSs offer something extra,

Table 3.1   UK Internet Service Providers

Company	Email address	Telephone	Monthly fee (£)
Atlas	info@atlas.co.uk	0171 312 0400	12.00
BBC	info@bbcnc.org.uk	0181 576 7799	12.00
Bogomip	info@mail.bogo.co.uk	0800 137536	12.00
Cityscape	sales@cityscape .co.uk	01223 566950	15.00
CIX	cixadmin@cix.compulink.co.uk	0181 296 9666	15.00*
Compuserve	70006.101@compuserve.com	0800 000200	6.50*
Delphi	ukservice@delphi.com	0171 757 7080	10.00
Demon	sales@demon.net	0181 371 1234	10.00
Easynet	admin@easynet.co.uk	0171 209 0990	9.90
Enterprise	support@enterprise.net	01624 677666	8.00
Global	info@globalnet.co.uk	0181 957 1008	10.00
Nethead	sales@nethead.co.uk	0171 207 1100	7.99
Netkonect	info@netkonect.net	0171 345 7777	10.00
Pavilion	info@pavilion.co.uk	01273 607072	12.55
PIPEX	sales@pipex.net	01223 25012	15.00
Star	info@star.co.uk	01285 647022	12.00
UK Online	sales@ulonline.co.uk	01749 333333	9.99
U-Net	hi@u-net.com	01925 633144	12.00
Zynet	zynet@zynet.net	01392 426160	10.00

* A certain number of free hours included

Source: Temple *Getting Started in Shares*, 1996, Table 8.1, p. 195. Reproduced with permission by John Wiley & Sons, Chichester

but charge more heavily for extensive Internet use. Check whether or not the ISP supports the operating system on your PC. Not all, for example, can provide a Mac-related service.

What You Get

What you get from your Internet service provider depends on whether or not you have opted for a direct or indirect connection.

An indirect connection should, as a minimum, provide you with:

❏ an email address
❏ an offline reader
❏ access to an IP prompt
❏ access to Internet newsgroups
❏ access to any internal bulletin boards and conferences.

Access to services such as FTP, Telnet, and the World Wide Web in these instances is best gained via the IP prompt and will necessitate some basic knowledge of UNIX commands (as discussed in Chapter 2). World Wide Web access will normally be via a Lynx text-based browser. This will not download images from Web pages but will enable the hypertext links on them to be activated using simple cursor key commands. Email messages are normally composed offline and uploaded via the offline reader software.

A direct SLIP/PPP connection should provide the following:

❏ an email address
❏ an email management program, such as Eudora (or equivalent)
❏ a graphics-based Web browser, such as Netscape (or equivalent)
❏ access to Internet newsgroups, normally via the Web browser
❏ specific programs to launch FTP and Telnet sessions.

FTP for downloading files in this scenario does not normally entail using UNIX commands. Assuming the connection and login is successful, the program will simply show a file manager interface at the remote computer and the file can be selected and downloaded within a Windows or Macintosh 'point and click' environment.

Telnet sessions can be set up in a Windows or Mac environment, but will require the use of UNIX commands once the login to the remote computer has been successfully accomplished.

Internet service providers should normally also make copies of all relevant software available on disk, although there may sometimes be a nominal charge for this. Some Net enthusiasts prefer the idea of downloading everything by modem, but in practice this can be time-consuming and less user-friendly than inserting a floppy disk and using the normal Run command.

Another drawback is that while ISPs will provide official copies of all the programs used, these are often not supported by full user manuals, but only by a basic instruction booklet. This provides information on the basic features of the programs but not much else. Although the programs are intuitively easy to use, some trial and error may be involved in using them, and buying a manual or guide from a computer bookstore may be a good investment.

Using a Browser

Much of the rest of this book concentrates on accessing Web sites of use to investors. It would be worthwhile, therefore, spending a little time becoming familiar with the basics of Web browsers.

My own experience is mainly limited to Netscape Navigator, but many similar comments can be made regarding other popular browsers. Netscape has, however, for the moment become the industry standard with about two-thirds or more of the market, but Microsoft's Internet Explorer is gaining ground.

Double clicking on the browser icon will dial up the appropriate service provider number and establish the SLIP/PPP connection that allows the browser to function. Occasionally a connection will not be made for a variety of reasons, usually because of a heavier-than-normal number of users at that particular time, which will mean you get an engaged tone.

The initial page brought up, by default, may well be the service provider's home page, which might contain a variety of background information. The home page for CIX is shown in Figure 3.1. Sometimes the browser software will default to the software company's home page, but these default settings can be changed easily.

Figure 3.1   CIX's home page

The basic Netscape screen also provides direct one-button links to lists of new sites, sites that might be of general interest, upgrades of the browser program, basic Internet directories, newsgroups, and search engines. (Using search engines will be covered in more detail in Chapter 5).

Other facilities in the browser, contained in a toolbar at the top of the browser, allow for skipping forward and back to previously visited Web pages—handy when in the middle of a Web browsing session—and for typing in known URLs (specific Web page addresses) from scratch. You can use the stop button to halt unduly slow downloads. The reload button retries a previously aborted transfer of data from a Web address.

It is worth noting that Gophers and FTP sites can be addressed through a Web browser such as Netscape, simply by entering the hypertext version of the Gopher or FTP address.

The speed at which Web pages download is linked to the capacity of the modem you are using and traffic on the net, but it is also a fact that Web pages that contain a lot of images will take much longer to access than ones with a more basic design. So for those interested in speed, there is a toggle button to turn off the images of downloading Web pages. Pages are still displayed in colour with the appropriate hypertext links, only the pictures are absent. Ease of navigation may, however, be lost as a result.

Another useful facility is the ability to 'bookmark' pages, saving the URL for future use. In subsequent sessions the site is simply selected from the drag and drop menu in which it has automatically been stored.

It is also sometimes convenient to be able to save the contents of Web pages for later use. This can be done either by saving the page to disk, printing it out there and then, or else, to save telephone charges, emailing it to your own own email address and viewing it offline later.

The real point about browsers is that they are intuitively very easy to use, once the essential point about using hypertext links is grasped.

None the less, browsers are changing all the time and new versions of browser software are likely to contain fresh functions bundled into them. Netscape 2.2, for example, allows email to be accessed from within the browser and has a secure mode for conducting transactions over the Web.

Although a lot has been made in the media of the supposed lack of security inherent in Web browsers, in reality they are rather more secure than reading a credit card number over a telephone line. However, for high-value transactions, using a browser in secure mode, as indicated by a solid 'key' icon in the bottom left corner of the screen (as you can see in Figure 3.1), is only prudent.

The Typical User

A recent survey of Internet users by Durlacher Multimedia contained some interesting statistics about the characteristics of the Internet market and its typical user.

The old stereotype of users being a mixture of crusty academics resentful of the incursion of commercial interests on to the online world, or spotty 'nerds' with nothing better to do, is giving way to a more rounded view of who uses the Net and why.

For example, the survey found that, far from being solely the province of the young, usage was spread fairly evenly among the 22–36 age group, with the 37–52 group also containing a substantial core of users.

Internet users are still predominantly male, although recent press reports of studies done in America suggest a significantly higher proportion of female users there. An NOP study reported in the *Guardian* (2 September 1995) came to similar conclusions. Annual income figures suggest that Internet use is largely, though not exclusively, a middle-class phenomenon. The bulk of respondents to the survey appear to have annual income in the £15,000 to £40,000 range, with significant proportions also showing up as blips at the bottom and top of the table, demonstrating the medium's use as a hobby both by the rich and by the student population, many of the latter having free access.

At any one time, around a fifth of users are new to the Net, but most acknowledge that finding their way around takes less than a week. Most are either satisfied or very satisfied with the service offered by their ISP. Slightly over half are surfing using Windows PCs, and 16 per cent use Apple Macs. The remainder use UNIX machines.

The majority of users spend 6–20 hours a week on the Net. Only 10 per cent spend more than 50 hours a week; a similar proportion spends under five hours. Most users spend around half their time on the World Wide Web. The rest of the time is spent on a range of other Internet-related activities, such as participating in discussion groups and sending and receiving email.

Traditional Internet applications such as FTP, Telnet and Gopher appear now to be used only occasionally, having been superseded by the user-friendly Web. Use of the Internet for business, research and educational purposes takes up about half the time spent on the Net, with games and entertainment making up a big proportion of the remainder. Shopping via the Net is still very much a minority pursuit.

Netiquette

There are a number of do's and don'ts related to activities on the Net, and it is as well to be aware of them in advance.

Some of these can be put in the category of avoiding wasting either time or Internet bandwidth capacity to the detriment of other users. But some are throwbacks to the non-commercial origins of the Internet. There are still purists out there who get offended at the solecisms unwittingly perpetrated by newer users.

A few obvious examples are detailed below. These cover some of the areas that we have discussed in this and the preceding chapters.

Telnetting and FTP. When faced with the choice, always connect to the server closest to you. It may be an attractive thought to log on to a server in Australia to conduct an 'Archie' search, but it is better to use the normal UK ones resident at Imperial College and the University of Kent.

Distant servers. Try to log on to a distant server at a time when local traffic can be expected to be light. Because of the time differences involved this may not be obvious. This is practical as well as good manners. Downloads will be quicker from a remote server if traffic is light.

Wasting bandwidth. Don't waste bandwidth by downloading high volume images to your PC. Far better to turn off the graphics section of your browser and download just text.

Signatures and repeat messages. Most email programs contain the option to append a personalised 'signature' (it may contain your address and phone number or be a—supposedly—witty quotation). Over-elaborate signatures are a needless waste of bandwidth. Other common practices that have the same wasteful effect are the attachment of the message to which you are replying to your new posting. Unless absolutely essential, this should be avoided.

Self-promotion. Internet purists frown on blatant attempts at self-promotion. I was once roundly chastised by email by an American academic by answering a question posted in a newsgroup by suggesting that the enquirer buy a book on the subject I had just published. Advertising your services in newsgroups can be done, but only in a discreet way via pointers to a relevant Web site, or through encouraging those interested to email you for details.

Asking obvious questions. This tends to be frowned on. Many newsgroups and other sites have FAQ (frequently asked questions) lists which can be downloaded to avoid posts that ask the obvious.

Spamming. By the same token, most newsgroup users (especially those in financial areas) get very irritated by postings which are flagrantly off-topic, or which self-evidently promote money-making scams—of which there is no shortage. Equally, cross-posting the same message to several related groups is also intensely irritating and generally frowned on.

Libel. Be careful what you write, especially to newsgroups and to other sites in the public domain. The general rule is not to write anything you would be embarrassed to see published in a normal daily newspaper with your name attached to it. Journalists are normally asked not to quote from newsgroup postings without getting the permission of the original poster, but don't bank on them doing so.

Keyboard style. Excessive use of upper case symbols, which sometimes do not translate well, is not encouraged. Brevity, on the other hand, is applauded. Use of block capitals is considered the equivalent of shouting to get attention, and is generally only done very sparingly. There are several standard abbreviations and acronyms that can be used: examples are IMHO (in my humble opinion), AIUI (as I understand it), FWIW (for what it's worth), RTFM (read the f****** manual), and so on. In general, however, these are used to abbreviate redundant phrases that add nothing to the communication concerned. They also promote the image of the Net as an organisation for insiders, which is counter-productive. Similarly, so-called emoticons or 'smileys'—groups of punctuation marks which, when viewed sideways-on, produce icons indicating emotions, e.g. :–) [happiness/irony], :–([sadness], ;–) ['nudge, nudge–know what I mean?], :–o [astonishment]—are considered by many to be naff and unnecessary.

In this chapter we have looked at how the Internet and World Wide Web can help the online investor, the Internet's origins, structure and the tools that can be used to explore it, how to get connected, and the pros and cons of different types of service. In the next chapter we will look at the investment-related information and investor services that can be gleaned from the online world.

CHAPTER 4

Online Investment News and Discussion

The stock market thrives on information. Yet even for private investors a live price and news feed (such as Market Eye) costs upwards of £1,000 a year. If you haven't got one—and most people haven't—you can be excused for feeling that all the information that filters down from the market via the press or teletext is second-hand and rather stale.

There is no perfect solution to this dilemma of cost versus the timeliness of information. But online investors have other advantages that make up for it, and having real-time information is not the be-all and end-all of investment. It's the quality of the information that really matters.

For example, in his various books the veteran US fund manager Peter Lynch makes much of the advantage the private investor has in being able to invest on the basis of his or her own experiences as a consumer or as a member of a local community. This experience, he argues, may very well include examples of successful, yet undervalued, businesses.

This can be applied to the online investor. The physical community you inhabit and the experiences you have are still there and still valid, but they are supplemented by the 'virtual' community and experiences represented by the Internet in its various facets.

Most successful investors thrive on hard news and gossip about investment subjects. And there are many ways in which the online investor can tap into both. As elsewhere on the Internet, much of the current content has a US flavour, but as time goes by an increasing proportion of it is about topics relevant to investors in the UK and Europe.

The information falls into several categories and this chapter is correspondingly split into several sections. Each section has a newsy bias, but will also point up the diversity of information available online.

The broad categories are as follows:

❐ bulletin board newsgroups
❐ Usenet newsgroups
❐ email discussion lists
❐ online news feeds
❐ online newspapers.

Newsgroups are a logical starting point because they often represent the first exposure to the Internet and its diversity experienced by users when they initially get connected.

Bulletin Board Newsgroups

Some Internet users tend to dismiss bulletin board systems, many of which pre-dated the rise of the Internet as a mass-market medium, as rather old hat. But for the UK online investor, bulletin board newsgroups (sometimes called conferences or forums) have the advantage that, in contrast to many other areas of the Internet, they can offer a source of comment and opinion that is specifically UK-oriented.

First, though, a word about how they work. Email is at the core of the way the groups function. Instead of sending email on a bilateral basis to a single correspondent, perhaps a friend or colleague whose email address you know, bulletin board newsgroups are simply a central point into which all the email discussion and opinion can be posted and where it can be seen by all the participants in the group. An example of a message posted to a Usenet newsgroup (*uk.finance*) is shown in Figure 4.1.

And, since the message contains the sender's email address, there is always the option for a particular discussion to be continued on a bilateral basis. The obvious analogy is that it is like pinning a card to a notice board in a public place, for example a library or a college; someone (whom you

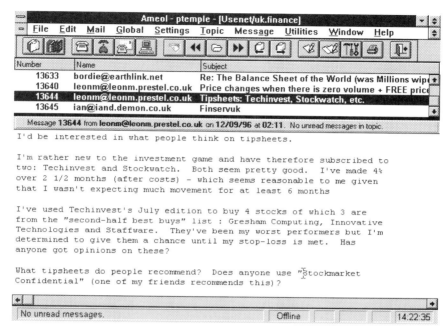

Figure 4.1 A message posted to a Usenet newsgroup

may not know) can reply either by leaving a message on the board, or by communicating directly with you.

Another advantage of bulletin board conferences is that they are often 'moderated' (refereed). This means that posts to the group which are irrelevant or abusive can be removed by the bulletin board operator. This is sometimes in marked contrast to the unmoderated newsgroups in the Usenet system (discussed later). On occasion these contain a big proportion of irrelevant information.

By convention, information in conferences and newsgroups is connected together in 'threads'. This is a collection comprising the original message and the responses to it. A potential poster to a bulletin board can therefore either initiate a new thread, or reply to an existing one.

The norm is for messages to be composed offline, using an offline reader (OLR). As explained in Chapter 3, this is like an autopilot which batches all the messages to be uploaded and downloaded and completes the task in the minimum time possible before disconnecting. By employing it, users do not need to waste valuable connection time either reading messages or composing replies while online.

However, the use of OLRs means that discussions can take some time to complete and the responses to an initial posting on a topic almost certainly will not be replied to immediately. This phenomenon is known as 'OLR lag'.

Why does OLR lag happen? A post to a newsgroup may not be uploaded immediately, for example. It may then take some time for the potential replier to note the message and respond. Then his or her reply may also not be uploaded to the bulletin board or newsgroup immediately. Days and weeks can sometimes go by before a discussion is satisfactorily concluded.

Most OLRs permit the configuration of messages in different ways. The reader can move either from one unread message to the next in chronological order, or from thread to thread. Most newsgroups also enable the user to identify which subscribers are joined up to that particular conference (i.e. receiving its messages) and therefore ready in the background to participate in discussions that interest them.

At the time of writing the leading bulletin board groups operating in the UK are CompuServe, Delphi and CIX. All offer access to Usenet newsgroups (of which more later) and all have internal conferences and forums. Since I am connected through CIX I will use their conferences as the main basis for the examples that follow, but other major bulletin boards offer a comparable service.

In CompuServe, for instance, a variety of forums exist for investors. These cover topics such as personal finance, tax, financial software, and so on. Each of these forums contain subdivisions on particular topics. CompuServe's investment forum, for example, deals variously with share trading, options, mutual funds and unit trusts, and a variety of other subjects. Delphi, although it has a smaller number of subscribers than CIX, has content provision similar to CompuServe.

We'll look briefly at CIX and the various investment-related conferences it operates, as an illustration of the way the system works and some of the topics discussed.

Under the heading of 'Money, investment and financial institutions' in the index of conferences operated in the CIX system are a range of conferences including, for example, Abbey National, banks in general, First Direct, handling debt, investment, money, tax and financial planning, options, money laundering, negative equity, and so on.

I'll look at a couple of these as I write. First, money. In CIX, the Money conference currently has 172 participants and is subdivided into a number of different topics variously entitled: making it; losing it; debt; general; contacts; enquiries; and practice. The 'enquiries' topic is the most active, with 17 messages in the past month, on topics including pension AVCs, transferring CGT between husband and wives, and several other issues.

Secondly, investment. The investment conference has 210 participants and rather more topics to go at. These include sections for: beginners; files; a 'general' section; and separate topics on penny shares, options, pensions, PEPs, shares in general, software, and technical analysis. The 'general' topic is an active one, with several messages daily. At the time of writing, subjects covered have included: the debate about building societies floating and how best to take advantage of the trend; which shares are included in the FT-SE100 index; how financial advisers justify their fees; a list of the TESSAs on offer; and information on a new finance-oriented Web site. Many of the other topics are more or less dormant. There is, however, a reasonable amount of interesting cut and thrust between participants, who range from professionals and experienced private investors, to beginners both to the investment scene and the Internet. As with many CIX conferences, the atmosphere is friendly, and helpful—with a touch of banter.

One general point about all bulletin board systems is that they often come with files available for members to download. In the case of the investment conference on CIX, for example, these files include demonstration disks for several different types of investment software, historic data on the FT-SE100 index, a list of suggested reading, and other useful snippets. In the money conference is a small file list which contains background briefing notes on various financial planning topics, and 'ten awkward questions to ask your financial adviser'.

An enthusiastic user can start up a conference at any time on a topic that he or she feels is worthy of discussion. First, though, permission from the system operator must be sought to start the conference. Then the user must be prepared to spend time moderating the discussion. OLRs supplied as part of a bulletin board conferencing package often have a special add-in program that enables the moderator to do his or her job, removing off-topic messages if need be, and commenting on others.

Newsgroups operated by BBS operators tend to be smaller and more participative than the larger ones on Usenet (see below). It is more difficult, for example, to hide (known in Internet jargon as 'lurking') and not participate. It is also up to the individual participant, if a topic that he or she might want to know about is not being discussed, to post a provocative comment to try to get a discussion going.

It is also worth bearing in mind that some of the less obvious conferences may include discussion on financial topics. For instance, in the CIX system there are conferences related to all the major broadsheet newspapers, magazines such as *The Economist* and *Private Eye*, and all the main political parties. If these are of no other use, they often provide a thought-provoking and humorous insight into current events.

To emphasise one important point: it is self-evident in a national bulletin board system such as CIX that all of those logged on to UK investment-related conferences will either be UK online investors or those with an interest in the UK finance scene. Most discussions do tend, therefore, to be of specific interest to UK online investors. This is not always the case with Usenet newsgroups, which we move on to look at next.

Usenet Newsgroups

History provides no definitive answer as to why Usenet is called what it is. However, by common consent it is reckoned to be a contraction of Users' Network, or USENIX Network, reflecting its origin as a spin-off from a large UNIX user group.

But don't panic at the mention of UNIX. You can read Usenet newsgroups using UNIX commands, but it is equally possible, and more normal for most users, to view and contribute to them using an OLR. In this respect they are similar to, and sit comfortably alongside, the conferences or forums operated by a BBS system such as CIX or CompuServe.

There are, however, other differences between the conferences and forums of BBSs and those of Usenet. These are manifested in several ways.

The first difference is in the sheer number of them. At the last count, for example, there were around 3,500 individual conferences in the CIX system, but more than 17,000 Usenet newsgroups.

The Usenet system is made slightly more manageable by the fact that the newsgroups operate in a broad hierarchical system, which enables a specific field of interest to be identified more quickly. There are, for instance, sections of the hierarchy for newsgroups devoted to particular US states, particular countries, to computer topics, to scientific topics, to social topics, to news about Internet-related matters, and to recreations of various types. Everything else, and for the most part this includes anything to do with investment or finance, is lumped together in a 'miscellaneous' (or 'misc'.) category.

For UK online investors, the choice of relevant Usenet newsgroups is a surprisingly small one. There are, for example, *misc.invest* categories with suffixes such as *.technical* (technical analysis), *.stocks*, *.futures*, *.funds* (to do with bond, equity and derivatives funds), *.canada* (investment in Canadian markets), *.real-estate*, and so on. Newsgroups with specific UK content are confined to one, namely *uk.finance*.

Investment topics relating to other countries may be available, although some may well be conducted in the host language. Where no country prefix is displayed in the Usenet index it can safely be assumed that the newsgroup will have predominently US content. Of course, US-oriented newsgroups need not be totally ignored. They may contain information (for instance about software or investment-related Web sites) that is equally interesting to non-US investors.

Before we go on to look at a brief sampling of the type of messages from these various newsgroups, however, we'll look further at some of the other differences between Usenet newsgroups and the typical bulletin board forum or conference.

One of these differences is that as well as there being many more Usenet newsgroups to choose from (although only a handful of really relevant investment-oriented ones), there is a vastly larger pool of potential participants. If you consider, for instance, that CIX's 20,000 or so subscribers can produce 100–200 people interested in an investment-related forum, think of the number potentially interested in an investment-related Usenet newsgroup, which is open to all those with Usenet access in the world.

This could be viewed as an advantage. But having more participants is a two-edged sword. Putting out a general request for information on a particular investment topic, for example, may be answered several times over. Or it may simply be buried in the welter of other information in the group, and therefore ignored. The trick is to give the posting a relevant and eye-catching lead-in and to make it succinct. This increases the chances that it will get read.

The second point is that most of the Usenet newsgroups are unmoderated. Hence they can contain a number of less desirable aspects of the

Internet. These include blatant self-promotion, various scams, totally irrelevant or abusive postings, stock pushing, and other nastiness which tends to be deterred or weeded out by BBS operators.

All this is best summarised as a low 'signal to noise' ratio. In other words, a lot of irrelevant postings may have to be waded through in order to catch information that is relevant and useful. There are ways around this, however.

One is that most offline readers will contain a simple command that can weed out, mark as 'read' or 'to be ignored' threads that are irrelevant. The other is that, with practice, most users become used to scanning through newsgroups quickly and skilled at detecting which items are of interest.

One plus point for Usenet newsgroups on investment topics is that they are invaluable informal sounding boards for the twists and turns of investor sentiment—and a good way of applying contrary opinion theory.

A good example of this has been the rather chequered ride that high technology and Internet-related stocks have offered, especially in the US market over the past couple of years. Using investment-related newsgroups it would, for instance, have been easy to spot these turning points by noting the opinion of the 'crowd' and take the opposite tack when the clamour reached its height.

There have also in my experience been several instances where newsgroups have highlighted stocks worthy of further research. Perhaps the best example was Unipalm, the Internet service provider taken over by UUNet Technologies in late 1995.

It needs stressing that the picking up of tips like this must be followed by solid additional research, since newsgroups represent an ideal forum for investors who have shares in a particular company to talk them up on pretty insubstantial grounds. Indeed, stock market regulators in the USA in particular have become concerned at the sharp price movements that have sometimes accompanied the tipping of shares in influential investment newsgroups.

With these cautions in mind, we'll look at the character of some of the finance and investment-related Usenet newsgroups mentioned earlier, shown in Table 4.1. This table demonstrates that logging on to Usenet newsgroups needs to be done sparingly. It is perfectly possible for some of the more popular newsgroups—such as *misc.invest.stocks* and *misc.invest*—to have well over 100, or in some cases over 200, messages per day. Wading through this quantity of mail does take some time.

Table 4.1 Investment-related Usenet newsgroups

	misc.invest. technical	misc.invest. stocks	misc.invest	uk.finance	misc.invest. futures	misc.invest. funds
Main subject	Software; technical analysis	Stock picking/pushing	General investment topics	UK personal finance	Mainly US futures and options	US mutual funds
No. of posts	30–35	250–300	60–70	30–40	35–40	50–60
Typical posts	Bollinger bands Recurrence IV—any views A new derivatives mag Market technicians seminar Shock analysis System testing software	16 yo wants invest. advice Yahoo! Symantec—any followers? DDIM—what happened? Stocks to explode in 96 IOMEGA up 3 at $35!	Holt optional stock report New Internet IPO HK market technical pos'n Need prof. financial planner Canadian mining newsletter Rant at Charles Schwab	Inv. Chronicle—subscribe? Remaing mutuals Building Socs and Bristol & W Profit from British beef? Loophole in inheritance tax Traded endowments	Dec. Corn/Wheat spread? OptionVue software for sale Commodit-E Journal 97 live hogs French Franc/Lira? KL options market—new?	Warning about mutual funds Performance of S&P 500 Buying cash at a discount? Alberta SE Fidelity's new qtly statement Load funds—less panic if crash
Signal/noise ratio	Medium	Low	Medium	High	High	High
Relevance to UK online investors	Moderate	Low	Moderate	High	Moderate	Low
Comment	Can be source of information on software download sites	Opinionated pushing, especially of technology stocks	Some useful information on investment related Web sites	Emphasis on insurance, PEPs and so on rather than stocks	Some theory; good on futures-related Web sites	Almost exclusively US-oriented

From the standpoint of the UK online investor, logging on to the *uk.fi-nance* group is essential, while the extent to which US-oriented groups are used is another matter. The *misc.invest.technical* group does tend to contain information that can be of use to an audience wider than just US investors. For instance, there is often information on new or existing software available for downloading.

As new Web sites are launched that are relevant to investors, they do also tend to crop up in newsgroups. This gives Usenet groups another handy function—that of alerting the investor to new material that has become available elsewhere on the Internet. It is not, however, necessary to log on to all of the half a dozen or so finance-related newsgroups to pick up these flags: many announcements of this type are cross-posted to all relevant ones.

The extent to which you make use of Usenet newsgroups will depend on the amount of time you are able to devote to the material, relative to the use you might get out of it. In my own case, I might spend up to half an hour most days participating in newsgroups, but part of my interest is professional rather than just to do with my personal investment activities.

Posting to newsgroups—rather than just passive reading—is obviously part of the process. You can reply to queries posted by other users, ask questions or make comments of your own. In *The New Internet Navigator*, Paul Gilster describes several 'rules of the road' that are worth reproducing here, and which echo the comments on 'Netiquette' made in Chapter 3.

Gilster's rules for posting to newsgroups are:

❏ Do you really need to post?
❏ Use email where you can.
❏ Know your destination.
❏ Use descriptive titles for your post.
❏ Avoid advertising.
❏ Avoid abusive discussions.
❏ Keep your 'signature' short.
❏ Exercise care in quoting earlier messages at length.
❏ Remember that news to you isn't always news to everybody.
❏ Clarity is all.

Readers familar with Usenet newsgroups will note that I have omitted any reference to those organised under the *clari.* heading in the Usenet hierarchy. ClariNet is an electronic publishing service that provides an edited feed of significant news stories taken from wire services such as AP and Reuters, and repackages them in newsgroup format on a 'read-only' basis.

Not all ISPs offer *clari.* newsgroups as part of their package (since subscribing to it costs them money). Because it is more in the nature of a news feed than a participative newsgroup it is included in a later part of this chapter along with other news services.

Finally, tracking all the newsgroups that might have potential relevance to an investment query is clearly a time-consuming business. So it is worth knowing that there is a search tool, known as DejaNews, available to give a bit of assistance for specific queries. DejaNews is easy to use and, given the right search terms to work with, should come up with interesting recent news on a particular topic.

DejaNews is located at the Web address http://www.dejanews.com and offers the facility to perform both a quick unsophisticated search across all Usenet groups, or a more tailored search across a selected list filtered by group, by author, by date, and so on.

The ease with which good search results are achieved clearly depends on how tightly you are able to define its terms, by excluding common words that might crop up in normal conversation. For instance, I recently performed a search on the small UK engineering company Thomas Locker, which produced a large number of hits—references—with a sporting theme (locker rooms and so on). But near the top of the list were references to articles posted in the *uk.finance* newsgroup—closer to what I really had in mind.

Searching is accomplished very quickly even with a very broad enquiry, and the results display the hit rate (the extent to which some or all of the words crop up in the post), a headline or part of headline, the newsgroup from which it is taken, and the author. Figure 4.2 shows a page from the results of a DejaNews search. The quoting of the newsgroup is particularly important. Given the limited number of finance orientated newsgroups, it is comparatively easy to spot from the search results which items are relevant to a particular enquiry.

In addition, the use of a search tool sometimes leads to serendipity in the form of posts in newsgroups that it may not have been imagined contained relevant information. For example, I recently searched DejaNews using the word 'Virtuality', for information on the company of the same name. This produced 245 hits, with hits number 75 and 76 being two posts from the UK finance newsgroup. These proved mundane, but another was a review of a product launched by Atari, involving technology

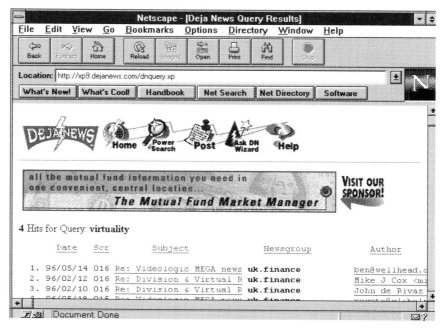

Figure 4.2   The results of a DejaNews search

developed by Virtuality. This post contained a lengthy discussion of the relationship between the two companies—good background information unlikely to appear in the company's annual report or corporate brochure. This is an example of the importance of quality information I referred to at the beginning of this chapter. It's not 'inside information', but equally it's not available to everyone, and thus can have solid investment value.

So Usenet, though it is the repository of a lot of trite and ill-informed comment and speculation, can none the less be made to work via intelligent searching. DejaNews is free to use, and is funded by advertising.

We will look in more detail at 'search engines'—as they are more commonly known in Internet-speak—and how to use them in Chapter 5.

There is, though, a trade-off to be struck between minimising the number of relevent 'hits', while keeping the search wide enough to include some element of unearthing the unexpected and the interesting.

In the same way, a happy medium can be struck between the potentially parochial BBS newsgroups with comparatively few 'subscribers', and the anarchic and uncontrolled nature of the Usenet system.

This comes in the form of specialist email discussion lists, to which interested parties can subscribe, and which we look at next.

Email Lists

Email lists are rather different from newsgroups and more akin to the conferences encountered in a BBS. They have a more limited number of participants than may be the case in Usenet, a referee, and a tendency to stick to the topic in hand. The reason for this is obvious. You don't subscribe to a list unless you are interested in participating in it.

Automatic mailing list management software means that joining lists like this is easy. The problem is that very few have a direct relevance to issues of specific interest to a UK online investor.

The character of these lists is more like a private discussion group than the boisterous and anarchic exuberance of the Usenet newsgroups. Many of the lists grew out of scholarly conferences on particular topics and are still run and refereed by academics.

First, we'll go through a little background about how lists like this work. The software that runs a mailing list is more often than not automatic, and can be manipulated by sending email messages in a strictly defined format.

There are at least three main types of list management software in use at present on the Internet, LISTSERV, LISTPROC, and MAJORDOMO. The commands for each are slightly different and it is worth consulting an Internet guide (such as Gilster or Randall) for the appropriate command structure. Signing on to a list will normally produce a return message giving the commands in brief and how to get help for more complex procedures.

If we take LISTSERV as an example, commonly used commands include *subscribe* followed by a space and name of the list (to sign on), *signoff* (followed by the listname) to un-subscribe from it, and so on. *Review (listname) by country* will produce a list of participants analysed by country giving their names and email addresses.

It is important when sending commands—as distinct from messages— that the correct address is specified in the email. This should be the address for the administrator of the list rather than the one that accesses all its recipients. When sending commands to LISTSERV or other similar software the subject header line is left blank and the message is typed in the message area below. It is also important to turn off any signatures that are automatically added to email messages. These can be misinterpreted by automatic list management software.

The subtleties are best illustrated with an example. For the mailing list *Electronic Journal of Finance*, the administration address is list-serv@vm.temple.edu, the message sent to join the list should be *sub-scribe finance*, followed by your first name and last name. When posting comments to the list, however, the address is fi-nance@vm.temple.edu. This distinction is important because it is irritating for members of the list to get commands via email that are obviously meant for the list administrator. Messages posted to the list address pop into the email boxes of every participant of the list. Rather as in a news-group, the recipient can choose to reply or not, as the case may be.

The real problem with mailing lists is actually finding out that they exist. Mailing list information is sometimes posted in newsgroups and given out in Internet-related magazines. However, an easier way to access some of the relevant information is via a number of Web sites specifically devoted to cataloguing them.

One is known as the Directory of Scholarly and Professional E-con-ferences. It is compiled by Nancy Kovaks and its Internet address is http://www.mailbase.ac.uk/kovaks/kovaks.html. There are also several other list directories available. One is PAML (Publicly Accessible Mailing Lists) located at the Internet address http://www.neosoft.com/internet/paml. Liszt, a searchable index of lists and newsgroups located at http://www.liszt.com (see Figure 4.3), is probably the easiest to navigate and search, and is the most comprehensive.

A selection of lists relevant to investors, extracted from these sources, is shown in Table 4.2.

Hunting down details of the lists can involve some detective work, with investment-related topics often categorised under finance, stocks, invest-ment, business, accounting, and so on. Most of the directories include in each case the name of the list, the topic under discussion, whether the list is moderated, whether it is a passive list simply for mailouts of informa-tion, or discussions, whether or not it has has archives, and who it is suitable for.

What topics are covered in lists of this type? Some lists are simply disseminators of information and are not designed for discussion. This is

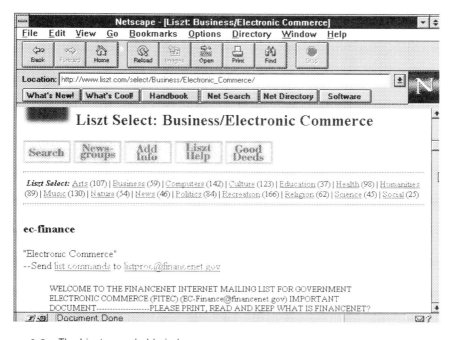

Figure 4.3 The Liszt searchable index

not to say they are not useful, though, and I will come on to a couple of lists like this that have a specific UK relevance later. Others are firmly in the area of newsgroup-style discussion—although perhaps at a more elevated level than is normally the case in Usenet forums.

I will use as an example a list I am familiar with. The *Electronic Journal of Finance* has included requests for information on the best business schools in which to study finance, erudite articles on socially responsible investing and whether or not it pays off, a heated discussion on the role of astrology in making investment decisions, and discussion about the impact of US investor holdings on the performance of non-US shares.

Many of these forums have a US orientation and there are comparatively few discussion lists available that cover UK finance and investment topics. Having said that, the spread of the Internet outside the USA will undoubtedly lead to lists of this type being set up in due course, so UK online investors need not despair that their interests will never be met in this way.

Table 4.2 Investor-relevant email discussion lists

List name	Topic	Active/passive	Moderated Yes/No	email address for subscribing
Accounting	US accounting topics	P	Y	listproc@financenet.gov
accounting-discuss	US accounting topics	A	Y	listproc@financenet.gov
Banking	Commercial and retail banking issues	A	N	list@cfonline.com
E-INVEST	Discussion of investing techniques	A	Y	listserv@vm.temple.edu
FINANCE	Discussion of finance theory	A	Y	listserv@vm.temple.edu
FinServ-UK	UK financial services discussion	A	Y	FinanceManager@silverquick.com
Foreign-futures	Futures price data	P	Y	listserv@pitstar.com
Futures-big-page	Futures price data	P	Y	listserv@pitstar.com
IPN	Discussion of investor protection issues	A	Y	listproc@essential.org
Mergers	Discussion of issues related to mergers	A	N	lists@cfonline.com
Quote-Page	Commodity futures prices	P	Y	Contact pady.smith@pitstar.com
SPACE-INVESTORS	Information on space-related stocks	A	N	space-investors-request@lunacity.com
Spot-page	35 US and foreign commodity futures	P	Y	listserv@pitstar.com
Stock-picking	Discussion of stock-selection techniques	A	Y	majordomo@listserv.nashville.net
Venture	Discussion of IPOs, venture capital etc.	A	N	lists@cfonline.com
WALLSTREET	Discussion of Internet-based investment products	A	N	wallstreet-request@shore.net
WALLSTREET-DIRECT-LIST	Information on Internet-based investment products	P	N	wallstreet-direct-list-request@cts.com

Who inhabits lists like this at the moment? In each of two popular lists, the Electronic Journal of Finance and the less theoretically inclined Electronic Journal of Investing, there are around 700 participants; roughly half are in the USA, and the remainder are spread around the world, with 10–20 participants in the UK. This doesn't sound a lot, but it is possible that use of discussion lists may well increase as Internet users and online investors become more sophisticated, and less patient with the haphazard nature of Usenet. One recently introduced feature of the FT Information Web site (http://www.info.FT.com), for example, is a series of passive email news retrieval groups.

Some investment-related Web sites operate mailing lists to keep interested investors up to date with what is happening at their site. One site that does publish information of this kind is the Interactive Internet Investor (http://www.iii.co.uk) which emails out periodic newsletters to those who are interested. Those keen to subscribe to this list, which has a distinct personal finance flavour, can do so by sending email to subscribe@iii.co.uk with the message *subscribe interactive investoralert*.

Another passive mailing list of interest to investors is the one operated by HM Treasury. This list emails out news releases and other announcements to subscribers. To get yourself added to the list, simply send an email message to maillist@hm-treasury.gov.uk with the message *subscribe press* or *subscribe whatsnew* in the body of the message, leaving the subject line blank.

It is worth pointing out that although we have used the words 'subscribe' and 'subscriber' throughout this section, this is simply shorthand to describe the process of logging on to the list. All of the lists are totally free to join.

One very obvious point is that automatic mailing lists represent an ideal way for companies to keep in touch with their shareholders and any other interested parties, and an ideal way of making sure that price-sensitive information is disseminated as widely and as quickly as possible.

Although there are few (if any) UK companies contemplating doing this at present, there is no reason why provision of information in this way should not eventually become commonplace.

LISTSERV software is cheap and easy to operate, and lists can be configured so as to be passive disseminators of information. In other words, there need be no worry about corporate computer capacity being clogged by unwanted email from irate investors or time-wasters.

Among US companies, passive email lists are now beginning to be used to communicate with investors, customers and business partners. High-tech companies appear to be in the forefront of this trend, which can be expected to gather pace as more of the population gets connected.

In the next section we will look at the way in which online investors can access news via the Internet and World Wide Web from conventional sources similar to those used by professional investors, and at little or no cost.

Online News Feeds

Newsgroups, discussion lists and BBS conferences are not the only way for the online investor to gain access to news and opinion. In fact, what newsgroups and conferences offer is strictly a mixture of opinion, questions and fact. Hard news is an altogether more precious commodity.

In particular, stock-specific hard news in an easily accessible form is a rarity even on the Internet, but there are many other helpful sources that can save money and time for investors, and give them a window into the types of services viewed by the professionals.

We can subdivide them into three main categories: passive hard news related Usenet newsgroups, such as ClariNet; online news services such as Reuters, CNN, and Bloomberg; and online versions of daily newspapers and magazines. These are covered in the remainder of this chapter.

ClariNet

ClariNet is an electronic publisher offering a series of newsgroups to which are posted (on a read-only basis) news stories from the main wire services, for example Reuters, UPI and AP.

Among its coverage of a huge variety of topics ClariNet has over 100 newsgroups covering items of general interest to investors, including stock market reports and economic news, some of which is specific to the UK or to European markets. There is also news relevant to specific industry groups, but this is generally dominated by US content.

Posts tend to be occasional, but specific and relevant when they do appear, with none of the opinionated dross that clutters up the normal Usenet investment forums.

The following handful of headlines simply gives a flavour of the type of stories the groups contain (the newsgroup and source is quoted in brackets after the headline).

❐ Gold investors look beyond six year high (*.biz.finance*/Reuters)
❐ Giant bank merger reflects efficiency drive (*.biz.features*/Reuters)
❐ Sega clicks onto battle mode with Euro-bid (*.biz.mergers*/Reuters)
❐ Greek state to sell more telecom shares (*.biz.privatisation*/UPI).

Remember, however, that because ClariNet is a service to which your ISP must subscribe to be able to include it in its Usenet feed, not all ISPs will carry these newsgroups. So check that this service is available before signing up.

Online News Services

A number of large news agencies provide services that can be accessed via the Web. These include Reuters, Bloomberg, CNN and others.

While many news-related Web sites are intended to tease those logging on to take out a more expensive subscription (displaying headlines but reserving the meat of the story for the subscription-based service), many do not take this tack and are essentially funded by online advertising.

One particularly good resource for the online investor is the IBM info-Market NewsTicker (see Figure 4.4). This is a piece of software that can be downloaded from an IBM Web site at http://infomarket.ibm.com/ht3/ticker.shtml.

The software comes in the form of a bar that sits across the top (or bottom) of a normal Windows display. News headlines can be updated as and when required or programmed to update at specific intervals. Once the software is activated, stories are downloaded and headlines scroll across the ticker bar. A single mouse click brings up a lengthy list of the latest stories, which can then be quickly downloaded and viewed via the Web browser. For the moment both the software and the service itself (which contains full-text articles) is free.

As with most Internet content, the majority of stories relate to US news, but there are also stories of general world news interest, and stories that may well be relevant to those with stocks that have major US interests. For instance, as a shareholder in BAT Industries, I have been able, through

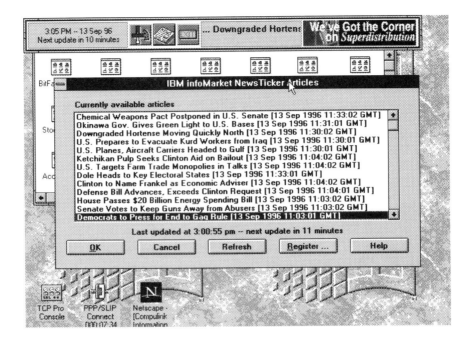

Figure 4.4 The IBM infoMarket NewsTicker

the news ticker, to keep close watch in the past year on the developments in US product liability lawsuits. Because it comes direct from wire services, the news is displayed in a way that is often more timely, accurate and comprehensive than TV news bulletins.

The following examples, taken at random from headlines current at the time of writing, give a flavour of the service:

❑ Stocks tumble: IBM down on earnings warning
❑ Coke profits up: stock split approved
❑ France says Britain breaks word on Mad Cow
❑ Hizbollah rejects US proposal on truce.

Reuters, Bloomberg and CNN all have sites containing financial news. The Reuters site periodically has a solid chunk of UK-relevant financial news stories updated throughout the day. However, this switches from week to week to news relevant for other countries, so Reuters stories in general are

Table 4.3 Online news services

	Bloomberg Personal	**Reuters Business Alert**	**CNNfn**
URL: http://	www.bloomberg.com	www.reuters.com	www.cnnfn.com
Basic character	News; World markets information; top story; personal finance	Financial and industry news sorted by date and country	General financial news; top story; briefs
Graphics content	Moderate	Minimal	High
Regn/login required?	No	No	No
Nature of content	Bond-oriented	Business and financial news and stock-specific stories	General news, non-stock specific interactive—comments welcomed
Links to other sites	Banks; bonds; Corps; FX; international business; markets; quotes	Web sites of Reuters-owned companies	Comprehensive
email feedback	feedback @bloomberg.com	newmedia @reuters.com	CNNfn.interact @turner.com
Overall rating UK online investor (1 = poor; 10 = good)	7	8	4

best accessed through the ClariNet newsgroups and services such as infoMarket.

A comparative assessment of some news service Web sites is shown in Table 4.3.

The Press Association also has a Web site, located at the URL http://www.pa.press.net, containing stories updated hourly. These tend mainly to be general news stories rather than those with a business, finance or investment angle. The press release distributor UNS also has a Web site (http://www.twoten.press.net) where verbatim press releases are displayed on a minute-by-minute basis. Like the PA service, many of these do not have an investment or finance flavour.

Other news organisations such as Telekurs have home pages on the Web, but at the time of writing these mainly function as sources of information on the organisations themselves, rather than providing news stories.

None the less, Web sites are developing quickly and it is worth regularly conducting searches to see whether or not these and other news organisations have more extensive operations under development.

Online Newspapers

Online daily newspapers clearly do not quite have the immediacy of wire service news or even such 'steam age' devices as teletext which, though crude in technological terms, none the less represent as good a source as any for investors to use to keep up with company news and share prices.

However, it is important for investors to be catholic in their business reading and the online editions of certain daily newspapers provide a good way of going about this without racking up a huge paper bill.

Table 4.4 gives a comparative assessment of the online editions of the main daily papers with quality business content. There are some obvious omissions from the list, namely the *Guardian* and the *Independent*. At the time of writing the *Independent* had no electronic edition of its newspaper, while the *Guardian* has several Web-related projects and an online edition of its *Guardian* Online supplement to Thursday's paper, located at http://go2.guardian.co.uk. This site has a searchable archive of stories.

The *Electronic Telegraph* and *The Times/Sunday Times* sites both essentially contain a full version of each day's paper, indexed for quick access. The only difference between the two sites is the rather more cumbersome graphics at *The Times* site. These can be avoided simply by turning off the 'autoload images' button on your Web browser.

A particularly useful feature at both sites is efficient and easy-to-use searchable archives for retrieving stories from previous issues. The *Telegraph* archive goes back to November 1994, and that of *The Times* site includes all editions published from the start of 1996.

The *Financial Times* site is slightly hampered by the fact that Pearson (the *FT*'s owner) has several other money-making services (such as its *FT* Profile and McCarthy cuttings services) which would be undermined by any broad-scale, Internet-based searchable archive. However, the *FT* site was extensively revamped in April 1996 and a search facility introduced, enabling users to search for stories previously published there.

The site now includes the Lex column and many other main features, although company news coverage is not comprehensive. The upgraded

Table 4.4 Online business newspapers

	Electronic telegraph	Times/Sunday Times	Financial Times	Wall Street Journal	Investors Business Daily
URL: http://	www.telegraph.co.uk	www.the-times.co.uk	www.ft.com	www.wsj.com	ibd.ensemble.com
Basic character	Verbatim version of normal paper; well indexed	Times and Sunday Times plus interactive supplement	Comprehensive highlights plus information on other FT services	Reasonable approximation to Money & Investing section	Comprehensive stories of relevance to investors
Graphics content	Medium/low	High (slow to download)	Medium/low	High	Low (v. fast download)
Regn/login required	Yes	Yes	Yes	Yes	Yes
Nature of business content	City headlines, links to full stories, prices, diary	Verbatim news stories, diary plus 2-hourly updates	Newsbriefs, plus selected top stories—some company news	Good company and investment coverage 'Heard on the Street'	In-depth news stories Briefer company comments
Links to other sites	No	No	No	Limited number	Yes, to companies mentioned in stories
Archive search	Yes, back to Nov. 94	Yes, from Jan. 96	Yes (search facility from April 96)	Refs to previous articles	Yes, plus search facility for corporate Web sites
email feedback	et@telegraph.co.uk	Yes (address not quoted)	Yes (address not quoted)	info@update.wsj.com	ibdweb@ensemble.com
Overall rating for UK online investor (1 = poor, 10 = faultless)	8	7	7	5	6

site is a considerable improvement over the earlier one, though, and worth checking out for researching back comments on particular topics. Registration and login is required, but the site is free.

Although principally containing US-oriented news, another good port of call is the *Investors Business Daily* site. This has a high degree of news and company comment, as well as links to the corporate Web sites (where available) of companies mentioned in the stories.

The *Wall Street Journal*'s Money and Investing Update site, effectively an online version of this section of the paper (including its influential 'Heard on the Street' column) is available via registering at the main *WSJ* site. At present this site is free of charge. Although there is no searchable archive, links in the articles do permit users to access background information on certain companies mentioned as well as previous journal articles with similar content.

The papers mentioned above and noted in the table are mainly dailies with a noted business content. A site called Newslink (http://www.newslink.org/) contains links to around 4,000 online newspapers, magazines and other publications, analysed on a geographical and broad subject basis.

The latest development in the news area is in so-called 'news filter' software. This can be set up to filter out stories of particular interest to you. The field is developing quickly and a list of the sources of news filters is available at the Strathclyde site. Some of the leading search engines (see next chapter) now have proprietary filters of this type which will constantly retrieve relevant news and other information. These use sophisticated word searches specified in advance; the user can indicate which of the retrieved information has proved useful, and the filter will automatically refine its future searches accordingly. Yahoo!, InfoSeek and Excite, among others, all operate personalised news filters of this type. The difficulty in using them is achieving precision while at the same time retaining the element of serendipity that comes from more general reading across a variety of investment-related sources.

Another approach is through software such as that developed by the UK company Autonomy Corporation. This is known as 'agentware'. Autonomy has a product, currently undergoing consumer testing, designed to apply this so-called 'intelligent agent' approach on a much broader scale. Details of the product can be found at the Web site http://www.agentware.com, from which the software can also be downloaded.

Using the Web Effectively

Whether you are an Internet enthusiast or not, it has been difficult to avoid becoming aware of the World Wide Web over the last couple of years. It can be a big help to the online investor, but its sheer size can be daunting.

There is a huge volume of commercial and educational content available at Web sites. More important, the medium of hypertext offers an easy way of moving quickly from one document to the next.

The rapid growth of the Web makes its size difficult to pin down. Darryll Mattocks of The Internet Bookshop recently guessed that there were some 24 million Web users and that this number could double inside a year.

Jim Clark of Netscape put those with Internet connections at about 40 million but growing at around 8 per cent per month, while Web users with graphics-based browsers were put at five million and growing at 15 per cent per month. Comparing these two very different figures with those in Chapter 2 shows how difficult it is to establish accurate statistics for Internet and World Wide Web use.

Others try to define the Web in terms of the computers distributing information. According to one estimate there are approaching 300,000 servers connected to the Web: a ratio of one server per 100 users is normally used to determine the size of the user base—which would make the figure 30 million. And each server may be host to several sites and even more pages. Some sources put the number of Web pages also at around the 30 million mark.

It can be assumed that the number of Web sites will grow in tandem with numbers of users, as more and more commercial organisations become aware of the marketing possibilities offered by the Web. And this isn't the end of the content available on the Net. The 17,000 Usenet groups referred to in the previous chapter also contain as many as four million recent articles and comments.

Though all of these figures should be treated with reservations, it is clear that there is plenty of information out there. The task is how to track down exactly what you need.

Fortunately there are some easy ways of taming this profuse content. These will be covered later in this chapter. But first, let's recap on some of the comments made in previous chapters relating to using the Web— including ways of getting connected, using a browser, downloading files, and other techniques.

We'll then go on to look at the characteristics of a typical Web site, how it's financed and the motivations of those operating it, and continue by looking at how to search for Web sites relevant to the topic you wish to cover. We'll also look at some Web sites of general use to the UK online investor and some 'jumping-off points' that can be used to gain quick access to other interesting investment-related sites.

Basics

What Type of Connection?

Earlier we drew the distinction between having a direct connection to the Internet via a no-frills service provider or having a connection via a bulletin board service such as CompuServe, CIX or Delphi. Remember that using a BBS does not preclude you having a direct connection to the Net, although it may cost you more.

Accessing the World Wide Web is possible, at one step removed, using an indirect Net connection. It will involve you using UNIX commands and a text-based browser, normally Lynx. But only by having a direct Internet link (known as a PPP/SLIP connection) can you use a graphics-based browser such as Netscape, Microsoft's Internet Explorer, or Mosaic. Most Web sites can be accessed using a text-based browser, but using Lynx to view a graphics-rich site could be frustrating.

The other key element in getting connected is to use the fastest possible modem. In practical terms for another year or two this means 28,800 bps.

The additional cost over a modem that runs at half the speed is a few tens of pounds, which would be recouped over a comparatively short period in lower telephone charges. Cheap ISDN connections and especially modems linked to cable systems offer the prospect of much faster connections in the future (see Chapter 3).

Which Browser?

The basic choice of browser is now between Netscape and Microsoft's Internet Explorer, although Mosaic does have its enthusiasts. Netscape's overwhelming early lead is now being rapidly eroded by Microsoft, but Navigator is still reckoned to be market leader. Many Web sites are specifically formatted to be compatible with Netscape and with Internet Explorer.

As the first widely distributed browser, Web site proprietors are keen to ensure that their sites are compatible with the most commonly used version of Netscape. At the time of writing this was version 2.01, freely available for downloading from Netscape's own Web site. However, the situation is clearly fluid, given the ease of availability of upgrades, and Microsoft's own initiative in this area.

Some key features that browsers should have are:

❑ the ability to turn off the loading of graphical images if desired to speed up the downloading of particular Web pages
❑ the ability to 'bookmark' favourite sites, to enable their URLs to be retrieved quickly. Bookmarks are particularly useful for sites that have a login and password structure
❑ the ability to move quickly back and forth between sites that have been downloaded previously, and speedy return to the home page
❑ the ability to check email from within the browser. Apart from convenience, this has the advantage that any quoted Web addresses are highlighted automatically as hypertext links.

How to Download Files?

Downloading files is comparatively easy using a browser like Netscape or Internet Explorer. Simply click on the desired piece of hypertext. The browser will then prompt you to save the file to a particular directory, which can be selected using a Windows file manager. It is worthwhile having an empty directory in which to save the file, especially if it comes in zipped format. Unzipping the file in a directory that already contains other items can cause confusion. Once the download is unzipped, the normal procedure is followed to install the file. This will usually be by clicking on a *.exe* or *setup.ini* file.

Some files can be viewed only by using a particular piece of software known as Adobe Acrobat. Acrobat enables the user to read files available in PDF (portable document file) format. The format presents a piece of downloaded text as a replica of the original document. For example the *New York Times* Web site enables the user to download a PDF version of the paper, an exact facsimile of the paper on the newsstand. For online investors Acrobat is also useful for viewing some statistical tables available at stock exchange and other Web sites. The software can be downloaded from the Adobe site at http://www.adobe.com.

Web browsers can't do everything, however; they do have their limitations for downloading files. Web site operators will let users download only the files they want exposed to the outside world. But there are many other sites where files are available. Here, using the UNIX commands described in Chapter 2, you will be able to move around the directories in the public areas of an FTP site and select the files that look promising.

How Web Sites Work

While the Internet may have begun as a co-operative and educational venture, the World Wide Web, best seen as the Internet's commercial offshoot, largely exists to pursue commercial, strategic, and above all profit-oriented goals.

Advertising

A typical commercial Web site may well contain items for sale, and it will often contain advertisements and links to advertisers' own Web pages, where goods and services may be offered for sale.

But the sheer number of Web sites means that each has to offer some unique content to attract visitors and therefore to be able to command good rates for advertising on it.

Popular Web sites will contain banner advertising at the top or the bottom of the page, and smaller online ads known as 'buttons'. The number of 'hits' each page attracts can be measured, as can the percentage of those hits (the 'click', or 'click-through' rate) which result in users accessing the advertisers' pages via the hot links provided.

Because Web sites contain multiple numbers of pages, what has become more important than the hit rate is the number of different pages (or impressions) that are viewed on the site during the course of a typical visit. The most popular pages may then command premium advertising rates, much as would the inside cover or centre-spread of a magazine.

Content

The fact that the Web is a medium in which it is easy to flick back or forward to another page with more interesting content, is another reason that dictates that quality of content is vitally important to the successful promotion of a Web site.

Quality of content does not mean heavy graphics. Indeed, most regular Web users would probably argue the reverse. A picture may be worth a thousand words, but a thousand words will download more quickly. So if a picture takes several minutes to download, the user may get bored in the meantime and move on.

A Web page that has simple graphics, downloads quickly and is well laid out with good content, will attract more users than Web pages that have been over-designed and are hard to get through.

Web site operators are, however, learning as they go along and there have been several instances where sites have been substantially upgraded and improved. So even a poorly designed site that might potentially have interesting information may be worth a repeat visit.

Cost

The cost of creating a simple Web site is negligible, but the point is that if the site is to be a credible one and to attract significant numbers of hits, then its design and layout needs to be good.

The result can be that the costs escalate alarmingly. According to Darryll Mattocks, who founded a site known as The Internet Bookshop (http://www.bookshop.co.uk), the minimum cost for a serious commercial Web site might be in the region of £1.5 million.

Mattocks' experience may be an exception. But consultants who design Web sites charge hefty fees, and space on the large server that might typically house the site will also not come cheap and may escalate according to the number of accesses the site generates. The advantage of connecting to a large server is in the speed at which pages will download to the user, and this is clearly important. Large organisations with big IT departments may, however, find that the process of setting up a Web site is considerably cheaper.

Rather like magazines, Web sites need periodic redesigns and this can add to the cost. Similarly, attention must be paid, particularly by those companies offering products likely to be bought by Net users, to portraying the right image of warmth and efficiency.

If, for instance, email addresses are given at the site and users invited to send messages and queries, then enquiries need to be replied to quickly and efficiently. A poor and inefficient Web site can have a negative impact on corporate image.

Links

Many Web sites have pages containing links to related sites. But remember that in the case of commercial organisations some of these links may have been paid for, rather than selected on their own merits. This is especially true if they are activated from a high-traffic page. Some established sites charge for links at advertising rates comparable to conventional media.

How to Find Web Sites

It is important for the diligent online investor to keep aware through conventional media and other sources, such as relevant newsgroups, of the advent of new Web sites that may be of interest. Their content may have merit, but they may not yet be linked to the more popular high-traffic sites.

Guesswork and deduction are also worth a try at the outset. Most Web addresses begin with the standard http://www prefix. Some omit the www part.

What comes next is where the guesswork comes in. Let's say you are keen to find out if a particular company has a corporate Web site. The domain suffix will narrow the field somewhat: if the company is a US corporation or an international organisation, then it is likely that its domain will be *.com;* if it is a UK company the suffix will probably be *.co.uk.* Hence it is a reasonable deduction that the Microsoft Web site is at http://www.microsoft.com and that Netscape is at http://www.netscape.com and so on.

However, if the address is not 'opened' absolutely correctly then the system is unforgiving and the user will simply receive an error message.

Trying a few slightly different alternatives may produce the right answer, but if these deductions fail the obvious next step is to use one of the several Internet 'search engines'.

Search Engines and How to Use Them

Search engines are sophisticated computer programs accessed via a Web site and used to find Web pages that deal with specific topics.

The term 'search engine' has been somewhat overused: some facilities described as such are mainly indexed lists of sites. These are sometimes called meta-lists. This is not to say that they will not be useful, but bear in mind the limitations they have.

The principle behind a true search engine is that by typing in a word or phrase and initiating the search, all the Web sites that contain that word or phrase can be retrieved and displayed, complete with the relevant hypertext links.

But the process is a haphazard one, and fine-tuning a search to produce a manageable number of correct hits is something of an art.

Search engines also differ in their ease of defining a search. Some offer, for instance a 'quick and dirty' search as an initial foray, which can then be further refined. Others allow search terms to be easily specified with a greater degree of accuracy at the outset, for example by restricting the search to a particular subject area or geographical region.

The key to specifying search criteria lies in the ease with which search 'operators' can be defined. This is not as straightforward as it might seem. It is perhaps simplest to explain why with an example.

Let's say you want to search for any Web sites that mention traded endowment policies. To those not familiar with the term, these are a tax-efficient investment medium offering attractive long-term investment returns. Policies that would be surrendered to the insurance company for a variety of reasons are instead sold to investors through market-makers, the sellers receiving an uplift over the surrender value, and the buyer keeping up the premium payments but reaping the investment returns that accrue at the end of the policy's life.

Simply typing in the words 'traded endowment policies' may retrieve a large number of spurious sites. These could mention, for example, methods of financing further education (another use of the word endowment), mentions of corporate or economic policies (rather than insurance policies), or sites to do with trading stocks and shares (rather than trading policies).

What is required is to be able to specify a particular phrase. And there are a number of conventional ways of going about this.

Putting plus signs between the words may work (words to be excluded from the search can be prefixed with a minus sign). Or a specific phrase may be sought by putting it between quotation marks.

Rather than plus and minus signs, some search engines work via specific words (known as Boolean operators) such as 'and' and 'not'.

Specifying, for example, traded AND endowment AND policies NOT college, may exclude sites that deal with university endowments. Similarly, you might expect that the search would also contain the words 'surrender value', or simply 'surrender', somewhere in the text. So adding 'NEAR surrender' might refine the search even more precisely.

Some search engines give easily selected alternatives explained in plain English. They might, for instance, use pull-down menus to allow you to select words separated by AND, by OR, or to select THIS PHRASE. This will allow the correct Boolean logic to be specified accurately yet easily.

Specifying the search criteria is not the end of the story, however. Another common problem is that a search may retrieve a list of sites that contains large numbers of duplications. Some search engines do remove duplicate sites to some degree, but more often the elimination process needs to be done intuitively simply by looking at the information thrown up in the hit list.

Some search engines perform their searches on the text contained in a particular site, and some merely on the words contained in the title of the site. The former may take a little longer to complete their search, but the results are likely to be better.

Accessing search engines and working out which is best for your purposes can be a tricky process. Those using Netscape can click on the 'net search' button on the browser to get an up-to-date list of search engines.

The home page of your Internet service provider may also have links to search engines. For UK online investors this should contain one or more specific UK sources. There is also a very good Web site—Business Information Sources on the Internet—at the University of Strathclyde (http://www.dis.strath.ac.uk/business/) which also contains a useful list of search engines and indexes, with a brief review of each (see Figure 5.1).

In the course of investigating this subject, I made a list of all the search engines I came across in the space of a few days. The list runs to several

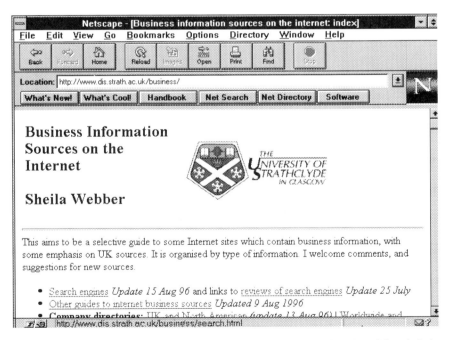

Figure 5.1 Business Information Sources on the Internet at the University of Strathclyde

dozen and is by no means exhaustive. Randy Reddick, an authority on the subject, reckons there are currently over 200 search engines on the Web. Here are some of the commonly used names (placed in alphabetical order):

Accufind
Aliweb
AltaVista
CNet Search
Excite
HotBot
Infoseek
Lycos
McKinley
MetaCrawler
Netfind
Open Text
Point
Savvysearch
Starting Point
Techweb
URL Search
WebCrawler
World Wide Web Worm
WWW Yellow Pages
Yahoo!
. . . and so on.

With this profusion of choice the key may be simply to find search engines with which you become comfortable through frequent use, those which enable searches to be done easily, quickly and precisely, or those which enable several search engines to be canvassed simultaneously.

The following are some brief comments on a few of the more popular ones. Their characteristics are summarised in Table 5.1. The list is far from exhaustive, and new search products are springing up quickly as time goes by. The useful DejaNews service, used for searching Usenet newsgroups for relevant comments, has also not been included here as it was covered in some detail in Chapter 4.

The comments below and in Table 5.1 are my own subjective ones made from the standpoint of a UK online investor.

AltaVista

AltaVista, operated by Digital, claims at the time of writing to offer 31 million pages on 476,000 servers and four million articles from 14,000 Usenet newsgroups as its database. Usenet updates happen in real time. AltaVista is fast, and a quick search may well produce what you are looking for. More advanced searches require correct use of Boolean operators but there is a good help page explaining clearly how to do this. The only slight drawback is that the Web and Usenet cannot be searched at the same time. AltaVista claims currently to get some 23 million accesses per weekday, which speaks for itself. AltaVista now also has a UK access point.

Yahoo!

Yahoo! is a large-scale index which has a search facility. The search facility extends to category titles and comments on sites only. For quick location of a large site this may be the easiest way to proceed. Boolean operators can be specified easily using simple checkboxes. Searches of the database can be narrowed down by subject or region to produce more precise results. Yahoo! is also now offering its users embedded links to Alta Vista, enabling broader-scale Web searches to be conducted. Yahoo! has a UK-based clone, accessible at http://www.yahoo.co.uk.

InfoSeek

InfoSeek is something of a hybrid too, but hitherto has had more emphasis on comprehensive searchability than Yahoo!. I have found it easy to use and the intuitive specifying of key words and phrases seems automatically to produce the desired result without undue fiddling around to specify exact operators. Regular users suggest that putting the terms required in [ ] will achieve the effect of the Boolean AND operator. A useful adjunct is a link to a searchable index of email addresses at http://www.whowhere.com.

Table 5.1 Basic search engine characteristics

	Open text	Yahoo!	AltaVista	InfoSeek	Lycos	WebCrawler
URL: http://	index.opentext.net	www.yahoo.com	www. altavista. digital.com	www2.infoseek.com	www.lycos.com	www.webcrawler.com
Operator	Opentext Corporation	Yahoo!	DEC	InfoSeek	Carnegie Mellon	AOL
Search/index	Search (simple and complex)	Searchable index	Search (simple and complex)	Hybrid	Both. Simple/ enhanced search	Both. Simple/ enhanced search
Open text/title	OT—any/all of 3 words/phrases	Category titles/ comments	OT or title if preferred	OT	OT	OT
Defining terms	Easy	Easy	Harder in advanced mode	Easy	Easy in enhanced mode	Conventional/ averagely easy
Geographical search	No	Yes	No	Can specify to some extent	No	No, but some enhancements
Topic search	No (except in search term)	Yes	No	Can specify to some extent	No	No, but some enhancements
Overview	Slightly quirky	Good starting point	Big, fast and comprehensive	Versatile, easy to refine	Comprehensive description of hits; fast returns	Good-looking; interesting features; fast

Lycos

Lycos, the self-styled 'Catalog of the Internet' was developed at Carnegie Mellon University. There is both a simple and enhanced search mode, with the option of defining how the hit list of results is to be displayed. Operators can easily be specified in the enhanced mode of searching and the system appears to produce comprehensive and rapid results. The claim is that more than 90 per cent of Web sites are indexed. Items indexed include titles, headings and subheadings, the first 20 lines of the document, and the 100 most significant words. Lycos also owns Point, an organisation which produces ratings of Web sites.

Opentext

As might be assumed, Opentext performs open-text searching of Web sites in both simple and advanced modes. It claims to index some 10 billion words. Considerable precision is possible in the advanced mode, with easy specification of quite subtle Boolean concepts, and ranking of results by occurrence. None the less, the system produces slightly quirky results, although there is good on-screen help.

WebCrawler

This was first developed at the University of Washington, but is now owned by America On Line (AOL). WebCrawler was the first full text search engine and the first I used on a regular basis, mainly because of its ease of use. It has simple and advanced search modes and offers the opportunity of browsing an index of popular categories. When a user identifies a Web site that looks interesting, the software prompts 'get more like this'—which can be helpful. Conventional Boolean operators are used and coverage is claimed to be especially broad, albeit at the expense of some precision. Some experts think WebCrawler is good for a quick search for a top level Web page. About 100,000 Web sites are indexed.

These brief comments display the ample choice offered by different search engines. Only familiarity and regular use can really produce the result that is right for you. There are some specific UK-related search tools, but several of the search engines listed above are good performers when it comes to identifying relevant UK-related pages from specific searches.

Meta-search Engines

The best type of search engine, however, is the one that searches several search tools simultaneously and produces a consolidated list of hits, with—as far as possible—duplications removed. These are known as meta-search engines.

There are two obvious contenders here: MetaCrawler and Savvysearch.

MetaCrawler can be found at http://www.metacrawler.com (see Figure 5.2). It was developed at the University of Washington. The interface allows an accurate specification of the search to be made easily, while the enquiry can also be limited by region, by domain, and by various other filtering criteria.

Figure 5.2   The MetaCrawler meta-search engine

The list of hits obtained from all the leading search engines are collated into a single list with duplications removed, and then displayed (as far as is practicable) on a single page. There is also the option to choose between a quick and comprehensive search.

Savvysearch, located at the University of Colorado, operates slightly differently. While the list of search engines potentially contactable is broader, this program searches only those deemed most likely to produce results. The system defaults to providing the results engine by engine, although a consolidated hit list is accessible. Savvysearch is accessible at http://www.cs.colostate.edu/~dreiling/smartform.html, an unwieldy URL that is best bookmarked.

As a way of comparing the respective merits of the various search engines these meta-search tools access, Table 5.2 shows the number of hits assembled by each respective search engine for a series of search tasks relevant to a UK online investor. Searches can be defined in terms of domain, strength of 'match' retrieved, and also in terms of the time the meta-search tool is allowed to take to complete its task.

The table shows the results of searches performed using a mixture of different words, including the 'traded endowments' example explored earlier, several company names both large and small, a reference to UK accounting standards, the CRESTCo settlement organisation, and the UK's Alternative Investment Market (AIM). Several searches, such as Chelsfield and CRESTCo and AIM, were restricted to UK only, some were performed on the basis of finding a medium match, and others on the basis of a strong match.

MetaCrawler appears to be programmed to seek the best 10 hits from each search engine it tries, but the relevance of hits is hard to gauge. Many hits will be duplicated. MetaCrawler automatically removes the duplication and presents a consolidated list.

While it is difficult to make concrete recommendations on the basis of so imprecise a trial, from the standpoint of the UK online investor AltaVista and Excite appear to come out as the best to use. On the other hand, there is little to be lost from conducting any search using a meta-search tool, since arguably one gets the best of both worlds.

Individual search engines may, however, be quicker and allow more precise specification of search criteria than is possible on the somewhat blunter meta-searcher.

The other lesson is that the more unusual and less generic the search term sought, the more relevant will tend to be the results. The most

Table 5.2 Comparison of search engine performance using MetaCrawler (Number of hits)

Search terms	Traded endowments	Foreign & Colonial IT	Chelsfield	BAT Industries	CRESTCo	UK Accounting Standards	AIM Market	Dixons Group
Yahoo!	1	0	0	14	0	2	0	0
Lycos	2	0	10	5	6	0	10	3
Open Text	5	0	2	6	0	1	0	0
Excite	9	10	7	10	1	10	10	10
InfoSeek	10	1	4	10	0	0	1	4
AltaVista	10	10	10	10	6	7	1	10
Inktomi/Hot Bot	10	10	2	10	0	10	10	10
Galaxy	0	0	0	0	0	0	0	0
WebCrawler	7	10	0	6	0	0	10	2
Total (excl. duplications)	48	7	25	65	10	5	40	18
Relevance of hits	Most relevant	Most relevant	Most relevant	Part relevant	All relevant	None relevant	Few relevant	Part relevant
Basis of search	Unrestricted Medium match	Unrestricted Medium match	UK only Strong match	Unrestricted Medium match	UK only Strong match	Unrestricted Medium match	UK only Strong match	UK only Strong match

accurate hit list of the group was for CRESTCo, with its unusual mixture of upper and lower case spelling, while 'traded endowments' also scored well.

There are other meta-search engines available including IBM info-Market, as well as special purposes search tools such as DejaNews and an MIT-developed search engine that derives email addresses from messages posted to Usenet. Other search engines can be found that are specific to single countries.

In the case of the UK the choice is not huge. UK Index (http://www.ukindex.co.uk) is essentially a searchable index rather than a true document search, although the search can be narrowed down to specific areas and operators are easy to specify. At the time of writing it appeared to lack the critical mass possessed by the search engines described previously, although it may be useful for finding information that is peculiarly British and therefore less likely to be found by broader-based tools.

Lastly, it is worth noting the availability of some sites that are collections of search engines, enabling access to a choice of searchable resources on various topics. One of the best of these is Internet Sleuth, located at http://www.isleuth.com.

Internet Sleuth claims to have over 1,000 different searchable databases. Some are devoted to business, finance and investment. These databases tend, however, often to have a US orientation.

Jumping-off Points

In a slightly different category are what can be termed 'jumping-off points'. These are not really search engines, but sites that represent a good point to begin a search for information because of the large numbers of related links assembled in one place.

Some well-known indexes, such as Yahoo!, really fall into this category. But there are also a number of sites that are of specific interest to UK online investors and which have good links to a range of investment related information.

Business Information on the Internet

A good starting point mentioned previously is this University of Strathclyde site. This is organised in a number of broad categories including, for instance, search tools and lists of business information sources, directories and lists of commercial sites, company profiles and financial information, country information, statistics and economic information, news sources and so on.

Taking the link to company profiles and financial information as an example, this section contains links to commercial providers of information such as FT Profile, and also to free sources such as EDGAR, the database of SEC filings on US listed companies, the Fortune 500 and Global 500 databases, which are searchable, information on companies in Scandinavia and Eastern Europe, and many other links.

The section on market, statistical and economic information contains a variety of links, including one to the UK government statistics database.

The 'directories' link is mainly taken up with US-oriented material, but also gives links to other sites including the only UK-specific Web site database and an Internet version of BT's Yellow Pages.

UK Web Directory

The UK Web Directory, located at http://www.ukdirectory.com, is a collection of Web sites which at the time of writing numbered 9,000. It claims to list all UK Web sites, and the site indexes all the conceivable interests it thinks UK surfers might have. It is not just business and finance-related, but it has specific links to business and finance topics as well as to government-related pages and others that online investors might find interesting.

Following the 'finance' link brings up a list of sites broadly grouped into banks, finance, and insurance. The finance link takes in investment related topics and connects to a number of useful sites. These include those operated by the AITC, Electronic Share Information, and several stockbrokers and investment exchanges. The overwhelming impression is, however, one of an orientation towards accounting and personal finance information. It is, none the less a good starting point.

Interactive Internet Investor

The Interactive Internet Investor site (http://www.iii.co.uk) has an extensive range of information of use to UK investors. It includes in particular a searchable database of unit and investment trusts including performance figures from Micropal, data from leading personal finance and investment management product providers such as M&G, Gartmore, and Fidelity, and a searchable index of articles from specific personal finance publications.

Moneyworld

This is also a good source of personal finance information and share prices for the UK online investor. The URL is http://www.moneyworld.co.uk. Sections include financial contacts, news, a daily business report, easy-to-understand guides, a UK personal finance directory, mortgages, savings products, rates and performance, and a glossary.

The 'financial contacts' section includes links to investment trust managers, insurance companies, unit trust managers, traded endowment policy market-makers, independent financial advisors, stockbrokers (including a clickable map to locate a stockbroker near you), telephone banking operators, and financial regulators.

The 'news' section includes a selection of personal finance-oriented stories updated regularly. It does not, however, contain news stories updated during the day and therefore cannot be considered a substitute for the services mentioned in Chapter 4. The 'daily business report' is a retrospective look at the UK market and closing numbers from other markets.

The 'guides' section contains articles on a selection of investment topics including bonds, derivatives, ethical investment, personal loans and so on.

The 'directory' section has a conveniently indexed collection of links to various sites of relevance to UK investors, including links to accountants, cash card services, commodities, derivatives, financial publications, offshore centres, brokers and fund managers, venture capital, and world stock markets.

The latter subgroup is a list of links to various world markets, indexed geographically. Price data on Moneyworld, arranged via a link to DBC Signal, has an interesting sideline. There are 15-minute delayed quotes available in the afternoon for UK stocks quoted on Wall Street and for the constituents of the Dow Jones Index. Normal UK intra-day prices may be added soon.

Both Interactive Internet Investor and Moneyworld will be looked at in more detail in Chapter 10, on personal finance aspects of the net.

Moneyweb

This is another personal finance-related site (at http://www.moneyweb.co.uk) containing links to a variety of articles on personal finance topics. There is more emphasis in this site on patient explanation of personal finance concepts, and fewer comprehensive links to other investment-related sites. The site is quirky, idiosyncratic and informative. The pages also include details of the *finservuk* discussion list.

Qualisteam

A useful jumping-off point with a European rather than US orientation is Qualisteam (http://www.qualisteam.com). This is a French site which has specific and comprehensive links to a range of banks, brokers, and exchanges around Europe and elsewhere. Qualisteam claims to have links to 95 per cent of banking Web sites worldwide, more than 1,000 in all, and to the stock markets of over 65 countries (see Figure 5.3).

It has an alphabetical index of all its links, 1,400 in all, as well as having sections on news-related Web sites and links relating to electronic cash and other Internet issues. This is a substantial resource and one which can provide many links to a range of different organisations. The site also includes an active finance-related bulletin board.

Lenape Investment Corporation

Richard Sauers of Lenape Investment Corporation, a US firm, has compiled an exhaustive list of sites of interest to investors. The site can be accessed at the URL http://www.enter.net/~rsauers/ where the abbreviated latest edition of his regularly published sourcebook is available in both text and hypertext mark-up format, the advantage of the latter being that links to the sites are automatically present in the text.

The links displayed in the site are indexed by the first letter of the second part of the URL (after the http://www. prefix), and a brief description is given. A more detailed classified list is produced in hard copy format at prices (for non-US residents) upwards of $16 plus post and packing.

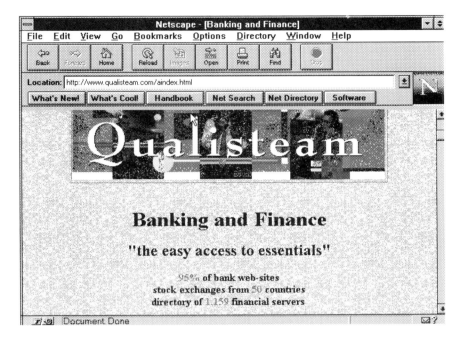

Figure 5.3 Qualisteam—a useful jumping-off point

Other Jumping-off Points

Global Trader at http://www.bluewave.co.uk/globaltrader has a comprehensive collection of links in a 'frames' site that is slightly hampered by fussy graphics.

Finance Online (http://finance-online.com) claims around 2,000 financial links, subdivided into broad categories, including quote servers and software download sites.

The so-called Financial Information Network (http://www.finetwork.com) has a limited set of US-oriented links.

Lastly, Investorama (http://www.investorama.com) has a well-ordered directory of links to a variety of different resources as well as a section specifically devoted to investment-related jumping-off points.

You can see that there are a number of ways in which the Web's mass of content can be tamed by intelligent searching and by 'bookmarking' a specific number of jumping-off sites that contain material that may be used regularly.

My own list of bookmarks, for instance, contains a number of news-related sites (the *FT*, the *Electronic Telegraph*, *The Times*) as well as Reuters. I also bookmark jump-off points such as the Strathclyde, Lenape, Moneyworld and Investorama sites plus the search engines I particularly favour (such as DejaNews and MetaCrawler). With these, most relevant general investment related sites on the Web are only a few mouse clicks away.

This list does not constitute a recommendation, since each online investor will have different requirements and interests. Only by experimenting can you really determine which sites may or may not be useful. Above all, it is necessary to be honest about how much use you might get from a particular site, and periodically to prune bookmarks that have not proved to be particularly well used.

Once a company has been investigated using some of the search techniques available, and you have decided it is right to buy the shares, the next question is whether it is desirable or necessary to conduct the transaction online, and how to go about it.

The subject of online dealing and related issues will be explored in the next chapter.

CHAPTER 6

Dealing Online

Until recently, all stock market dealing was conducted on the basis of personal contact. A client would instruct the broker to buy or sell some shares, by letter or by telephone. The broker's dealer would then go on to the Stock Exchange floor and deal face-to-face with a jobber, the wholesaler of shares, at the best price available.

Very often a wealthy client would meet the broker face-to-face, perhaps over a City lunch table, to review shareholdings and plan a dealing strategy for the following few months.

This system changed in 1986 in the Stock Exchange's so-called Big Bang. Dealing migrated from the Stock Exchange floor to large dealing rooms and trades were conducted over the telephone with electronic displays giving price information.

Floor trading continues in many markets. London's futures exchange (LIFFE) is one example, as is the New York Stock Exchange. But in many financial centres, electronic trading has all but replaced face-to-face contact.

There are many reasons for this change. One is cost. Electronic networks, once set up, are cheaper to run.

In many markets, electronics allows deals to take place in comparative anonymity. With the old method of trading, a dealer would scurry around a crowded market floor to check a price with a number of different jobbers (now called market-makers) to ensure that the best price was obtained. An order being entered over a screen has less impact on the market than a dealer from a large broker checking a particular share price prior to dealing. Electronics can also permit the process of price setting to be conducted automatically, with a computer setting the price that best accommodates the highest numbers of bids and offers entered for a particular share.

This is known as 'order driven' trading, distinct from the 'quote driven' system of competing market-makers for each individual share. Its introduction in London has been the source of some controversy, with objections from market-makers, whose livelihood it threatens.

The Stock Exchange authorities in London spent a long time attempting to arrive at a solution which best accommodated the interests of all parties, although only time will tell whether the system, introduced in August 1997, will prove workable, or whether compromises have left it flawed.

Aside from this aspect of electronic markets, large market-makers and the brokers who trade with them have developed a system whereby orders received from small investors can be transacted automatically at the best price available. This is clearly advantageous to all concerned. Investors are guaranteed 'best execution'—still a fundamental principle of most major exchanges—while the Stock Exchange firms concerned are spared the labour-intensive process of dealing with a large number of small orders.

Once this system of automated order execution developed—not only in the UK, but also in the USA and other advanced markets—it allowed a new category of broker to develop: one who could site his or her premises in a low-cost area and offer a no-frills dealing service to clients.

Which Broker?

Private investors can go to brokers who offer to take a client's existing investment portfolio and look after it without the client having to make any investment decisions at all.

This type of broking service, known as a discretionary account, in effect makes the broker the individual's personal fund manager and is only really economic for wealthy individuals with large portfolios. In this instance deals are done by the broker and the client is informed about them some time later. Clearly the onus is on the broker to perform well and 'beat the market'.

While the broker would once normally be rewarded in the form of commission, in the case of many discretionary accounts the broker is now paid a percentage annual fee, which rises as the value of the portfolio grows.

For many individuals a discretionary broking account is either too expensive, or the antithesis of what investment is all about.

Those with a limited amount of money to invest who do not want the bother of picking investments can always buy a unit trust. Some are indexed to the market, removing the risk that particular share selections will underperform the index. Funds are also available that are insulated against any drop in the market and will capture a certain percentage of any upward move in the index. These can be a good option for investors whose priority is preservation of capital.

Those investors who want to make their own investment decisions, picking shares they like the look of and deciding when to buy or sell, have two alternatives when it comes to choosing a broker. These boil down to whether or not the individual concerned wants investment advice or not.

Many brokers offer a 'portfolio advice' service. The client retains the final say over what to buy and sell and when, but may ask the broker for advice about a particular course of action, or ask his or her opinion about a particular share or other investment. At the up-market end of the scale the service can include advice about the client's tax position and other relevant matters, but more often than not the service is based on an exchange of ideas between the client and the individual broker servicing the client's account.

The broker makes money out of dealing commission from the client's orders and from fees charged for additional services such as portfolio valuations and the like. The service the client gets will depend to a degree on the frequency with which deals are done.

The most recent innovation, however, has been the advent of execution-only broking. This means that the client is not offered any advice (execution-only brokers are prohibited by City regulations from offering advice of any description), and the broker will simply transact an order without question at the best possible price.

The quid pro quo for the lack of advice is that commission charges will typically be much lower than the dealing-with-advice or the discretionary service. Charges are kept low because of the high-tech systems at the heart of the execution-only brokers' operations, which route calls to a team of dealers, who can then deal electronically using the order-execution systems operated by market-makers.

Administration is also kept streamlined. Many execution-only brokers insist that clients keep their shares in a nominee account and link their purchases and sales to a high interest cash management account. This account can simply be debited when a purchase is made and credited with sale proceeds—without the need for cheques to flow back and forth. The advent of the CREST electronic settlement regime is also tailor-made for a system of this type.

But the real push behind the establishment of execution-only broking services came in the 1980s with the plethora of privatisation issues. These left many individuals with small parcels of shares. Often they had not dealt with a stockbroker before. Brokers competed to sell these shares in the hope that the individuals concerned would stick with the investing habit and become regular clients.

In many instances this proved a vain hope. None the less, many regular investors who might previously have dealt through a higher-cost dealing-with-advice broker discovered that execution-only services offered a way of cutting their dealing costs. This was provided they were independent-minded enough to make their own decisions and research their own shares.

Seeing the advent and success of execution-only firms, led by ShareLink and quickly followed by Fidelity Brokerage, many other brokers—offering a range of other services to their clients—have since also begun offering an execution-only service as an option.

Why Deal Online?

The real point about the development of execution-only broking is that it is tailor-made for online dealing. While most of the point of having an account with a full-service firm is conversing with the broker, exchanging ideas and advice, for the execution-only client this is not the case. Here, communication between client and broker is restricted to giving an order and having it confirmed that the transaction has been done at a particular price. Human intervention in this process is not essential.

Although in my experience most staff at execution-only brokers are sympathetic and patient with clients who may not be fully conversant with Stock Exchange jargon and the intricacies of dealing, some people—particularly those who deal infrequently—find calling up a broker a forbidding prospect. Others are irritated by the fact that calling up the broker may result in the call being held in a queue until a dealer is available.

This scenario adds to the pressure on the client. Having got through to an obviously very busy dealer, originally intending simply to ask a price, the client may feel some obligation to deal anyway. This is not conducive to good investment decision making. A client should feel able to deal only when required, and the process of dealing (sometimes characterised as the glamorous part of investing) should in fact be reduced to the status of a functional transaction, no more or no less significant than ringing up a cinema box office to book a couple of tickets for Saturday night.

The most important part of the investment decision is deciding which share to buy and when. The act of placing the order should be simple and quick, and is not the end in itself.

This being the case, any execution-only broking client ought to consider the possibility of transmitting orders to and receiving dealing confirmations from the broker by electronic means, as an alternative to the disembodied voice of the dealer on the phone.

Later we will look at the alternatives currently on offer for electronic dealing through a UK broker. But let's look first at some of the points that need to be established at the outset.

These can be summarised as follows:

❒ You need to be comfortable making your own investment decisions without the benefit of any advice or research from the broker.

❒ To use electronic order inputting software, you need to be familiar with normal dealing vocabulary. For instance, the software may offer the opportunity to input orders either 'at best' (the best price then ruling), 'limit' orders (where you specify a limit above which a purchase or below which a sale will not take place), and orders which are 'good for the day', or 'good until cancelled'.

❒ Shop around. Investigate whether software or other facilities are provided as part of the online trading service, and whether commission charges are competitive. Brokers who offer online accounts ought by rights to charge less than they would for a telephone-based service, since there is less (costly) human intervention involved. But this principle has yet to be firmly established.

❐ Establish at the outset whether order confirmation is received while online, or whether you might have to wait for a subsequent email message to provide information that it has been completed. Brokers differ in this respect.

❐ Make sure the service you choose offers the ability to check the current best bid and offer prices prior to an order being entered. The ability to check your portfolio's value, and the amount of unused cash in the account, is also handy.

❐ Security is also a vital concern of many contemplating online trading for the first time. Does the service transmit orders over the World Wide Web, or is it based on a private network? How good is the password protection and encryption? Can orders be sent in secure mode from a browser? Security issues can be overstated but in view of the sums involved you may wish to have the reassurance that access to your investments is secure.

❐ Online dealing services in the UK are at present confined to brokers which already offer telephone based execution-only services. At the time of writing, and unlike in the US, there are no purely online brokers. If going electronic entails a change of broker, make sure first that the dealing and administration service being offered is at least as efficient as the one operated in the conventional way by your existing broker. If, for example, you are happy with your existing execution-only service, it may be better to wait until your broker offers online trading as an option, rather than switch to another's electronic service whose dealing and administration is an unknown quantity.

Later we'll look at how the services currently on offer in the UK stack up. First, though, since this innovation in the sphere of online trading originated in the USA, we'll check on how services have developed there, what type of product is typically offered by US online brokers, and how much it costs.

The US Experience

Click on the appropriate page in Yahoo!'s Business and Economy/ Investing index and you find a list which, when printed off, is about five pages long. This gives some indication of the number of brokers that have a presence on the World Wide Web.

Some of these brokers have established a Web presence as an advertisement for, or a precursor to offering online order execution. But in most cases these sites are simply cyberspace commercials advertising the more mundane services they offer investors.

There are about five or six prominent US brokers offering online trading at present, including one, E*Trade, which trades only this way (see Figure 6.1 for E*Trade's home page). The others are established discount or execution-only brokers which see online order entry as simply another way of tapping into their customer base while at the same time paring their administration costs.

Electronic trading of this type is not new. Large broking firms servicing the institutional market have offered their clients the option of dealing electronically for some time, either over a proprietary network or using the widely diffused networks of third parties, notably information providers such as Bloomberg, Telerate and Reuters.

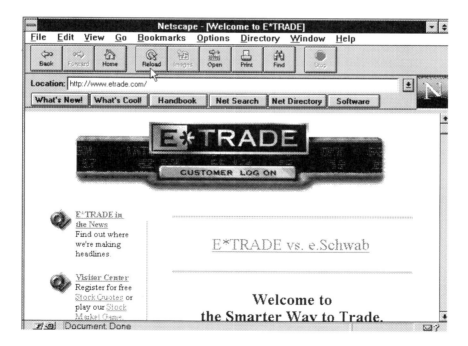

Figure 6.1   E*Trade's home page

Now, the online broking revolution has reached the ordinary investor. In the USA it is reckoned that approaching 500,000 individual investors now have online dealing accounts, a number that is growing in leaps and bounds.

PC Financial Network, a subsidiary of the Wall Street firm Donaldson Lufkin & Jenrette, is generally thought to be the biggest with around 150,000 online accounts, aided by its initial link-ups with the bulletin board services operated by Prodigy and AOL.

Charles Schwab, the big US firm which also owns the UK's ShareLink, has over 100,000 customers for its online StreetSmart service. Other players include Fidelity, which also has a presence in the UK, Quick & Reilly, E*Trade, Accutrade, National Discount Brokers, and Lombard.

Yahoo! also lists CompuTel Securities, Ceres Securities, eBroker, Jack White & Company, and Aufhauser among those offering an online trading services.

One lesson of the US experience is that competition is likely to drive down dealing costs as the online trading habit expands. Since the essence of the services is that the customer can in effect tap directly into the automated execution services used by the brokers themselves, the broker becomes no more than a conduit for orders, and a site for processing bargains and ensuring that trades are settled correctly.

The corollary—one that will hold good in the UK too—is that the marginal cost to the broker of doing the trade is extremely low. No highly paid dealers need be involved, and the charge to the investor can in theory just represent the cost of processing and settling a trade, moving cash and stock back and forth, plus a profit margin on top. Indeed, price cutting has recently become a more prominent feature of the online dealing scene.

The more subtle question is whether this is the type of service that should be bought solely on the basis of price. Seeing the downward pressure on commissions that the electronic era brings with it, many execution-only services have tried to add value to the package they offer by bundling in information services, either free or at a discounted price. They fall short of offering advice, but represent useful information for which the investor might otherwise have to pay a full price.

Schwab's Street Smart package, as well as including access to account information, price quotes, and search facilities, also includes an hour's free time on Dow Jones News Retrieval, an hour's free use of S&P Marketscope, a free one month's subscription to Reuters Money Network, and other products.

The US service from Fidelity, known as FOX (Fidelity Online Xpress) includes an investment software package, free real-time quotes on stocks and options and mutual funds (unit trusts), and some fundamental company research and technical analysis.

Quick & Reilly has over 100 offices throughout America and operates a no-frills service and deeply discounted commissions. It is claimed that charges can be as little as 30 per cent of brokers such as Schwab or Fidelity that are generally catering to the more affluent investor. Q&R's online service offers quotes, electronic order entry, account monitoring, plus a free bank account.

For those investors that have developed other ways of accessing fundamental and technical information on the shares they wish to invest in, and therefore simply require a standard, no-frills dealing facility, the Quick & Reilly package works well.

E*Trade is perhaps the most interesting phenomenon of all. The firm is based in Palo Alto, California, in Silicon Valley. It began life not as a broker but as an electronics firm designing systems for other brokers, including Schwab and Fidelity. Its Web site at http://www.e-trade.com offers background on the company, share and mutual fund prices, links to other relevant Web sites, details of how to open an account and place an order, an electronic investment game, and information on its commission structure.

The service also offers context-sensitive news retrieval. Those interested in a particular stock can click a button for the latest news on it. A passive email list keeps account holders up to date with developments at the site.

This effort has been rewarded by substantial numbers of customers—so much so that from time to time there have been complaints that the site is hard to access, growing pains that are likely to be quickly rectified. The plus point is that many of E*Trade's customers are highly educated, above-average income earners, and (most important of all) active traders.

Table 6.1 gives a brief comparison of the services offered by leading US discount brokers, and Table 6.2 notes the commission charges of different brokers.

It is unlikely that the online revolution will stay confined to the USA for long. There are already several examples of brokers outside the USA with a Web presence, although few of these as yet appear to offer full online trading.

Table 6.1 US online brokers and their services

	Fidelity	Aufhauser	E*Trade	Quick & Reilly	Lombard	NDB	Schwab
URL: http://www. …	fid-inv.com	aufhauser.com	etrade.com	quick-reilly.com	lombard.com	pawws.secapl.com/ndb	schwab.com
Graphics content	Low	Low	Low	Medium/heavy	Low	Low	Medium/heavy
Regn/login required?	No	Yes	Yes for part	No	Yes	Yes	No
Nature of content	Broking a/cs; comm. rates; information, automated services; S&P research	One page only; restricted access to rest of site	Trading demo; technical information; comm. rates; a/c opening; visitor centre	Background news; chairman's message; a/c opening	Limited information on comm. rates; demo; information on company	News; comm. rates; price comparison; calculator	What's new; software; investment tools service; a/c opening
Links to other sites	No	No	No	No	Yes	No	Yes
Overall rating for online investors (1 = poor, 10 = good)	6	3	6	7	7	7	7

Table 6.2 Comparison of Commission Charges*

	100 shares @ $10	500 shares @ $15	1,000 shares @ $20
NDB	28.00	28.00	28.00
Lombard	36.50	36.50	36.50
Q&R	37.50	69.98	98.10
PCFN	40.00	80.00	110.00
FOX	41.85	90.90	129.15
Schwab	42.30	91.35	129.60
Accutrade	48.00	48.00	48.00

* Correct at time of writing

None the less, brokers with sufficient interest to build and operate a Web site include several firms in Canada, and ones in countries as diverse as Russia, Greece and Sweden. There are also several in Britain, and we go on next to look at the state of the online trading revolution in the UK, and where it might go from here.

Online Trading in the UK—the ESI Story

It is often the case that what takes place in the USA will happen in the UK five years later, and this looks like being the case with online dealing. Execution-only broking was a US idea that caught on in a big way in the UK after being extensively developed on the other side of the Atlantic. Online trading is its natural extension.

It also has an additional selling point to offer in the UK. Here, stock-broking, and dealing, was once regarded as the preserve of the affluent middle and upper classes.

Since almost everything in Britain is deemed to have something to do with social class, it would be unrealistic to expect this attitude to disappear overnight. But the advent of ShareLink and other execution-only services in the past 10 years or so has done a lot to democratise and demystify the process of share dealing.

It is natural therefore to expect companies such as ShareLink to have been in the forefront of moves to introduce online trading to UK investors. The problem within the UK has lain, however, in the vested interests of more conventional Stock Exchange firms and in the conservatism of the London Stock Exchange itself.

The reason is simple. In the 10 years or so since Big Bang, the Stock Exchange has been struggling to find itself a new role, and to preserve as much as possible of its old one. It has been singularly unsuccessful. Its role as market regulator was subsumed into the Securities and Futures Authority (SFA) and the Securities and Investments Board (SIB), its role as a standard-setting and examining body into the Securities Institute, its role as a disseminator of price display hardware and software into firms such as Reuters and ICV, and its role in settlement, after the TAURUS debacle, into CRESTCo.

The Stock Exchange does, however, still have an unofficial policing role, attempting to detect instances of insider dealing. It also controls the admission of shares to listings, and it controls the dissemination of raw price data input by its member firms. It was in the latter area that a major showdown between the old and the new era occurred.

Electronic Share Information (ESI) is a comparatively young company set up by Herman Hauser, the entrepreneur behind the founding of Acorn Computer. Its mission has been to allow its users access to share price information and other company information via the World Wide Web (http://www.esi.co.uk) and to provide the links to brokers to allow its subscribers to transact orders electronically. It offered the first online dealing service in UK stocks for private investors.

The Stock Exchange's well-chronicled objections to the ESI service did not lie in its making available electronic trading to the private client, but in the way in which ESI was disseminating price information. The Exchange withdrew permission for the company to distribute live price information over the Internet two days before the launch of the service.

In the event, the threat was withdrawn soon after, at the cost of some embarrassment to the Exchange who, though it clearly feared that the system might be used as a way for some ingenious individuals to obtain expensive share price information on the cheap, failed to understand precisely how the service might be used by individual investors.

Most investors understandably want access to a dealing price before inputting a trade. In other respects, and in its most basic form, the ESI service, in terms of the price information offered, is similar to teletext services. More expensive subscriptions (£20 per month for the top-end Silver service) offer unlimited checking of live prices for a selected portfolio of shares.

From the dealing standpoint, though, how does the ESI service work? The key is an electronic gateway to ShareLink. To use the service you must previously have opened a ShareLink Marketmaster account. This is a trading account linked to a cash management facility with a leading high street bank. The system is password protected and, once the account has been approved, orders are routed via your browser's secure mode. The encryption involved in passing information across the Net in this way is many times that of the security systems used by the Stock Exchange to transmit price information to its member firms and data vendors.

ShareLink's service, accessed through the World Wide Web in this way, is virtually identical to that used by its telephone clients. In other words, rather than speaking to a ShareLink order-taker and giving an order over the phone, it is simply placed electronically. The system allows for an order to be checked before it is sent. Instead of receiving a verbal confirmation, email notification is sent to the user that the deal has been transacted.

ShareLink guarantees that an order will be completed within the hour, and normally much more quickly. Once the order has been confirmed the system automatically updates the portfolio details stored in the user's account.

Innovative though it may have been, the service is not particularly cheap. On top of the ESI joining fee and monthly subscription, the Marketmaster account operates on the basis of £10 minimum and £50 maximum commission plus a £6 per quarter administration fee. There is now a £15 flat rate commission for frequent traders.

The service is OK as far as it goes, but it does have some of the drawbacks that the ShareLink service has always possessed, notably the lack of instantaneous confirmation that an order has been transacted. ESI is, however, using the power of its growing user base—now estimated to be 26,000 strong—to pull in other information services which make its package more attractive.

At first the ability to download full market prices over the Net for a comparatively modest monthly charge was regarded by many investors as highly attractive in its own right. But recent changes to the pricing structure of the service means that this is no longer included as part of the main service and requires an extra subscription.

Additional information provided includes Extel news headlines. Links are also provided to software short-cuts to make downloading share prices into a variety of proprietary chart packages relatively easy.

Details of ESI's services and tariffs are available from its Web pages. The Scottish-based execution-only broker Stocktrade has also recently become accessible through the ESI trading gateway. Similar conditions apply.

Other UK Online Dealing Services

Pure deep-discount electronic brokerage has yet to appear in the UK and it may be that the ingrained habits of the British investor prevent it developing for some time.

The other online services currently operating or about to be launched (at the time of writing in early 1997) include services from Infotrade and Fidelity Brokerage.

Infotrade

Infotrade is an online information and dealing package developed specifically for the personal finance market and backed by Mitsubishi Electric. Its home page is shown in Figure 6.2. The service is gradually being enhanced but the idea is an attractive one. It offers the integrated provision of technical and fundamental information on companies, as well as access to online trading through a choice of (at present three) brokers.

The service does not operate over the Internet or World Wide Web, but via direct dial-up. Initial data and software is provided on CD-ROM and then updated via regular online downloads. There is an initial cost for the software (around £70), a £25 connection fee and then a subscription of £10 a month for the regular service. An enhanced service (at £12 a month) is also offered. This provides price updates in the evening rather than after midnight, but in all other respects the service provision is the same.

The service offers Internet email, online customer support, the last three years' abbreviated company results for every listed company, as well as a basic activities description. In addition there is information on directors' dealings, corporate actions, broker forecasts, closing prices, *FT* headlines, a two-year share price history, a basic charting module, and online trading. Pay as you go services include *Financial Times* news stories, brief details on companies from the Hambro Company Guide, real-time prices and electronic Extel cards.

This is pretty attractive for those who want the convenience of all the information in one central source. The software is also intelligent enough to make accessing all the relevant information intuitively very easy. The main drawback being that the charting module is basic, and certainly would not suffice for those accustomed to more sophisticated systems.

Take-up of the service has been slow, partly perhaps because of the need for users to have a CD-ROM drive for the initial loading of

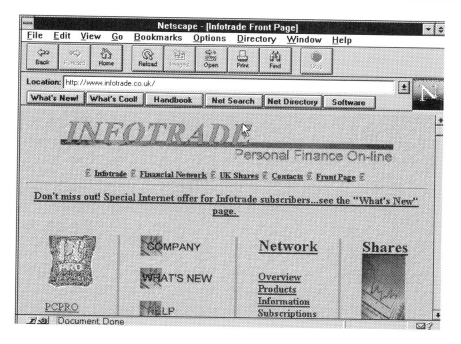

Figure 6.2 Infotrade's home page

information. This will be less of an objection as time goes by. But a more fundamental problem is that much of the information (the *Hambro Company Guide*, news headlines and so on), are already available from other Web-related sources. The cost-effectiveness of the product therefore diminishes somewhat for those with an existing Internet connection.

The system is likely, however, to be steadily enhanced. Current plans, for example, call for the introduction of other personal finance products and advice on to the network, including insurance, tax and legal services, and PEPs. The service also has a Web site at http://www.infotrade.co.uk, where more information is available.

Fidelity

The UK execution-only brokerage arm of Fidelity is also in the throes of launching an online dealing service for its clients. Like Infotrade it will use a private network rather than the Internet. The aim is to give its users access to the same information that its telephone dealers have at their fingertips when a client calls up.

The service will allow users to view their account data and statements, a transaction history, view the balance in their money market account and to enter orders and receive confirmations electronically. In addition, up to 10 snap quotes will be available at a time. Links to portfolio management software such as Quicken and perhaps even to popular graphics packages, as well as fundamental information and news services, are also likely to be made available in the fullness of time.

Information on the service, including a demo download of Fidelity's Vision software, is available at Fidelity's UK Web site at http://www.fidelity.co.uk.

UK Brokers Online

The World Wide Web is now coming to be used more and more by brokers wishing to interact with their computer-networked clients.

Full-blooded online trading may take time to gain acceptance, by brokers themselves as much as by their clients. But once a broker has accepted the power of the Web—as an increasing number have—as a way of communicating with clients, extending the service to online trading is a natural progression. So other brokers will almost certainly offer online dealing in the future.

Aside from the brokers already mentioned as operating in this way, the following also have Web sites for investors: Cazenove; Charles Stanley; Durlacher; Killik & Co.; Options Direct; Redmayne Bentley, the Share Centre and others.

The content of some of these sites is looked at briefly below.

Cazenove

The Cazenove site, at the Internet address http://www.cazenove.co.uk/cazenove, is in fact operated by Cazenove Unit Trust Management. Despite its source it is, however, an extremely interesting site for the general investor in UK shares, not just individuals who might be interested in Cazenove's in-house unit trusts.

The site includes 'technical information', charts, contact names, general dealing information, and has a large section giving details of the firm's unit trust and PEP products, including performance data, asset allocation, and the largest holdings in each of the portfolios.

'Technical information' available at the site includes the FTSE index constituents, and which have been the best and worst performing world markets in the course of the year, as well as some information on UK tax legislation relevant to the investment scene.

The chart section has 30 charts including all major indices, and those of some minor and emerging markets, currency rates, and bond yields in major markets. The charts are well drawn and provide useful perspective. Other than the charts, the site is largely graphics-free and downloads quickly.

Charles Stanley

Charles Stanley (http://www.charles-stanley.co.uk) is a large private client broking firm and was one of the first to launch a Web site. It is essentially a 'commercial' for the firm's services but does contain the latest FTSE index value, closing prices from the day before, and information on the range of services provided by the broker.

The broker claims to have plans for an online dealing service and some other enhancements to the site, although none is as yet apparent.

The text is written in clear English and, like the Cazenove site, gets by on the minimum of graphics, and downloads quickly.

Durlacher

This broker is primarily known as a traded options specialist and the site (http://www.durlacher.com) is designed to showcase this ability. It also highlights the firm's research and corporate finance specialisation in multimedia and the Internet. Durlacher's welcome page is shown in Figure 6.3.

The site also contains a list of services the group provides, which is brief in the extreme. But the options section is more informative, and a section covering the Multimedia offshoot contains links to the summaries of major reports the group has prepared on a variety of topics.

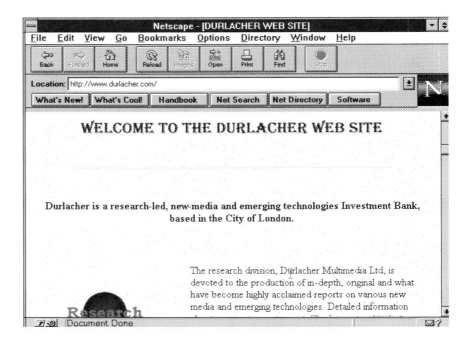

Figure 6.3 Durlacher's home page

Options Direct

Options Direct is also, as its name suggests, an options broker orientated towards (although not exclusively so) the private investor. The home page (http://www.options-direct.co.uk) displays a range of contents, including general information on the company, its people, the services it offers, commission rates, client-only pages, a monthly review, a daily option market report, and other relevant links.

The 'people' section contains brief CVs of the company's personnel, while the daily market report includes statistics relating to the day's options turnover, quotes from dealers and information on significant market trades. The links section includes only the predictable ones to newspapers and exchanges. The graphics content of the site is minimal, enabling rapid downloading.

Killik

The broking firm Killik & Co. also operates a Web site (http://www.killik.co.uk). Its initial page contains several links including a welcome area, which includes comment on the Killik & Co approach to private client broking, stock news (a daily market bulletin with some interesting features), details about the company's branches, and a form to request further information.

Barclays

The Barclays Stockbrokers site can be found at http://www.barclays.co.uk/stock/home.htm. Accessing has in the past been rather forbidding, with a huge graphic taking up the whole of the home page. The user had then to click on flags to call up other pages. The site has recently been redesigned and includes a welcome page, information on services, an information request form, stock opinions, and news releases. The welcome page has more precise links. Stock opinions simply give details of Barclays' telephone-based opinions, while newsdesk is actually not news, but a compilation of features of general interest to investors.

Despite the revamp, the result is that the site promises rather more than it actually delivers, even though much of the information is interesting and useful.

These brief illustrations demonstrate that although some UK brokers are beginning to dip a toe into the online dealing scene, many are waiting to see how the initiatives begun by ESI, Infotrade, Fidelity and others work out before committing themselves to the investment a move like this might require.

If you want to deal online, however, there is now a decent choice of broker and commission rates are competitive—even if the level of service varies from one to the other.

Even if you choose not to place orders through an online medium, an important ingredient in any investment decision is the accessing of up-to-date price information and other data in a cost-effective and timely way. The next chapter shows how to acquire it and what it costs.

CHAPTER 7

Prices and Data Online

A cynic, claimed Oscar Wilde, was a man who knew the price of everything and the value of nothing. The City is full of them, and serious online investors need to beware. Value, rather than price, is what the investment process is all about.

Professional investors almost have too much information on which to base decisions, making it difficult for them to arrive at a detached judgement. Private investors may often feel the reverse. When markets are moving quickly, they are frustrated that they do not know, up to the minute, what is happening to the market price of their shares.

How to get hold of cheap, high-quality price data has long been a problem for private investors. It is also one which pre-dates the popularisation of the Internet. Yet although many of those selling price data to private investors do not rely on the Internet for disseminating it, almost all delivery methods are electronic, and therefore fall within the scope of this book.

So 'online', for the purposes of this chapter, is defined as anything that comes either via broadcast media or down a telephone line, rather than necessarily over the Internet and World Wide Web.

Knowing the price of a share without having some means of assessing its value, by comparing its price with the accounting numbers that back it up, can be dangerous. But fortunately the sources of online data on these so-called 'fundamentals' are increasing, albeit slowly.

Assessing Your Needs

Data is available at a price. The issue is less about how to get hold of what information is available, and more about working out exactly what you need and how much you are prepared to pay. Unlike many of the information sources that have been outlined in previous chapters, price data can be expensive. Shopping around may be necessary.

One reason is that price data is a product ultimately controlled by exchanges which, rather than acting as passive disseminators of the price input supplied by their members, generally claim that by passing through their hands the data has had value added to it and can be priced accordingly.

Exchanges levy charges for price data supplied to data vendors, who subsequently pass it on to their customers. How much is charged depends on how timely the data is. Real-time price data is regarded as the most valuable; day-old data has only limited value and is therefore often available for free. Even prices that are 15 minutes old have little economic value to market professionals.

At this point I must state my biases, which have been built up over a lengthy spell trading the stock market with varying degrees of success. For me, the key elements any online investor has to consider when working out what price data to use and how much to pay are:

Do I really need real-time data? In my view, real-time data is expensive for the advantages it gives the average private investor. For most 'retail investors' investment performance comes from careful selection of stocks, spotting value, and astute timing of major market moves. Trading on an intra-day basis is expensive for those not dealing in large amounts (by which I mean a £50,000 trade rather than a £1,000 one) and is best left to the professionals. I have also found the presence of a real-time screen can have a disruptive effect on trading decisions, pushing the investor into unwise moves.

Do I really need an intra-day display at all? Personally, all I like to have is an indication of which way the market is moving and, since these are available at minimal ongoing cost from sources such as Teletext, they are as easy to have as not.

What kind of end-of-day data do I require? This is the critical question. The answer really is 'the most comprehensive you can afford'. In particular, it is important that every investor has (as a minimum) the ability to access stored data on, say, the 300 or 400 stocks he or she is most likely to deal in, to be able to change the components of the list easily and at minimal cost, to substitute new and interesting stocks for those looking tired or which have disappeared. It is crucial to be able to see (after the event) the extent of the intra-day movement in a stock *and its trading volume.*

So the decision is a complex, two-stage one.

Real-time data is not essential, but the end-of-day data to be down-loaded into the investment software packages that most PC-literate private investors use should be the most comprehensive and flexible you can afford. But this does not necessarily mean that data on all the stocks in the market must be stored and updated every night. Although a Pentium PC will make light of the task of processing this data, and software packages can scan data on this scale to pick out interesting stocks, to my mind this reverses the natural process of investment.

You may be stimulated by a news item, or a report in a newsletter, or for that matter a tip in a Usenet newsgroup, to seek out more information on a particular company. Among the relevant information will be the pattern of price movements over the past few years. A cost-effective means of down-loading or viewing an instant price history is more valuable than being able to watch share prices in real time.

The next part of this chapter looks at the options available for those who want real-time or near real-time price data, and what each of the options costs. In this context we will look primarily at UK sources but also at some World Wide Web-based Internet sources of US stock quotes. These offer clues on how similar services will develop in Britain and elsewhere.

Then we go on to consider the various options available for end-of-day downloading, and the way in which the Internet can be used to access online company 'fundamentals'.

Intra-day Data Sources

We'll look first at the various methods of getting online price displays in the course of the trading day.

Teletext

This is the classic intra-day data source, used by many UK private investors. It is a generic term for the rival services offered by the BBC (Ceefax) and Channel 4 (Teletext Ltd). Each offers prices of the largest stocks and a (slightly different) selection of smaller ones updated up to seven times daily.

Teletext services can be accessed from any TV equipped to receive them, and use what is known as the vertical blanking interval, or VBI, the spare lines at the top of a TV picture, to transmit data. It is an unsung technical marvel. Simon Waldman wrote in *Media Week* (26 August 1994): 'I have this incredible bit of technology at home. With the press of a button I can call up any one of more than 3,000 digital pages offering the latest news, sport results, and even a dating service. It costs nothing to use and, unlike my Internet connection, it never crashes. You may have heard of it—it's called teletext.'

The services differ between the two main providers. The BBC version, for example, includes an index (the Dow UK) updated minute by minute, and until recently also had several pages of option prices as well as its roster of share prices. Teletext, the Channel 4 service, is a commercial offering and therefore has advertising interspersed in its pages. It also only updates the index every 15 minutes. Teletext also has two pages dedicated to end-of-day prices for all the stocks listed in London. The result of these differences is that the two services combined add up to more than each of the services represents on its own.

As an aside, the Dow UK index replaced the FT-SE100 as the main index on the teletext services when the index owners, FT-SE International, demanded a per-user-based charge for its real-time dissemination, thereby rendering it uneconomic for teletext operators—with their millions of users—to continue with it.

The main advantage of teletext is that it is free, other than the initial cost perhaps of buying a dedicated teletext TV set that can permanently be tuned to the service.

Teletext services also have pages of risers and fallers, popular stocks, new issues, and a limited amount of news, including company results.

You can also download share prices direct from the teletext services into a PC share price charting package. But, for reasons I will explore in more detail in the next section, this does have some drawbacks.

Having used other real-time price displays over the years, both professionally and as a private investor, though teletext is not ideal in many respects, to my mind it probably represents the optimum intra-day price service for most investors, at least until other forms of data come down in price.

Market Eye

At the other end of the scale, but still popular with investors, is ICV's Market Eye service, which also works off the TV signal. ICV has around 3,000 subscribers for this service, which offers a real-time price feed from the Stock Exchange, and will enable you to get up-to-date price data in the form of the best bid and offer in the market at any one time for all listed stocks. These can be built into custom pages so that different portfolios can be carried on separate pages, for example, or a 'watch list' of stocks built up. In addition the service includes company and market news, a ticker of stock exchange trades as they happen, the biggest risers and fallers in the day, and a lot of other information.

At the time of its launch, Market Eye was available only via a dedicated terminal and decoder box, which the customer had to buy or rent at the outset. A few years ago ICV launched a PC version of Market Eye. Initially this had comparatively little impact, perhaps because users were reluctant to abandon the equipment they had paid for. More recently a greater proportion of users have begun to convert to the new system. Though this version will sit on any normal desktop PC, to make full use of the system may necessitate having a dedicated PC for the display, so there could be a hardware cost involved.

The advantage of Market Eye is that you have live prices at the touch of a button, and the ability to have a genuine feel for the market as it unfolds in the course of the trading day. I have mixed feelings about how useful this really is for many private investors. But one big plus point of Market Eye is that you can save on data download costs. End-of-day data and, for the real aficionado, real-time data can be downloaded into most popular software packages at no extra cost.

The disadvantage is that it is expensive. The basic services costs around £1,000 pounds a year, on top of which has to be added a near £200 exchange fee, and more if you choose also to take option prices from LIFFE. An optional licence fee for Market Eye for Windows software, which pretties up the display, is an extra £195 per annum, while you initially need to spend about £400 on the datacard to enable the service to be received and, if necessary, the PC hardware to slot it into.

Even allowing for the advantage of free end-of-day data downloads, this puts the whole package beyond the reach of many investors. A 'data download only' option is available at about half the price of the main service, but competing services of this type are now much cheaper.

Market Eye's few thousand subscribers compare with a combined nearly 30 million accesses a week for the two teletext services combined. Even if only 5 per cent of these are accesses of the financial pages—and there is evidence to suppose it may be more than that—it is clear that the teletext services are genuinely valued by the average private investor.

Satellite Systems

Stock market data by satellite has been around for some time but has its drawbacks from the standpoint of private investors. One is that it is expensive and only a limited number of services offer information on UK equities. The second drawback is that domestic satellite dishes will not normally receive this data and there is extra expense buying and installing suitable equipment.

Some companies offer a 'buyback' policy to take the risk out of the process, but a service such as Tenfore, the obvious choice for a UK online investor since it includes comprehensive UK coverage, still costs in the region of £170 a month, and you may receive a considerable amount of data that is not really required. DBC Signal, the other main satellite-based price feed, did not at the time of writing include UK equity prices as part of its service, although there may be plans for it to do so.

Pager products

Another way of keeping in touch with share prices is via pager-based products. At present there is a choice of three products of this type, respectively from Futures Pager, Hutchison Telecom (proprietors of the Orange mobile phone network) and from Sprintel.

Pagers really come into their own for investors on the move, and especially if you simply want to check the progress of the index, futures prices, or a few selected shares. Technological advances have meant that pagers now update much more frequently than they used to and to all intents and purposes can be considered real-time products.

The main problem is that the physical size of the pager means that there is a limit to the quantity of information that can be displayed in an intelligible form. Pagers also developed as a way of keeping dealers in touch with fast moving futures and foreign exchange markets, and still concentrate in large measure on this type of information.

Futures Pager has recently introduced a service which in effect turns the pager into a mini-Reuters screen that can capture data on specific shares. The tariff, however, is expensive for the average private investor. The best product in this area is arguably from Sprintel, which took over an established price display service known as Financial Alert. This was a portable product the size of a personal organiser that could both be carried around and also plugged into a PC, to give a real-time display on around 1,000 shares.

The Sprintel pager product, Real Time Alert, offers the ability to have paged prices of a selected list of up to 45 stocks. This service is also linked to a real time news feed from AFX Examiner, and you are fed general news and bleeped when a news item is announced that relates to one of the stocks in the pager's 'portfolio'. Pre-set price limits can also be set on the pager so that you are alerted when these limits are breached.

Other pager firms have developed a product which allows the unit to be used as a datafeed for a real-time PC price display. Other refinements include a joint venture between Vodafone and Market Data Centre which allows price displays to be received via a digital mobile phone display. This service also offers both standard sets of data (futures prices, indices and so on) as well as a specified list of share prices. More mobile phone-delivered services of this type have recently been launched, including entries from MAID and Tenfore. In the case of the latter, however, the messaging charges are high relative to those of conventional pagers.

Pager products suffer from the disadvantage of not quite national coverage, although most suppliers are moving to address this problem. On the other hand, they tend to be charged at a flat rate per month, while the mobile phone-based products are based on call time and therefore can be relatively costly. Sprintel's Real Time Alert costs around £45 a month including VAT, while Futures Pager, which aims at a different user base, costs roughly double this figure.

Dial-up Data

Another alternative for private investors is Prestel Citiservice. This is accessed by modem (and, more recently, via the Web) and enables you to tap into real-time prices as well as news headlines, electronic banking, text retrieval, and other services. Day-long background use would probably rack up hefty telephone charges but the company does offer a flat fee for its share price service, making periodic 'dipping-in' to a selection of live prices a real possibility.

The price of this service, around £300 plus VAT per annum including exchange fees, looks cost-effective compared to other real-time screen products, and includes all UK equities and gilts. Options and futures prices are extra and the additional charges are hefty, partly because of exchange fees. End-of-day downloading is included at no extra charge.

Alternatives to this as a way of accessing live prices periodically during the course of the trading day are via premium rate telephone services such as FT Cityline. Here you dial up a number and add in a four digit share code corresponding to the share price to be checked. Services of this type normally give price and volume information, plus the number of mid-price movements and the index level at the time. They are expensive if used frequently.

Prices in 'Bundled' Services

Until exchange fees for real-time data come down, accessing unlimited price data of this type will prove expensive for the ordinary UK private investor. Limited databases of up to, say, 50 stocks can, however, be monitored at lower cost. This can be done either through a pager like Sprintel's Real Time Alert, or via Web-based and other dial-up services that bundle other facilities in with a monthly subscription.

We'll look at some examples of this, before going on to see how the web can be used by US on-line investors in search of intra-day prices.

Electronic Share Information (ESI)   This UK pioneer of online share dealing provides a means for investors (who may not necessarily even have an online trading account) to access real-time prices, as shown in Figure 7.1.

Previously the company offered only a teletext-style price service accessible free of charge, but now also operates a system whereby its bronze

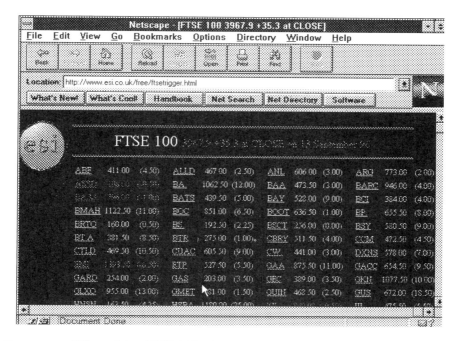

Figure 7.1 ESI—real-time FT-SE 100 prices

service, available for a subscription of £5 a month, permits a customisable page of 25 real-time snap quotes to be downloaded for £1 a time. In this service, too, the FT-SE100 'trigger page'—a single screen display of the latest prices for all the top 100 stocks—is updated eight times daily. News services are available at 10p per story, or £10 per month for all stories. The service also allows you access to charts and price histories.

The more expensive silver service has the FTSE trigger page updated every minute and allows unlimited updates of snap quotes for a customisable page of 25 stocks. This costs £20 a month plus VAT. The service is accessed from ESI's Web page at http://www.esi.co.uk.

As well as the normal teletext list updated on the usual intra-day basis, free services available at ESI include end-of-day share and unit trust prices for the whole market. The advantage over teletext is that the service is arranged so that the top 100, mid 250 and other popular shares and recent issues are available in alphabetical order on different pages, obviating the waiting on teletext for several different pages and sub-pages to cycle round.

What ESI is prevented from doing, however, is offering the ability for its subscribers to browse an unlimited number of real-time share prices on a continuous basis.

Infotrade Infotrade charges for real-time data on a time-related basis at the rate of 20p a minute, with a minimum charge of one minute. In practice, the service offers access to the prices of a portfolio chosen from a list of up to 800 securities. You can set up your software to grab a snapshot of the desired prices and then log off—or else to stay on line and watch prices updating in real-time for as long as you wish.

This is a useful facility for those who wish to use Infotrade as a catch-all source of information, but using the service solely as a price feed is not a realistic option.

UK and US Web Sites

Aside from Web sites such as ESI's, where prices might be viewed partly as an adjunct to a dealing service, there are several other Web sites which offer investors an economical insight into price movements.

Moneyworld (http://www.moneyworld.co.uk) has a section devoted to 'British Stocks Quoted on Wall Street' (see Figure 7.2), which includes not only large companies with US listings and ADRs (American depository receipts), but also some smaller companies with a US presence. Data for this site comes from DBC Signal, the satellite broadcaster, and the quotes are delayed by 15 minutes.

Though delayed and expressed in dollars, the price display does show the trend in the shares concerned, many of which are popular with private investors, in the afternoon period when the two markets overlap and in the evening period when Wall Street is open after London has closed. This can provide a pointer to the likely movement in these stocks at the market opening in London the following morning. Moneyworld is also now offering a free teletext-style price service with detailed end-of-day data and information on 30 overseas market indexes updated on a delayed 15-minute basis.

Useful though this is, it falls short of what the average investor ideally requires from an intra-day price display. In effect, the ideal most investors seek is the ability to access free live quotes for the relatively small number

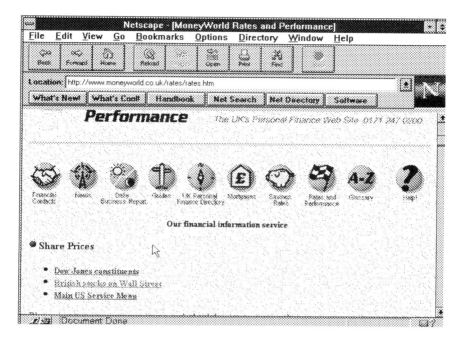

Figure 7.2 MoneyWorld's UK prices on Wall Street

of stocks they may hold or may be watching, and to revisit these quotes periodically in the course of the day. US online investors have become used to being able to do this through a variety of online services offering stock quotes.

Yahoo!'s 'markets and investments—stocks' index lists over 80 sites offering quote information of some kind, many of which offer free snap quotes on a limited number of stocks per day, or a variety of prices on a 15-minute delayed basis.

The best-known examples of this type of service are probably Quote.com and Security APL, but the range of services offered is expanding all the time. One recent innovation, for instance, is PC Quote Europe, which offers a quote service on a 'watch list' of five stocks which can be selected from a variety of European and US markets.

These offerings are not entirely altruistic. At Quote.com for instance (http://www.quote.com), there are a variety of other services available, including Standard & Poors-style balance sheet and profit and loss account summaries. These and other services are chargeable on a low-cost pay-as-you go basis.

By comparison with the UK scene, the services are cheap. In Quote.com's case, for example, its basic package priced at $10 a month includes 100 quotes a day, automatic portfolio updates at the end of every day, portfolio alerts to pick up unusual movements, selected company financial information, and newswire headlines.

Interquote (http://www.interquote.com) is another supplier whose pricing structure betrays the different levels of economic value perceived to be offered by different levels of data. Broadly speaking, interactive data costs more than data in a standard display (which may not include the stocks in which you are interested), while real-time data costs more than 15-minute delayed data, which costs more than end-of-day data.

At Interquote, the top-end interactive service with real-time data costs over $80 a month, while at the bottom end of the scale, simple end-of-day data costs only $5. A limited number of quotes, displayed on the software that Interquote supplies free to its users, costs $10–20 per month. Once downloaded the data can be imported into your own technical analysis software.

Many of these Web-promoted services offer a choice of real-time, 15-minute delayed, end-of-day and email quote services. Most require you to register to be able to receive fuller information. Registration normally requires parting with basic contact details.

The central point to bear in mind with services like this, as with other aspects of the Internet, is that free information is generally used as a hook to sell subscriptions to more expensive services. But the private online investor does not necessarily need the level of detail that the professionals demand. Delayed prices (with the option of the occasional snap quote on a stock in which you may wish to deal), is available at comparatively low cost.

The lesson is that information for which existing professional subscribers pay heavily will not normally be available in a form that can easily be accessed. Commercial organisations, such as stock exchanges and data vendors, do not normally behave in an altruistic manner. If they appear to be doing so, there is invariably a catch.

The lesson from the USA is that online price displays for all the securities that an investor might need are coming down in price. And despite the seeming efforts of the London Stock Exchange to price data outside the reach of the private investor, the time is coming when Internet-delivered price data (albeit perhaps slightly time-delayed) should be available for a configurable list of stocks for a very modest price—and certainly for less than the £20 a month currently charged by ESI—good value though this service is compared to many others.

End of Day Downloads

While many investors are rightly ambivalent about their need for real-time quotes during the trading day, for the serious investor the ability to download share prices into a graphing package is a must.

Even if you do not perform sophisticated technical analysis on the price data, the ability to see a snapshot of the share's movement over an extended period has considerable intuitive value. Interpretation is still important, but even at its simplest level the information is of value.

As mentioned before, the ability also to download open, high, low, close and volume (OHLCV) data is important. The volume of trading in a stock is an important guide to the significance or otherwise of movement in the shares and to do without this is false economy, even if you do not wish to perform sophisticated technical analysis with the information.

A range of alternatives for downloading price data is available to the online investor, with varying costs, and these are examined next.

Teletext Downloads

Teletext downloading works in a comparatively simple way. You buy a normal PC expansion card which has a standard TV aerial socket. This allows a spur off your TV aerial to be connected to your PC. Then, other things being equal, the computer can be tuned to read the teletext signal on the prices pages. An expansion card like this costs less than £200. But it suffers from the drawback that teletext prices are closing mid-prices only, and do not contain any intra-day or trading volume information.

Downloading from Teletext also has a reputation for being less than wholly reliable, and can suffer in particular from poor TV reception and unusual atmospheric conditions. Coping with updating during absences from home can also be tricky.

An earlier drawback to teletext, that stocks were dropped from the list for no reason, has been circumvented by the fact that Channel 4's Teletext service now includes end-of-day prices for the whole market, while software programs have been developed, such as Updata's Teleshares product (there are others, too), which smarten up the display of this information and ease the process of downloading. Changes to price retrieval codes, another bugbear of the old system, are amended by this type of software through periodic disk updates.

Modem Updating

It is possible to group several forms of data in this category. One example is the several proprietary databases available, either through independent entities or maintained by some software suppliers. Updating by modem enables more complex forms of data to be downloaded than is possible via teletext, and especially OHLCV data, the basic raw material of most sophisticated technical analysis packages.

This type of updating has hitherto been considered an expensive luxury, but prices are coming down fast. Prestel On-line, for instance, offers a high-speed download of OHLCV data for all UK equities and gilts for only £125 a year in a format compatible with popular software packages. Complete London Stock Exchange price histories are also available.

Instead of charging prices at one time running well into four figures for its data, Synergy Software now has a system whereby you can have a bundled package of data and software for an annual subscription starting at £395 per annum. This system, known as StAR, enables you to monitor a database of up to 400 stocks via a regular daily download, but also enables the database to be changed and new stocks selected as often as needed free of charge. The price histories of new selections can be downloaded as and when required, and then subsequently updated.

This is arguably more manageable than keeping files on all 3,000-odd listed companies, although it is now being undercut by other more comprehensive services.

Downloading from Real-time Datafeeds

The various real-time feeds mentioned above offer the facility for downloading of OHLCV data at the end of every trading day. In the case of

Market Eye, for instance, around 20 software packages, including all the popular ones, now offer an interface to the system, enabling price files to be updated at no extra charge.

Downloading is also possible from DBC Signal, Tenfore and other real-time feeds. In most cases the process of importing the data is comparatively simple. Data download options usually allow data to be converted into ASCII or CSV format, which most software packages will accept, and software manuals will give instructions on how this can be done.

Before signing up for a data package, however, it is vital to ensure that the software you use is compatible with the data you propose to download. Software suppliers can usually offer a range of options and will allow you to pick one that represents the right combination of detail and price.

Downloading from Web Sites

A restricted number of UK Web sites offer the opportunity of downloading stock market data. More will undoubtedly develop as time goes by. The best known is clearly ESI. ESI Data originally could be accessed for a minimum subscription of £5 a month plus VAT, which represented one of the best bargains around, but more recently the company has begun pricing the service somewhat differently, although Silver service level subscribers can still access it relatively economically.

The data is supplied in ASCII, CSV or Indexia (a commonly used chart package) format and can be imported easily into most popular investment software. Previous days' data is cached for a month, allowing users to catch up on any prices that might have been missed through absence. It can be supplied either in the form of a compressed *.zip* file, or in uncompressed form.

Downloads by Email

Downloading share price data is also possible by email. In fact, ESI offers you the option of receiving its data in this way on an overnight basis. Other organisations, including some software suppliers, offer a similar service. OHLCV data for the market is available at around £125 per annum for an evening download, or around £50 for a next-day service. Mid-price data is usually free.

Provided you are confident of your ability to convert data received via email into the appropriate format for importing into a software package, this represents a perfectly acceptable and invariably trouble-free method of delivery.

Downloading Fundamental Data

The distinction between downloading share price and trading volume data on the one hand and fundamental information on the other is an important one. The online investor is much less well served in the latter area.

In this context fundamental information means earnings forecasts, directors' dealings and other sensitive information, and all the standard financial information to be found in company accounts.

For the moment the UK online investor has to fall back on a number of tried and tested sites for information of this type. Subscribers to the ESI site mentioned in the previous section, for example, can access fundamental data from Hemmington Scott, publishers of the *Hambro Company Guide*.

This gives abbreviated balance and profit data for all UK companies, including some unquoted companies, and is available through ESI at a cost of £1 per access. Good though the *Hambro Company Guide* is as a product, it does not match the level of detail most investors need for a thorough investigation of the basic financial data on a company.

Infotrade, another online service mentioned previously, offers a rather more comprehensive package. Here, for a regular subscription of £10 a month, users can get (in addition to downloadable share prices and electronic share trading) information on dividends, other corporate events like rights issues and scrip issues, brief company descriptions, three years' abbreviated company results and two years of forecasts, information on directors dealings, and *FT* headlines.

Further levels of service are available within the Infotrade package, including the AFX Examiner news service, which costs a further £12 a month and provides company news, market and economic news, and political, general and sports news. The service is compiled by City journalists who understand the needs of the market, and therefore the coverage is usually pertinent for the private investor. Additional pay-as-you-go services include the real-time share price service alluded to earlier, *Financial*

Times articles, AFX company reports (in effect an electronic Extel card), and *Hambro Company Guide* entries.

Hemmington Scott itself has a Web site—UK Equities Direct (the URL is http://www.hemscott.co.uk/hemscott/) (see Figure 7.3)—at which data, mainly from its normal Hambro Company Guide publication, is currently available free of charge. This includes consensus earnings forecasts, recent P&L and balance sheet historical data, share price charts, contact details, recent official comments on company prospects, and a variety of other information including rankings of corporate advisers and public relations companies, lists of index constituents, sector constituents, option stocks, and a variety of other useful information. One recent and laudable extension to the service is the provision of an electronic version of selected company annual reports and/or interim statements.

Companies have to co-operate with Hemmington Scott for the Web site to be able to supply this information, but at the last count there were nearly one hundred sets of company accounts on the system, and more

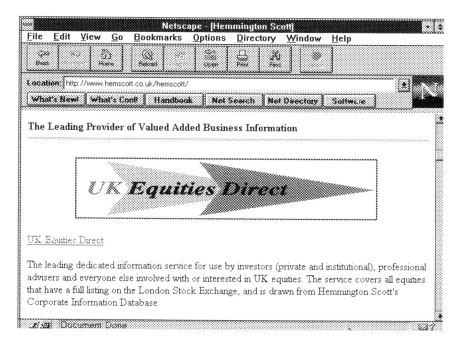

Figure 7.3 Hemmington's Scott's UK Equities Direct

should be added as time goes by. Clearly, reading such documents on screen can be cumbersome. But having the data available in this way avoids the necessity of contacting the company if all that is required are some basic figures and a glance at the chair's statement.

A similar annual reports service is offered by Corporate Reports at its Web site (http://www.corpreports.co.uk) although so far the choice of companies is more limited than on the Hemington Scott site.

If it takes off, this aspect of the service would carry faint echoes of the EDGAR site in the USA, now operated by the SEC. This is a searchable index of official SEC filings, including annual and quarterly financial statements and other data. Electronic filing of company information has now been extended to cover the whole gamut of publicly listed securities in the USA. Although the EDGAR index is slightly quirky to use, the availability of what in UK terms is tantamount to an electronic Companies House for listed stocks is a superb resource for the investor and one that is widely used. The URL for EDGAR is http://www.sec.gov/edgarhp.htm.

It remains to be seen if such an initiative would get off the ground in the UK. With Companies House now an executive agency and talk of its privatisation, the notion of it providing even part of the information filed there free to online users may not be commercially acceptable. Even as a pay-as-you-go electronic service there would be considerable demand from those who do not relish the expense (and tedium) of a trip to its City Road premises.

At the time of writing, a useful and welcome addition to the FT Information Web site (http://www.info.ft.com/companies) has been the ability to search the FT's database and retrieve basic information on 11,000 companies worldwide, together with links to relevant news stories from the paper.

The Problem of Choice

Keeping the supply of information to a relevant and manageable size—long a problem for the professional investor—is a task which demands some skill.

As the preceding pages indicate, there is a complex pattern of services available online through which you can access real-time price data, delayed price data, and end-of-day data through a variety of channels.

Sometimes it is provided on a stand-alone basis, and sometimes in conjunction with other services which may not be needed.

Corporate financial information is also available in both free and paid-for forms, again often bundled in with other services.

Working out what is worth paying for and what isn't depends on you. However, do bear in mind the following:

❐ The cost of micro-billed services tends to add up, and although the data provided can be convenient to access from one source in this way, in many cases it is available online elsewhere for free.

❐ Real-time price data is an expensive luxury for all but the keenest investor or those committed to active trading on a minute-by-minute basis. Teletext services provide adequate intra-day information for most investors.

❐ Up-to-the minute news is comforting to have, but in practice even the most assiduous investor will be unable to beat the market reaction to price-sensitive announcements.

❐ Potentially more useful are services such as the Hemmington Scott's UK Equities Direct, which gives access to useful information on every listed company, and also to annual reports on an expanding number of companies.

❐ Investors should therefore concentrate their spending on paying for quality data for end-of-day downloading, paying particular attention to getting OHLCV data and loading this into a good quality charting package. The cost of this data is coming down rapidly.

Fundamental information can normally be acquired free or at low cost from other sources, and buying a 'bundled' service that includes it risks clouding the issue. If information is to be paid for, then it should merit purchase on a stand-alone basis.

Costs are falling. And what appears expensive now may be within reach of even the most modest budget in a few years' time.

CHAPTER 8

Online Software

One of the main features of the Internet is the ability it offers to transfer files from remote computers.

Using file transfer protocol (FTP) tools, an online investor can log into another computer anywhere in the world and gain access to the files that its owner has designated as accessible to the online community.

Before looking at the opportunities this presents, how to go about accessing these files, and what's available, let's consider for a moment what this means.

Even the most complex computer programs are simply collections of files. So computer software can be downloaded via FTP from a remote computer by any online investor who wishes to do so.

In the case of the UK user this is a very important attribute. The majority of computer software originates in the US. This goes for investment software as much as for any other type.

The result is that (in theory) an online investor can get access to software online at US prices and, with some adaptation, use it with UK data. Since software prices are significantly lower in the USA than in Europe, downward pressure on UK investment software prices is likely to be the result—at least in the long term.

In reality most software users will probably opt for buying a package from a UK supplier—if only because of its familiarity, and the more certain knowledge that the data generally available in the UK can be used to drive it.

But investment software does not just mean chart packages. There are several spreadsheet-based programs that perform useful functions for the investor. These can be downloaded from sites in the USA and easily used with UK figures.

Before looking at these different types of software package and where they can be found, we'll briefly review the mechanics of FTP.

FTP Reviewed

We had a look at the way in which files could be downloaded from remote computers in Chapter 2. Here is a brief recap of this topic.

FTP tools are used to gain access to files stored at a remote computer and transfer them to your own. A remote computer will usually have a login procedure that requires the user (who might be an employee of the organisation concerned) to enter a user name and a password.

Using FTP, you can log in to those sections of the computer's store of files which the operator has designated as open to the general online user.

How you do this varies depending on the type of Internet connection you have and the programs it supports. Those with an indirect connection via a bulletin board system may do so by following simple instructions to get to an Internet Protocol (or IP) prompt and then inputting recognised UNIX commands.

Some offline readers supplied by BBS operators can automate this process using scripts (sequences of computer commands that are activated automatically), although using the scripts supplied with offline readers can be a hit and miss process.

Those with a direct PPP/SLIP connection are generally able to use a Windows file manager interface, not only to log into the remote computer, but also to find and select the precise file to download, and to configure their own computer to put the download in a specific place.

Since the FTP programs supported by different Internet Service Providers are all different, it is not really possible within the scope of this book to outline how they all work. As usual though, a little experimentation goes a long way.

The normal procedure runs something like this:

❒ FTP to the desired site.

❒ Enter a user name (normally 'guest', or 'FTP').
❒ Enter a password (normally your email address).
❒ Once successfully logged in, access the file directory menu.
❒ Enter the appropriate directory to view the file list.
❒ Select the file you require to download.

Directory lists will often contain text 'readme' files giving guidance on where to find files on particular topics and, within directories, brief information on what the files within them contain.

By far the easiest and most common way of downloading files, however, is through the hypertext links on the World Wide Web.

Typically, a Web site such as one operated by software providers like Microsoft or Netscape will have a series of pages devoted to programs, each of which can be downloaded simply by clicking on the hypertext link. In these circumstances the browser will produce a normal dialog box asking where and how the downloaded file is to be saved.

As a general rule, but particularly with compressed (or 'zipped') files, it is best to create an empty temporary directory in which to store the downloaded file. Once the program files are unzipped and the setup procedure run, the program will be installed in a separate directory and the temporary one, or the files in it, can be deleted.

Although downloading using a hypertext link represents the easiest option of all for downloading software, using UNIX commands is not especially difficult.

The procedure for downloading using UNIX is likely to be described in the manual provided by your Internet Service Provider, and the process is also described in some detail in Chapter 2. The most commonly used UNIX commands can be easily learnt and files acquired relatively easily in this way.

The basic UNIX commands and what they do are summarised in Table 8.1.

We'll look next at some general software sites, and at why many thousands of software programs are available free.

Why Software is Free

There are several ways of getting a feel for the extent to which free or low-cost software is available on the Internet, but perhaps the easiest is to visit

Table 8.1 Basic UNIX commands

Command	Followed by	Meaning
bye		Quits the system
cwd	directory name	Changes current directory to indicated directory
cat	filename	Displays file
dir		List contents of current directory
get	filename	Retrieves file from remote computer
help		Displays help information
quit		Quits the system
ls	file/directory name	List files/directories
mget	filenames	Retrieves multiple files from remote computer
more	filename	Displays file page by page (using spacebar)
man	command	Describes command function with example
pwd		Shows current directory name
status		Checks whether file type is ASCII or binary

the index provided by the Yahoo! search engine and the home pages of well-known software companies such as Microsoft, Netscape and Adobe.

In the case of the latter three sites, there is a range of software available for download by the online community. The sites also show the extent to which software developers gain assistance from these major companies via their provision of software development tools and other aids.

At the Microsoft home page (http://www.microsoft.com), for instance, there is a range of options available, including browsers, viewers (for viewing documents in the form in which they will appear in products such as Word and PowerPoint), authoring tools, software for servers, games, and a variety of free software.

At the Adobe site (http://www.adobe.com), there are the latest versions of the company's well-known Acrobat reader, which allows Web pages to be viewed as though they were the original document. This is useful, for instance, in the case of an online newspaper. The program can be downloaded free in versions suitable for several different operating systems, including Windows and Macintosh. Installing Acrobat allows PDF (portable document file) formatted files to be downloaded and viewed.

At Netscape (http://www.netscape.com), as with Microsoft, a range of programs and tools is available. Selection of the download required is made easier by a pull-down menu which allows the user to select the product required, the release version, the operating system, the desired language, and to specify the location of the download site so that the most appropriate one can be used.

Although nominally companies like Netscape appear to charge for their software targeted at individual computer users, in reality you can use it free of charge 'for evaluation purposes', although this means that manuals are not available, and no technical support is offered.

How do companies such as Netscape make money doing this? The reason is that the business model for software like this is rather different from that of other industries. A product such as Netscape Navigator has gained broad acceptance as a de facto industry standard through its free distribution to a wide range of users, as well as 'wholesale' sales through ISPs who offer it as part of their signing-on package for new users.

This means that the real target market—corporates requiring network software and the wherewithal to create Web pages that can be viewed by the browser—have the assurance that the product is widely distributed and the customer base represented by the users readily accessible.

There is, however, no such thing as a free lunch, and users may find they need to buy one of the many guidebooks produced, which use language slightly less dry than most computer manuals, in order to get the best out of the software.

This brings us to the question of shareware, demos, and buying software over the Internet.

The shareware concept allows you to download software 'for evaluation' and, if you like it and find it useful, places a moral obligation on you to buy a registered version and thereby get a manual, news on upgrades, and access to user support if appropriate.

This moral obligation may be more honoured in the breach than anything else, however, and one result is that, for investment software at least, the downloads available often take the form of 'demo disks', versions of the program which can only be used a fixed number of times, or versions which have their functions crippled so as to hamper normal use.

The sheer volume of choice available can be gauged by looking at the Yahoo! software index, which lists about 50 different categories, each with multiple numbers of entries. Many of these are not relevant for the online investor, but they do show the degree to which the Internet is becoming a recognised major distribution channel for software.

Yahoo! lists over 370 shareware sites, some of which will be worth exploring. A search option is also available. The next section will look at some central resources for tracking down investment software and other related financial programs. We'll then look in turn at some individual examples of downloadable programs for online investors.

Searching for Software

There are several ways in which online investors tend to come across useful software programs.
The main ones are:

❐ mentions in Internet-related publications
❐ mentions in investment related Usenet newsgroups
❐ via software search engines
❐ through specialist investment-related Web sites.

All have their merits and drawbacks. So let's look at each in turn.

Publications

Mentions in publications are a less attractive option, on the grounds of cost. Internet-oriented magazines can be interesting but, from the standpoint of the online investor, their content is normally of limited use. And cover prices of up to £3 a copy make something of a hole in the paper bill.
Until specialist investment-related Internet magazines begin to appear, a development still some way away, the online investor is probably better advised to seek information elsewhere.

Newsgroup Mentions

When I began to use the Internet and the World Wide Web seriously three or four years ago, my initial tips on downloading software came via Usenet newsgroups.
These are still a good free source of information. But the problem with using recommendations from newsgroups is that, although the posts concerned usually give details of the program, they may be posted by people with an axe to grind.

They could be the program developers themselves, friends, and other related parties. And many posts often omit to say whether or not the software comes with a price attached, or whether the advertised download is a full version of the program, or one that has restricted functionality.

Software Search Engines

Search engines are generally a more fruitful avenue of enquiry. Internet Sleuth (http://www.isleuth.com/soft.html) includes a list of nearly 30 search engines that can be used to find a piece of downloadable software.

Many of these search engines have pull-down menus that enable the user to specify the search more accurately and so increase the chances of finding the right item.

The links include a large number of freeware and shareware sites, as well as search engines that identify the whereabouts of particular products and software produced by specific companies. Sites are available for Amiga, Windows, Macintosh, and other operating systems, and the index also contains links to news items and details of uploads in the last seven days.

From the online investor's standpoint, the drawback to this is, first, that there is no search engine at the site specifically devoted to financial software. Secondly, it is generally necessary to know in advance the program name or the file name of the piece of software desired before a search can be started. But these objections are comparatively minor ones, and can be overcome.

Some (though not all) of the search engines listed are browsable, which helps if you are not quite sure what it is exactly you are seeking, and some contain a huge number of software items.

Because my Internet connection is on conventional Windows PC, I have concentrated on those that specifically look at this platform, but there are also extensive libraries of Mac-based software at other sites.

But it is important to distinguish between what the different software search sites do.

Some offer links to sites where the software can be downloaded, some simply give reviews of software, some list products produced by different software developers (essentially searchable indexes that will cross reference products and/or producers). Most of the sites are free to use. Those that aren't will allow a search to be conducted, but will not permit a download to be performed unless a fee has been paid and a user name and password entered.

In this case, the obvious course of action is to make a note of a file name and program name that looks promising, and go to another search engine, one which does not charge, to locate the file.

The World File Project (http://www.filepile.com) operates in this way. Users pay a registration fee per quarter or per year to download from it. The project is an ambitious one, aiming to index as much of the world's freeware and shareware as possible. At the time of writing, the site contains over a million different pieces of software.

Perhaps because of its scale, the search engine used does not (in my experience) identify the appropriate piece of software sufficiently precisely, and a list of hits from any search may contain several levels of duplication. The site is browsable, however.

Another rather more fruitful avenue, and a 'toll-free' one, is WinSite (http://www.winsite.com) a site solely devoted to software and add-ins for Windows and Windows applications. While the site can be searched, it is also browsable. This may be the best option. Two specific parts of the directory will probably prove of interest to on-line investors: an index devoted to Microsoft Excel files, and one devoted to what are called 'personal information managers'.

Among the Excel files, for instance, is a file (*astute.zip*), which contains a variety of statistical add-in functions for the spreadsheet program, one (*bpmwin10.zip*) which will help create business plans for small businesses, another (*mpm155.exe*) which is a simple portfolio data organiser, and several others. The much larger number of personal information managers includes electronic phone books, diaries, bank account managers, and simple bookkeeping programs.

Another large site is Shareware.com (http://www.shareware.com). This has more than 190,000 software titles available, and is searchable and browsable. The interesting aspect of this site is that the search engine appears good at identifying the appropriate shareware from the huge list at its disposal, and also displays a choice of several alternative sites from which to download the program, with an assessment of the efficiency and accessibility of the site concerned on a 1–5 ranking. An estimate of the download time for different modem speeds is also given. Shareware.com's home page is shown in Figure 8.1.

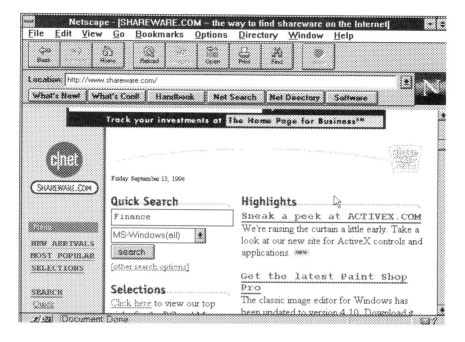

Figure 8.1   Shareware.com's home page

Both Winsite and Shareware.com are well worth bookmarking for future use.

Initiating Web Downloads

Downloading from sites like this is comparatively simple, especially where an alternative number of download venues is given. However, it is worth reiterating in plain language exactly what to do to ensure a smooth-running download. It boils down into a simple 12-stage process.

1. Create an empty directory. Call it (say) `c:\download`.
2. Launch Netscape (or whatever other browser software you are using) and open the URL of the software site. Let's say you go to http://www.shareware.com.
3. Search for the software you require.

4. Download the software by clicking on the hyperlink in the text. If offered a choice of sites from which to download the software go for the nearest most reliable site. If this fails, go for one of the large US sites such as Simtel or Oakland.

5. The browser will ask you how to configure the download. Choose *save to disk*.

6. A File Manager style interface should then appear and the empty directory can be selected as the place where the download will initially go.

7. The download will then take place.

8. Exit the browser, go back into File Manager (or its equivalent) and select the download directory. The downloaded file should be sitting there, probably with the suffix, *.zip* indicating that the file has been compressed to save on transmission time.

9. Empty the zipfile using the PKZIP utility referred to previously, or another decompression program. Deleting the shell of the original *.zip* file should then reveal its contents in the form of several other files with different suffixes.

10. One of these should be a *setup.ini* (or possibly *.exe*) file. Clicking on this will install the program into a separate new directory. The files in the download directory can then be deleted, leaving it empty and ready to receive the next set of zipped files.

11. Ensure that downloaded zipfiles are only emptied one at a time and then installed and the temporary directory's contents are then deleted. This ensures that confusion is avoided. Downloading and emptying zipfiles into the main *c:*\drive should also be avoided, since the newly downloaded items and their respective *setup.ini* files will be hard to identify.

12. The new application can then be used for the first time. Limited on-screen help is often provided with shareware programs, and the program will exhort the user to pay the fee necessary to obtain a registered version. In the main, these programs are good value, often priced at less than $20.

Specialist Finance and Investment Software Sites

Interrogating general software sites hoping to hit on the right package can be frustrating for the online investor. So it makes sense wherever possible to seek out specialist sites you know contain investment and finance programs. Here all the relevant information on different types of software can be assembled and compared with greater ease.

In the course of researching this chapter I came across two sites that are outstanding in this respect: one of the Wall Street Directory and the other at the University of California at San Marcos. They are described in more detail below, but it is the nature of the Internet and the World Wide Web that by the time this book is published others may have appeared.

Nowhere is the USA's lead in Internet-related activity more clearly visible than in this area.

To my knowledge there are no Web sites yet devoted to indexing UK investment software producers and their wares. Some of the more general applications found in sites such as Shareware.com can be found in the normal FTP sites in the UK. In the investment software sphere, however, UK online investors must for the moment resign themselves to downloading US programs and adapting them for UK use, paying the bill by credit card to obtain the software either by download or, in some cases, by mail.

Because of the remote nature of the transaction, it is very important that a demo or trial version of the program can be downloaded prior to any funds (plastic or otherwise) changing hands. This restricts the choice somewhat, but not so as any UK investor would notice. The couple of dozen investment software suppliers in the UK compares with more than 10 times that number in the USA.

The most comprehensive investment software site can be found at Wall Street Directory (http://www.wsdinc.com). This is a multi-purpose site covering links to many different categories of goods and services that the online investor could need, of which software is just one. As the size of the site has grown, the formerly indexed pages have been replaced by search engines which identify the product required. This has been made necessary by the growing number of links the site contains. It does, however, make the task of identifying suitable products through casual browsing and comparing them with other similar ones a little difficult. If you know what you are looking for, though, the site is very useful.

Each link contains a five-line description of the software, its price, and contact details, including an email address. Some links go direct to the Web page of the software company itself, where the software may be available for download directly and more information can be gleaned about it as well as other products marketed by the software company.

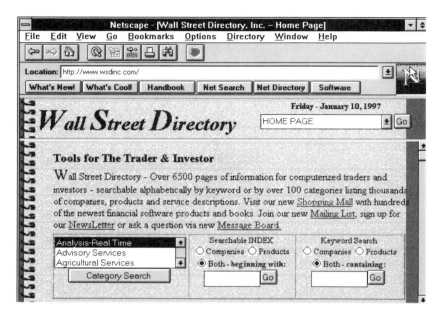

Figure 8.2 The Wall Street Directory site

The image reproduced in Figure 8.2 demonstrates the comprehensive and diverse nature of the site.

The other useful collection of directly downloadable finance software is held at the University of California at San Marcos (URL http://coyote. csusm.edu/winworld/diverse.html) where a regularly updated list of a variety of finance-oriented shareware programs is held.

While many of the packages have universal appeal, some are of more parochial interest, including, for example, a software package designed to calculate the required child support payments specified in California law for divorcees.

In total there are around 50 financial software packages, around the same number of specialist calculators and some 25 different Excel add-ins for a variety of functions.

Another site where investment software can be found is Wall Street Software at http://www.fastlane.net/homepages/wallst/wallst.html. This is a commercial site that offers a variety of downloadable utilities and demo programs, including Metastock and software-related to the US online service Prodigy. For UK users, however, its content is currently rather more limited than Wall Street Directory.

Individual Downloadable Investment Shareware Sites

Sites that offer a range of investment software downloads are only one way of accessing software. Most of the packages mentioned in brief below have been found via mentions in Usenet newsgroups. I make no comment either way on their usefulness or otherwise. It is up to you to check out the Web page, download the software if it seems likely to be useful, and make a judgement for yourself.

This section contains some examples of packages and sites which cover technical analysis in its various guises, and some concerned with financial planning and personal finance. They are generally packages that are not available at the time of writing at sources such as Wall Street Directory or UC San Marcos.

TCM Trading Systems (http://www2.interaccess.com/home) have developed a suite of six Windows-based, fully comprehensive, predictive trading programs. These are programs for those interested in active trading of the futures markets and the site offers information on all the programs, each of which covers a different futures instrument. Only a limited number of the programs will be sold, although the cost, at around $3,000 each, is arguably beyond the reach of many private investors.

Dataform (http://home.earthlink.net/m/dataform/software.html) offers a simple chart drawing program and investment data management module capable of being configured to accept UK data. A demo is available for download and the fully featured version costs in the region of $35.

Owlsoft (http://ourworld.compuserve.com/homepages/owlsoft) has a site where the visitor can see the basic characteristics of several programs, including Master Investor for Windows, a good-looking technical analysis program which again appears to be capable of taking data from the normal UK data sources (user-defined data formats can be specified). A demo version can be downloaded of this and of the company's other products. These include bookkeeping and other business related software. No prices are quoted for the registered versions.

ThinksPro (http://weber.ucsd.edu/rtrippi/books/rtthinks.htm). This program is a neural network development system which appears to be adaptable to the stock market scenario and works on the basis of complex statistical analysis of share price data. There is a brief description of the product and 30-day trial version is available. Again no prices are quoted for the registered version.

BioComp Systems (http://www.bio-comp.com/financia.htm) also offers a neural network program called the Neurogenetic Optimiser. This is claimed to have predictive power for any form of financial time-based information. A lengthy description of the program is contained at the Web site. At the time of writing is was not clear whether or not a demo version was available. No price was quoted for the registered version.

Centre for Elliott Wave Analysis, based in Australia, can be found at http://www.iinet.com.au/~cewa/. It is dedicated to popularising this venerable specialist method of share price analysis. The site contains links to relevant shareware on the topic.

Goethe (http://www.wiwi.uni-frankfurt.de/AG/JWGI) is a German site with several software-related links. Most are links to packages available in other sites such as Wall Street Directory, but there are also connections to other hard-to-locate software directories.

There are many examples of personal finance management software available at the large sites such as San Marcos and Shareware.com. Some others I have come across are shown below.

Planware (http://www.planware.ie/resource/planware) is an Irish site specialising in software to help with personal financial management and the planning needs of small and medium-sized businesses. There are download facilities and screen shots of a variety of DOS-based packages as well as links to other sites. Only a limited amount of price data is given.

TaxCruncher (http://www.lookup.com/homepages/55461/home.html) produces software—mainly for the North American market—to aid individuals filing their annual tax returns. A number of packages are produced and can be downloaded, and there are links to other producers of similar software. However, TaxCruncher's promised tax return software for the

UK market had at the time of writing been put on hold pending news of an Inland Revenue-sponsored version which may be priced to undercut commercial software suppliers.

Some Useful Packages for the Online Investor

There are plenty of technical analysis and charting packages to choose from. But the right package for one investor may not help another who has a different level of understanding of the subject, relies on charts to a greater or lesser degree, or has access to a different type of data.

In this section, therefore, I will confine my remarks to packages that can help the online investor come to grips with the fundamentals of a particular share. I have selected three that I use myself on a regular basis. You may well be able to find other equally useful ones.

Mathwiz

This is a sophisticated financial calculator produced by Informatik Inc. and downloadable from the San Marcos site's 'calculators' directory. The product includes a number of features including the calculation of days from dates (useful for determining bond interest payments and the number of days to an option expiry), amortisation schedules, which can be used to calculate loan repayments, and a financial calculator that provides the functions associated with discounting back a future stream of income to produce figures such as net present value and internal rate of return. This can be used for both steady and irregular flows of cash. Full on-screen help is provided.

StockQuest

This is also downloadable from the San Marcos site and at the time of writing the filename was *stckwz22.zip*.

The program is a deceptively simple tool for working out the correct value for a security. The model assumes that the investor knows the total return (i.e. capital growth plus dividend yield) he or she wishes to derive from an investment over a specified time period. For a given stock, the investor will also know the historic earnings per share and dividends. An assumption needs to be made about the likely growth potential for the company.

The basic questions the investor must ask are:

❏ How fast will earnings grow?
❏ For how many years (i.e. over what term) is it expected or required for this growth to continue?
❏ What return is required from the investment?

For the last question you need to bear in mind the yields available on other forms of investment, and that higher returns are normally also accompanied by higher risks.

Clearly none of the three questions above can be answered with any certainty, but comfort zones can be established. The model may work particularly well with a certain type of growth stock, perhaps a retailer with a formula for which there is potential and where a predictible number of new sites will be opened each year, producing a reasonably reliable estimate of earnings growth.

But the real value of this software is that the user is able to see how the three parameters—growth, term, and total return—interact. The three combine to produce a per share value for the security. This can then be compared with the share price to determine whether the stock is cheap or dear if the assumptions being made are correct. The impact of changing any of the assumptions while leaving the others unchanged can also be seen instantly.

How does it work? Earnings are compounded at the growth rate specified for the term of the investment to produce the estimated annual earnings at the end of the projected period. These earnings are then capitalised at the specified rate of return to arrive at the expected future stock value at the end of the term.

This future stock value is then discounted back at the yield rate to produce the net price for the shares. Dividends are assumed to grow at the same rate as earnings and the stream of dividends over the term of the shares is discounted back to arrive at their present value. This is added to the net price of the shares to produce the indicated total value.

It is probably easier to explain this using a concrete example as shown in the screen shot in Figure 8.3. The figures show the current values (at the time of writing) for the carpet retailer Carpetright. Earnings per share are

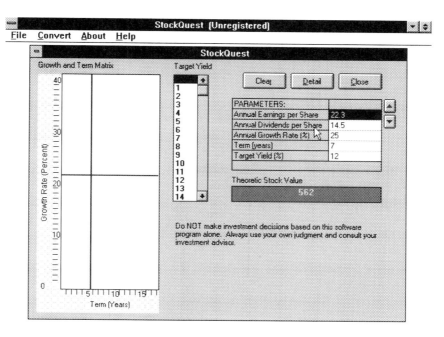

Figure 8.3   Using StockQuest to estimate the value of an investment

22.3p; dividends are 14.5p. We assume that profits will continue to grow at 25 per cent for at least the next seven years, the term of the investment we require. We would be happy with a total return in the region of 12 per cent per annum.

The model produces a stock valued of 562p compared to the present share price in the region (at the time of writing) of 590p, suggesting that these are the assumptions the market has currently factored into the share price. Put another way, if the market's valuation is correct, then buying the shares at the current price ought to give us roughly the return we require.

The advantage of this model and ones like it is that if assumptions are changed—new profit figures are disclosed, the assumed growth rate changes, bond yields (say) rise and therefore the return demanded from an equity investment also increases—then the impact on the share price can be seen easily.

Equally the required change in one variable needed to compensate for a change in another can also be determined. What improvement in the growth rate for instance might be needed to offset a half-point rise in yields?

StockQuest uses a simple form of discounting to arrive at its conclusion. A more sophisticated, yet still easy to use, version of the same concept is the Warren Buffett Way Spreadsheet.

Warren Buffett Way Spreadsheet

In his book *The Warren Buffett Way*, Robert Hagstrom describes the well-known American investor's penchant for investing on the basis of 'owner earnings'. This really means assessing a company on the basis of the long-term cash flow it is capable of generating under a comparatively frugal management regime.

Bob Costa, the operator of a Web site known as InvestorWeb (http://www.investorweb.com/) has taken this one stage further and devised a spreadsheet which works with Microsoft Excel Version 4 and upwards. It can be used to value shares with the entry of a minimum of data. The spreadsheet is located in the 'Other Investment Information of Interest to Investors' section of the InvestorWeb site.

Figure 8.4 reproduces the spreadsheet display. Only 12 lines of data need to be entered. This can be done quite quickly from an annual report or press release that normally accompanies a company's preliminary results announcement and which usually now give cash flow and balance sheet data. The table shows the data filled in for Carpetright on the basis of the same historical numbers used for StockQuest in the previous section.

The most important features of the spreadsheet, however, are the assumptions entered in the lower part of the table, which determine how cash flow is likely to pan out in the future. The difference between this spreadsheet and the more basic calculating tool represented by StockQuest is that a much more subtle pattern of future cash flow growth can be assumed.

This can take in ups and downs in the economy, or peculiarities specific to the company involved. The example shows that the assumptions entered for Carpetright, however, produce much the same result as was achieved by the simpler model.

These are just three detailed examples of the types of software on offer on the Net. The Warren Buffett Way Spreadsheet is free but requires you

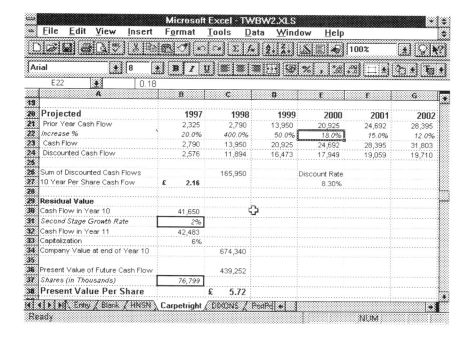

Figure 8.4 Using the Warren Buffett Way Spreadsheet to value shares

to have a recent version of Excel, while the other two products are low-cost shareware that function on a stand-alone basis.

Both the registered version of the StockQuest product and the MathWiz product cost $22.50. Details of how to register both products can be found at the Informatik Web site or by emailing info@informatik.com.

CHAPTER 9

Exchanges, Governments and Regulators Online

This chapter looks at the Web sites maintained by stock markets and derivatives exchanges around the world, and at the resources they provide for investors. It also covers some similar sites maintained by the finance arms of governments, and by financial market regulators.

Even though the UK's representation in this area is relatively minor in terms of the number of available sites, it is likely that it will grow in time. Examples from overseas point the way.

The expansion of the Net is also likely to lead to a greater degree of international share buying by the more sophisticated retail investor, and Web sites maintained by exchanges, governments and regulators, especially in the more developed stock markets of the world, are one way for them to find out more information before investing. This is true even if they choose to invest through an investment trust or unit trust, rather than direct.

Exchanges on the Web

Parallel to the rise of the Internet and World Wide Web over the past few years has been growth in the numbers of world stock markets. Many have sprung up in parts of the world hitherto closed to the brand of capitalism epitomised by share trading.

Most have been the result of the collapse of communism as a significant political force and the division of the formerly unified countries—previously held together artificially by totalitarian regimes—as differing national identities are reasserted. Rather like airlines, stock markets have come to be regarded as a symbol of legitimate nationhood.

Another factor has driven these developments along. This is the relative ease with which, in the information age, electronic markets can be set up and regulated, and the facility with which trade settlement and registration can be accomplished by the same electronic means.

The UK may have spent several years of heart-searching and substantial expense (amounting to more than £100 million) before arriving at its electronic settlement regime last July. But good though CREST is, and venerable though the London stock market is too, London's new electronic system has only enabled Britain to catch up settlement-wise to where some of the infant markets were at their birth.

Along with the growth in the numbers of stock markets has come an equivalent increase in the Web sites devoted to them. At the time of writing, the Yahoo! index of stock exchanges listed some 70 share markets on the Web, and a further 24 or so futures and options exchanges (see Figure 9.1). The Qualisteam site, mentioned in Chapter 5, also contains links to a range of stock exchange sites.

The Oslo Stock Exchange keeps a list of global stock market Web sites. This currently has some 60–70 entries, not all of which are on Yahoo!.

If you want information on, say, the Rio de Janeiro stock exchange, or the Kuwait stock exchange, you will have to go to Norway rather than to Yahoo! to find a link to take you there. Some of the links in both Yahoo! and the Oslo index also relate to market data on particular exchanges, not necessarily to official exchange Web sites.

Exchanges face a dilemma when it comes to Web sites. Typically, they make money from listing fees and memberships, and from selling real-time information. Visitors to Web sites, on the other hand, expect to see charts and data, and be able to download share prices without having to pay for them.

The exchanges, therefore, have to make sure that the data provided at the Web site does not undermine their own commercial interests, while still providing enough information for online investors to encourage interest in the market itself.

Most square this circle, if they do provide price information, by providing it free but on a time-delayed basis, with perhaps just an overall market

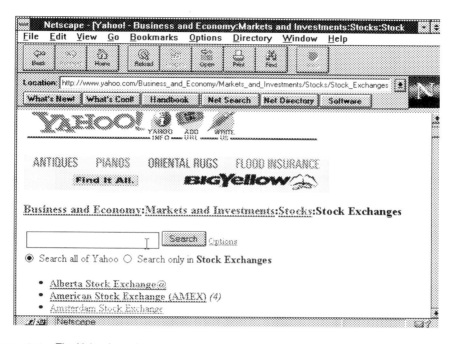

Figure 9.1 The Yahoo! stock exchange index

index available in real time. The London Stock Exchange, which is recognised as having among the highest charges in the world for data, has solved this problem by simply not having a Web site at all—with the exception of the one for the smaller company share trading system, the Alternative Investment Market (AIM).

There is little point in investors visiting exchange Web sites if the information there is inadequate or poorly maintained. This does not mean, of course, that the sites have to have sophisticated graphics or lots of pages. Investors need relevant information, presented concisely and updated frequently. The essence of a good stock market Web site comes down to a few key features:

❏ *The graphics content.* Elaborate graphics make what could be a quick visit to a site turn into a major excursion and detract from the experience.

Some stock market Web sites are particularly prone to this. The problem can be avoided by turning off the 'auto-load images' button on the browser, but sometimes ease of navigation is lost as a result.

❏ *Registration and login.* Many Web sites adopt this both as a way of controlling over-enthusiastic visitors and as a way of finding out information about those logging on. This is more a feature of sites that have heavy advertising (not normally the case with exchanges) and the monitoring in this case is more likely to stem from the desire—if price data is being uploaded to the site—to see who is accessing the data and how frequently. On the other hand, some regulators do not like too much information to be gathered from users, for fear that this will be used in inappropriate forms of promotion. Collecting your email address may be one thing; but regulators appear to draw the line at postal addresses.

❏ *Exchange press releases.* Many exchanges make press releases available online, and provided the site is frequently updated, this can be a useful source of statistics on market turnover and trade in individual stocks and instruments. Downloading and viewing statistics may be a complex process, however, requiring software such as Adobe Acrobat or other specialist viewers.

❏ *Publications list.* Exchanges often supply lists of publications and training courses, which can be a useful background guide. Many exchanges regard this as the *raison d'être* of their sites.

❏ *Member details.* This is crucial if you are contemplating dealing in the market concerned. Tracking down a broker through which to deal, or checking that your own broker has membership of the market concerned can be an important detail.

❏ *Price data.* Most investors want to have the ability to check prices, at least daily. As already noted, often exchanges have reservations about putting prices on the Net, for fear of undermining the lucrative sales of the information to professional traders. On some sites the price information available is simply the previous day's close; on some, time-delayed quotes are provided; a few exchanges provide real-time data.

❏ *Company details.* Some exchanges—mainly smaller ones—provide details of companies listed on the market, with basic fundamental data, contact numbers, and brief descriptions of activities. Some also offer company news, as announced to the exchange. This provision also tends to be confined, for obvious reasons, to the smaller exchanges. It would be unrealistic to expect, for instance, that the London Stock

Exchange would be able to make details of its several thousand listed companies available in this way.

❏ *Charts.* Some exchange Web sites contain charts of the main market index, and subsectors. Some have charts of leading companies or index constituents, or links to sites that do provide them.

❏ *Live index.* A good feature of several exchange Web sites is a real-time index figure, refreshed minute by minute. This can be good way of gaining a feel for how the market moves.

❏ *Links to other sites.* Although often owned by their members, exchanges are fiercely competitive and jealous of each other's territory. It is unrealistic, therefore, to expect them to provide easy links to each other's Web sites. None the less, a few do provide links to other local resources of interest to investors. This can be valuable, especially in emerging markets.

❏ *Frequency of updating.* This is sometimes hard to establish with precision, but clearly sites offering daily data need to be updated with daily frequency. Though a real-time feed of the index may often be present, the real key is how often the guts of the information on a site—press releases and historical statistics—are updated. Exchange Web sites vary hugely in this respect.

The next section provides some examples of exchange Web sites comparing these attributes, in as objective a manner as possible. Though it is clearly impossible to mention every site individually, the sites are grouped into leading exchanges, developed markets, new and emerging exchanges, and derivatives sites.

Major Exchange Web Sites

Table 9.1 summarises the characteristics of the Web sites of two US and four European stock exchanges. These are taken as simply a random cross-section of the sites available.

It is probably not immediately obvious from this table that the sites vary hugely in the ease with which they can be accessed and the speed with which the pages download. The French site of the Paris Bourse (SBF Paris) is particularly irritating in this respect, with heavy graphical content that serves no particular purpose, and for which navigation is completely absent if the images are turned off at the browser.

Table 9.1 Web sites of major exchanges

	AIM	Amsterdam SE*	SBF-Paris	Madrid SE	NYSE	NASDAQ
URL: http://	worldserver. pipex.com/aim	www.financeweb. ase.nl	www.bourse-de-paris.fr	www. bolsamadrid.es	www.nyse. com	www.nasdaq. com
Graphics content	Medium	Medium/ heavy	Heavy	Medium	Medium/ heavy	Light
Regn/login required?	No	No	No	No	No	No
Press releases	Yes	Yes	Yes	No	Yes	No
Publications list	No	No	Yes	Yes	Yes	No
Member details	Yes	No	Yes	Yes	No	No
Prices [mins delay]	No	No	No	Yes [15]	Yes (historical data)	Yes [15]
Company details	Yes	No	Yes	Yes	Yes (via links)	Yes (via links)
Charts	Yes	No	Yes	Yes	No	Yes
Real-time index	No	Yes	No	Yes	No	Yes
Links	No	No	No	No	No	No
How often updated	Infrequently	Infrequently	Daily	Daily	Weekly	Daily
Overall rating for online investor (1 = poor, 10 = good)	4	3	6	7	7	8

* Site recently redesigned.

Having said that, the content available on the listed companies is up to quite a high level, with links to charts and to company information and Web servers where appropriate. Statistical data is, though, limited and poorly presented. No intra-day prices are available.

When the first draft of this book was prepared neither the German nor the Italian stock markets had official Web sites. Both have recently launched one. The German site is accessible at the URL http://www.exchange.de and the Italian one at http://www.borsaitalia.it. A good chart service on Italian companies is also available from the URL http://www.linknet.it/borsa, with the underlying share price, a choice of two moving averages and some other technical indicators available in each case.

Elsewhere in Europe, the relatively new Madrid Stock Exchange site looks to have some promising innovations, with 15-minute delayed prices, a generally low graphics content except on the home page itself, all the usual statistics and charts, brief details of company figures, and indices.

It is something of pity to have to record that, so far as the UK is concerned, AIM's Web site does not measure up to these Continental initiatives. Although in theory the contents look good, with space for prospectus details, company press releases and announcements, charts, details of listing requirements and lists of nominated advisers, what has let the site down is poor updating and a large number of links in the index to the site that contain virtually no information of use to an investor.

It is possible that this problem may be rectified in time. In part it may stem from the success of the new market and the consequent large number of companies that have been admitted in the course of the past year or so.

The Amsterdam Stock Exchange site has recently been revamped. The old site was worthy but rather didactic, with little detail on companies and few statistics other than a real-time link to the AEX Index. Much of the space on the site was taken up with explanations about how the exchange had developed in recent years and with technical detail on exchange systems, much of which is certainly not relevant to potential 'retail' investors in the market. The new effort is a considerable improvement.

Sites in the USA are more highly developed. The New York Stock Exchange (NYSE) site, albeit slightly hampered by some pages with an overly heavy graphics content, does provide a useful amount of data and information, although not prices. It appears to be updated on roughly a weekly basis and has some links to company information.

The best site of the exchanges surveyed in this section was undoubtedly the NASDAQ site, which has a highly efficient server with a speedy response time, comprehensive performance data on the market as a whole, best and worst performers, and sector breakdowns. The site is set up basically as a quote server, but it has extensive links, especially to the corporate Web sites of the exchange's listed companies and to the relevant sections of SEC's EDGAR database. It is updated daily with index information provided real-time and all other prices delayed by 15 minutes.

Other Long-established Markets

There is a significant number of other long-established markets operating Web sites in the USA, elsewhere in North America, the Far East, Africa and Australasia.

Table 9.2 analyses each of these on the same basis as the ones above. Again, there are some surprising omissions. For instance, there is no official site for the Toronto Stock Exchange at the time of writing, although there is a commercial site, Telenium, at the URL http://www.telenium.ca, which offers a solid package of information on listed companies and their shares—including price charts, financial information, as well as Reuter news and other services. This is operated on a subscription basis.

Elsewhere in Canada, there is a stock exchange in Montreal listed in Yahoo!, but while the Vancouver Stock Exchange site is well constructed, it gives the impression of wishing to keep a lowish profile. The difference is stark between this rather sombre site and the all-singing, all-dancing NASDAQ one, for example.

Across the border, the Chicago Stock Exchange (formerly the MidWest Stock Exchange) has a site with good content, including 20-minute delayed prices and a schedule of company information that is brief but informative and which includes Web links to corporate home pages where available.

Table 9.2 Second tier exchange Web sites

	Australian SE	Chicago SE	Johannesburg SE	SE of Singapore	Vancouver SE
URL: http://	www.asx.com.au	www.chicago stockex.com	www.jse.co.za	www.ses.com.sg	www.vse.ca
Graphics content	Medium	Medium	Low/medium	Medium	Medium/low
Regn/login required?	Yes, for prices	No	No	No	No
Press releases available	Yes	Yes	Yes	Yes	Yes
Publications list	Yes	No	Annual Report	Yes	Yes
Member details	Yes	Yes	Yes	Yes	Yes
Prices [mins delay]	Yes (daily)	Yes [20]	From www. sharenet.co.za	No	No
Company details	No	Yes (+ Web links)	Brief	Web links to some company press releases	No
Charts	No	No	From www. sharenet.co.za	No	No
Real-time index	Hourly	No	No	No	No
Links	No	No	Yes	Yes	No
How often updated	Daily	Daily	Daily	Daily	Daily
Overall rating for online investor (1 = poor, 10 = good)	6	8	6	7	5

The Australian Stock Exchange has a useful site with daily closing prices, an index figure updated hourly and all the usual links to publications, member lists and press releases.

More interesting is the Singapore Stock Exchange which, like the Chicago Stock Exchange, makes full use of the 'frames' facility available within Netscape to present a good set of informative pages.

Where data such as company announcements has been sent electronically to the Singapore exchange, this is accessible at the site via hypertext links. As not all companies in Singapore do this, the Exchange stresses, the press releases available in this form are not representative of the market as a whole. Some links to corporate Web pages are also offered.

Price and index information is conspicuous by its absence, but the site does have links to other local resources related to investment.

Lastly, the Johannesburg Stock Exchange site has most of the usual facilities—including links to other sites, especially the Web sites of local banks. There is no price information or charts, but a link is provided to Sharenet (http://www.sharenet.co.za) which operates a low-cost subscription service of this type aimed at retail investors.

These sites show what can be done on relatively modest budgets with a little imagination. They highlight even more starkly the London Stock Exchange's conspicuous failure to respond to this challenge.

An even starker contrast is offered by the Web pages of some newly emerging markets.

Emerging Markets

Although there are a number of nascent stock exchange sites listed in Yahoo!, the list is more impressive than the content in some cases.

Checking out the Colombo stock exchange site, for instance, produced error messages on every single attempt, while some of the Eastern European stock market servers contained no English version. The following sites, analysed in Table 9.3, are some of those that remain.

The site for the Santiago Stock Exchange in Chile is a conventional effort, although at the time of writing it had no share price or company details, and only weekly index numbers. Some links are provided, mainly to local sites and others in the USA.

Table 9.3 Emerging market exchange Web sites

	Santiago SE	Budapest SE	NSE India	Thailand SE	Tel Aviv SE	Zagreb SE
URL: http://	www. bolsantiago.cl	www.fornax.hu	www.nseindia. com	www.set.or.th	www.tase.co.il	www.zse. com.hr
Graphics content	Medium/heavy	Light	Medium/heavy	Medium	Heavy	Heavy
Regn/login required?	No	No	No	No	Yes, for price service	No
Press releases available	No	No	Newsletters	Company news	Yes	Yes
Publications list	Yes	No	No	No	Yes	No
Member details	Yes	Yes	Yes	Yes	Yes	Yes
Prices	No	Daily	No	Real-time	Daily	Weekly
Company details	No	Brief accounts data	Contact numbers	Yes	No	No
Charts	Indices (weekly)	Yes	No	No	Yes, indices	No
Real-time index	No	Yes	No	Yes	No	No
Links	Yes	No	No	Yes	No	Yes
How often updated	Daily	2–3 days	Infrequently	Real-time	Daily	Weekly
Overall rating for online investor (1 = poor, 10 = good)	6	5	4	9	5	5

The Budapest Stock Exchange site is probably typical of many of those of the newly emerging Eastern European markets, with light graphics, daily prices, but no press releases or publications information. Contact information is provided on member firms and there is brief accounts data on the still small number of listed companies. However, there are charts of share prices and a real-time index is provided. Apart from its real-time features, the site appears to be updated every 2–3 days.

The site of the National Stock Exchange in India, the more aggressive of the main stock exchanges in the country, is a disappointing affair, with heavy graphics and contact details only for members and listed companies. There are no charts, no prices, no publications list, no real-time index and no links, and it is unclear how frequently the pages are updated. The only form of communication from the Exchange comes in the form of online versions of its member newsletters, which give some information but which do not appear either to be particularly up to date or to include every issue published.

By contrast the Thai Stock Exchange site is a model of informativeness. Although hardly a new market (it is more than twenty years old) this site should be taken as a blueprint for any aspiring market looking to construct a Web site. The graphics content is average, and listed company press releases are available, as well as other company data. Real-time prices of securities and the relevant indices are also displayed on the same basis. The site also includes a comprehensive set of links to a wide range of information sources on the country and its economy, and even includes information on Thai culture, cuisine and tourism.

The site of the Tel Aviv Stock Exchange suffers unfavourably by comparison with this model. The graphics content is excessive, although the site does make use of frames and audio. Press releases, publications and member details are available as well as daily updated prices. Some charts are available but there is no real-time index. To get meaningful price information you will be required to log in and pay a fee. There are no links.

The Zagreb Stock Exchange site also has relatively heavy graphics but not much information. Press releases from the exchange are available, as are member details. But prices are updated only weekly and no data is available on listed companies, nor are there any charts of share prices. There are some links to local sources relating both to the economy and to the government of Croatia. The site appears to be updated weekly.

Futures and Options Exchanges

Differences in the quality of futures and options exchange Web sites seem, on cursory examination at least, to be much less marked than is the case with markets trading the underlying shares.

Table 9.4 examines a random cross-section. We need to look at characteristics slightly different from those in the previous tables when comparing futures and options exchanges: whether or not there are detailed contract specifications available; whether the exchanges offer a variety of educational material, including software demos; whether or not they offer price data.

Typically derivatives exchanges have offered downloadable end-of-day data but not, on the whole, prices updated during the trading day.

LIFFE may eventually prove to be the exception to this. At the time of writing, London's futures and options exchange was proposing to provide

Table 9.4   Derivatives exchange Web sites

	CBOE	MATIF	LIFFE	NYMEX	SAFEX	Sydney
URL: http://	www.cboe.com	www.matif.fr	www.liffe.com	www.nymex. com	www.safex. co.za	www.sfe. com.au
Graphics content	Light	Very heavy	Heavy	Light	Medium	Very heavy
Regn/login required?	Voluntary	No	No	No	No	No
Press releases available	Yes	Yes	Yes	Yes	No	Yes (and newsletters)
Publications list	Yes (+ on-line ordering)	Yes	Yes	Yes	Annual Report	No
Member details	No	Yes	Yes	Yes	Yes	No
Prices	Yes (daily downloads)	Yes	Yes (1 day delay)	Yes (real time)	Daily	Yes (2 hours after close)
Contract specs	Yes	Yes	No	Yes	Yes	Yes
Software	Yes	No	No	Charts	Yes	Yes
Educational material	Yes	No	Yes	No	No	Yes (FAQs etc.)
Links	Yes	No	Yes	No	Yes	Yes
How often updated	Daily	Monthly	Daily	Daily	Daily	Daily
Overall rating for online investor (1 = poor, 10 = good)	9	5	7	7	7	8

registered users at its site with quotes on UK equity and index options updated every 15 minutes.

The sites covered in Table 9.4 differ considerably, not so much in the information they offer as in the speed with which it downloads.

As was also the case with the Paris Bourse, the French derivatives market has particularly heavy graphics at its site. These make navigating around it a time-consuming business. Each page contains large and pointless icons that take a long time to download. The MATIF site also contains little in the way of educational content and no links to other net resources.

This contrasts sharply with the Chicago Board Options Exchange (CBOE) site, which has light graphics and a rapid response, easy availability of press releases, online ordering of publications, and downloadable prices, educational software, and links to other sites. The daily updating of the site contrasts with what appears to be more like monthly updating for MATIF.

The LIFFE site has many of the same features of the CBOE site, but suffers slightly from over-elaborate graphics. Site redesign may eliminate this. Daily end-of-day prices and open interest figures are available in downloadable form for most instruments including equity options, time delayed by 24 hours, and there is a significant amount of information about the Exchange's educational initiatives. There are links to other sites included.

NYMEX has an interesting site with light graphics and the full complement of services available, including what appear to be real-time prices, or at least prices updated for the time of last trade. Charts are available. The site also contains details of NYMEX members, press releases, publications, but there are no links to other sites.

SAFEX, one of the newer derivatives exchanges, has a useful site. The Johannesburg-based exchange does not have press releases or publications available, with the exception of a full version of its latest annual report, but the site includes membership details and contract specifications. There are also daily price files and other historic information that can be downloaded, and extensive futures related links.

The Sydney Futures Exchange site is hampered with very cumbersome graphics which take a long time to download, but the content on the site is probably superior to all the others mentioned—with the possible exception that membership details and publications are not included.

That said, the site includes an extensive guide to the subject of futures and options, and to the exchange's contracts suitable for private investors. There is also detailed price information available daily two hours after the market close.

Longer-term statistics available for downloading from the site are also very comprehensive and there are extensive links to other sites, including a large number of other exchanges. Press releases and exchange newsletters are also available.

Case Study: LIFFE's Web Site

LIFFE's involvement with the Internet began in 1991 when access to it was made available to employees in selected areas of the exchange. At that time the objective was to offer those staff that needed it the option to use Internet email, as well as providing access to Gophers, FTP sites, and to certain newsgroups related to technological subjects.

Given this embedded knowledge at the Exchange, when Web sites for these markets came into vogue LIFFE was able to get its site off the ground relatively quickly and with minimum cost in terms of management time and financial expense.

The site is seen internally as part of LIFFE's publications department. The exchange's publications are essentially designed to be educational material for users of the market, and potential users. But it is acknowledged that presentation for the Web site requires these publications to be given a special design treatment to make their display as user-friendly as possible.

One advantage the exchange possessed compared to other organisations contemplating a similar move, was that it had no technophobia from management or staff to get in the way of the smooth implementation of the project. Moreover, no outside design effort was required—the site was assembled using an in-house design team. Getting the site up and running took around three months from start to finish, although it has since gone through several redesign exercises.

Other organisations may run up cost in designing foolproof security systems to prevent outsiders from breaking through from the Web site into internal computer systems. Because of the nature of its business, LIFFE has already had to be extremely security-conscious. Consequently the mechanics of organising the security for the Web site did not prove too much of a technical headache.

From the start, and in large measure for regulatory reasons, LIFFE determined that the content of the site should primarily be educational rather than marketing-driven. Part of a recent redesign was, without altering the nature of the site, to make it easier for specific user groups—for instance, retail investors interested in equity options, to drill down and get precisely the information they require, bypassing the rest of the site.

One of the most popular aspects of the LIFFE site is the opportunity it offers for users to download price and volume data on a range of futures and options products. This facility is used by private investors and professional traders around the world. LIFFE has, for instance, concrete evidence that futures traders and trading advisers in the USA regularly download its end-of-day data into technical analysis programs.

In terms of the popularity of the site, it is estimated that the Web pages currently get around 4,500 hits a day with a regular 300 or so users accessing an average of 10 pages or more per visit. Separate figures for the FTP sites (from where the data downloads are accessed) represent 50 per cent or more of this usage, and have demonstrated to management that the operation of the site can lead to extra business being transacted through the Exchange.

Aside from the home page, visited on 16 per cent of hits, the next most popular area is the publications section, which accounts for 8 per cent of hits. Publications are now available here in full in PDF format. The news pages account for 7 per cent of hits (this section is essentially an electronic archive of exchange press releases), general exchange news accounts for 9 per cent of hits, education pages for 5 per cent, and technology pages for 4 per cent. However, the figures are based on usage since the site started and the pattern may have shifted slightly as regular users become more accustomed to using it.

In terms of the origin of the 'hitters', around 27 per cent of them have a .com domain address (suggesting US origin), 18 per cent a .uk address, 17 per cent appear to originate from numbered addresses such as Compu-Serve, while 5 per cent are educational and academic users. Of the remainder, around 4 per cent of users originate in Germany, 2 per cent in Italy, 2 per cent in Japan, and a similar percentage in Australia.

Email responses to the site from users, a concern of many companies contemplating setting up a Web site, have been comparatively few in number (around 30 a week) and mainly related to users requesting further information from the Exchange's publications department, or asking to receive the detailed exchange data available on CD-ROM.

Lastly, one area that all exchanges are touchy about has also provoked lengthy debate within LIFFE. This is the issue of legal liability for the information displayed on the site. With a potential 250 jurisdictions involved, LIFFE has been careful to word a comprehensive disclaimer and to make it impossible to access the site without passing the page that contains it.

The legal issues centre on whether the Web site operator is transmitting the information to the user, or whether the user is taking a metaphorical journey to the physical location, picking up the information, and then returning home.

The latter seems the most sensible way to treat the issue, but good sense has not necessarily always been translated into solid case law. As it is,

LIFFE's disclaimer is generally held up as a model of how to treat the issue, and yet it is surprising how many exchange sites around the world can be accessed without encountering one.

Lastly, from the standpoint of users, LIFFE is well aware of the premium that many regular Web users place on ease of use, relatively light graphics content, and easy navigation back and forth through the pages. The last two redesigns of the site have been done with this very much in mind. The most recent, in January 1997, has segmented the site more clearly into the exchange's different product groups (bond products, equity products, commodity products and so on), increased the number of days of historical data held at the site, and also introduced a sophisticated search engine.

Governments and Regulators

Governments and regulators in many countries have proved quick to latch on to the communications benefits of the Internet, and the UK is no exception in this respect, somewhat in contrast to the state of affairs at the Stock Exchange whose interest in the Web as a means of promoting itself is strictly limited and, where it has been attempted, poorly executed.

The best starting point for investors is arguably the Treasury site. This is located at the URL http://www.hm-treasury.gov.uk. It contains a comprehensive table of contents, which guides the user to a variety of information including Ministerial biographies, speeches by the Chancellor, statistics on the running of the economy and the managing of public finances, press releases, news and links to other government departments.

One particularly attractive feature of the Treasury site is the ability to subscribe to an email list that ensures that Treasury press releases are despatched automatically to a subscriber's email address. The service is free and, though intended for the press and other interested professional parties, there is no reason why serious private investors cannot log into it.

This service is an efficient means of disseminating information and, as mentioned earlier, the list server system merits attention by corporates wishing to disseminate results and other announcements to broad constituencies of individuals who might be interested. This constituency includes analysts, institutions, private investors, and the press.

Other treasury-style sites are available, too. An interesting one is the French Treasury, which has a well laid-out site at the URL http://

www.tresor.finances.fr/oat/. This gives details of French government bond issues and other related statistics. It is mercifully free of the heavy graphics that plague other French stock market Web sites. Among other European central banks or treasuries, the Bundesbank does not yet have a home page.

Among the other links at the UK Treasury site is the Central Office of Information (http://www.coi.gov.uk). This acts as a central point for distributing information and press notices relating to government departments and other quasi-governmental organisations, such as the Bank of England, the OFT and other regulatory organisations. COI also runs a searchable database, based around the MUSCAT search engine, that allows the easy identification of items of government information from the mass of published data.

Another UK government-sponsored site is the CCTA (Central Computer and Telecommunications Authority) at URL http://www.open.gov.uk. This is also a collection of home pages and links to other government and quasi-government organisations, including public bodies, local councils, and agencies such as Companies House and HM Customs & Excise.

Yet another site that investors may feel tempted to check out is that of the Office for National Statistics, formed by a merger in 1996 of the Office of Population Censuses and Surveys and the CSO. Thoughts of reams of free statistics can be dismissed, however. For the moment this information is available only by subscription.

The UK's policy in this respect is somewhat at variance with the rest of the world, in both the accessibility of company information and official statistics. Taking the latter first, for example, many other government statistical organisations make an at-a-glance page of economic statistics readily available on their Web sites.

The Dutch official statistical organisation, Statistics Netherlands, has an extensive page of links to other government statistical organisations around the world. Its URL is http://www.cbs.nl. While some of the organisations listed adopt the UK model, many have useful information that can be accessed without payment.

Company filings are also more readily available in countries other than in the UK. In this case the benchmark to which all other countries should aspire is that set by the USA. While in the UK the most practical way of accessing company information is a visit to Companies House on City Road in London, the system costs £3.50 each for a company search and, though search ordering can be done online, retrieval is in the form of microfiche which must then either be copied or viewed through a special microfiche reader.

By contrast, the USA has the EDGAR service operated by the SEC. The Securities & Exchange Commission, America's stock market regulator, now requires all listed companies to file their annual returns electronically, and makes this database of returns available to investors over the Web in a searchable form. The EDGAR database, as mentioned in Chapter 7, can be found at http://www.sec.gov/edgarhp.htm.

The search engine used for accessing company filings at EDGAR can be quixotic. Searching for a company may turn up several spurious references to the company in the filings of competitors and other companies, for example, but among the listings will be the document you are looking for. This can then be viewed with relative ease by clicking on a hypertext link.

In addition to this database, the SEC site includes several other pages of interest to investors, including many relating to general investor protection issues.

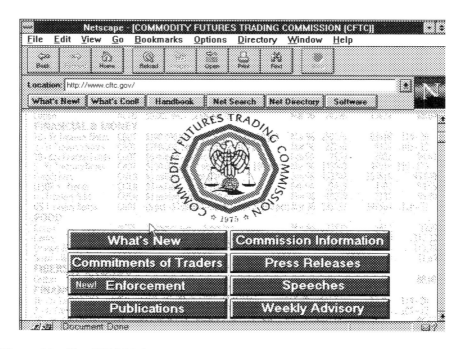

Figure 9.2   The CFTC Web site

The US futures industry regulator, the Commodity Futures Trading Commission (CFTC) also has a Web site, accessible at http://www.cftc.gov, (see Figure 9.2). This includes a variety of information, including press releases relating to the agency's regulatory activities, background information, details of speeches by Commission officials, and other material.

UK stockmarket regulators, by contrast, have been slow to set up Web sites, even though this may represent an effective way of communicating with their members and the public at large. At the time of writing, only IMRO, of the main UK investment regulators, had a Web site. It gives the normal information such as press releases and other data. The URL is http://www.imro.co.uk.

What the contents of this chapter indicate is the variance in the provision of information in different countries and across different exchanges around the world. It is not necessarily the largest countries or the most prominent exchanges that have the best Web sites.

From the standpoint of the UK online investor, however, it is disappointing that the UK's provision is so poor. Not only does the Stock Exchange not yet have any sort of presence for the main market, and the AIM Web site is poorly updated, but government sources of information are only available in a rather spotty fashion, and company filings and official statistics are only accessible by subscription and not yet available online.

The contrast with the USA, with its generous provision of official statistics and the outstanding SEC database of corporate filings, could not be more stark. An honourable exception in the UK is the Treasury site.

The next chapter deals with an area likely to contain Web sites more consistently informative to the UK online investor, those devoted to personal finance and banking.

CHAPTER 10

Online Personal Finance and Electronic Banking

Quite apart from the provision of cost-effective information on investment in shares, the World Wide Web has its uses for those in search of information on other personal finance matters.

Personal finance is a loosely defined term. Here, we will take it to mean anything related to your savings and investments, but excluding investment in individual listed company shares. So, personal finance can encompass banking, the merits of different types of savings accounts, savings and investment vehicles such as life assurance and personal pensions, PEPs, TESSAs, taxation, collective investments such as unit trusts and investment trusts, and many other topics.

It is easy to neglect this crucially important aspect of your finances. If you have a demanding job, there are never enough hours in the day to sort out the best deal on a savings product, to work out how best to minimise your personal tax bill, or how best to provide for an adequate (not to say generous) personal pension—one of the biggest financial decisions you can make.

The events of recent years, especially the furore over the mis-selling of personal pensions, have led to a climate of some mistrust between product providers, independent financial advisers and their clients. You want independent advice, but you may very well be searching for a truly objective source, rather than one that might be driven by the commissions offered on particular products. And you need an easy way of comparing the relative merits of different savings and investment products.

The Internet and the World Wide Web offer a number of ways of resolving these problems and issues. A few of them are:

❏ There are several sites on the Net where the basic nuts and bolts of personal finance are outlined in plain language and where issues can be raised and discussed.
❏ Over the past couple of years several large UK personal finance Web sites have been launched which offer the opportunity to explore some of these issues, and to search databases of performance statistics to select investment trusts, unit trusts, and other funds and products that fit your specific criteria.
❏ An increasing number of product providers are setting up Web sites to promote and eventually to direct-sell their products.
❏ One of the most basic personal finance services is a bank account, and the notion of online Web-based banking is slowly gathering pace.

The operation of bank accounts on the Web raises the issue of security and how sensitive information can be protected from the determined hacker, who is motivated either by a desire to subvert the financial system or by straightforward personal gain.

Regulators are also concerned that the growth of electronic personal finance activities in banking, insurance and investment could lead to practices which might harm savers and investors, by making regulatory monitoring more difficult.

Personal Finance Guidance

In parts of this book it is very apparent that a big chunk of the Internet and World Wide Web's content originates in, or is relevant to the USA. US Web sites often illustrate the way things may develop in the UK and Europe. Using US sites to illustrate the type of services that stockbrokers offer online is one thing, because the service they provide is essentially a generic one. Its features are similar across borders.

For personal finance advice the generic approach will not work. The different ways in which the tax system operates in the UK versus the USA, and different types of financial products available, and even different traditions relating to personal finance, and differences in attitude to various types of investment, all mean that we must consider UK sites alone in this section.

UK-oriented sites in this part of the investment scene are quite numerous. We'll look first at those which offer a general grounding in personal finance topics.

It is always possible, of course, to buy one of the many publications that deal with personal finance topics or to subscribe to magazines and newspapers that cover them. Personal finance is routinely covered in the quality week-end press, for instance, and there are many personal finance books that look at the different options open to individuals in this area.

The problem with this approach is partly cost, partly the way the content is presented, and partly the assumption made by many writers of a greater degree of knowledge than the reader may possess.

What the World Wide Web offers is the opportunity to satisfy oneself on basic questions and concepts in a sufficiently detailed but relatively anonymous manner—with the minimum of effort and cost.

Three or four sites currently stand out as ones where general grounding is available.

The first is Moneyweb, which is accessible at the URL http://www. moneyweb.co.uk (see Figure 10.1). Moneyweb is the creation of Ian Dickson, a one time independent financial adviser and now a personal finance writer and Internet consultant.

The Moneyweb site is primarily educational in content, and includes FAQs (frequently asked questions) on a variety of personal finance topics, including investments, mortgages, insurance, and so on. The only weakness is in the area of tax, where Dickson suggests contacting an appropriately qualified adviser. Answers to FAQs are given in direct and clear language and cover most of the topics on which individuals are likely to want to seek clarification.

The site also includes a large number of essays and articles on a wide variety of investment and finance topics.

Another good site of this type, but which includes more links to other sites of interest, is the AAA Investment Guide at the URL http://www. wisebuy.co.uk. Again the creation of a financial journalist and author, the site has clearly worded explanations that run the gamut of investment and personal finance topics, linked together in logical chapters.

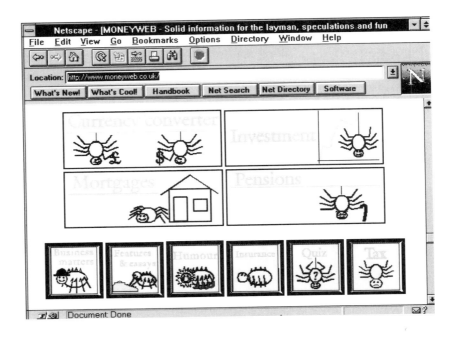

Figure 10.1   The Moneyweb Web site

The chapters include: best advice and how to get it; keeping down your tax bills; spreading your money around; saving towards a pension; a change in plan, and so on. One helpful adjunct to the site is a page that gives links to a wide range of Web sites created by producers and marketers of financial products, such as banks, building societies, fund management and unit trust groups, and stockbrokers. We'll look at some of these Web sites later in this chapter.

The third site that offers some basic guidance of this type is Moneyworld. This site, at http://www.moneyworld.co.uk, primarily offers hard information on financial products, such as interest rates, yields, and share prices. But it also has a series of brief guides to different aspects of personal finance, a glossary of personal finance and investment terms, personal finance news, and an extensive library of links to personal financial product providers, advisers and other sites of interest. This list is also searchable.

If you want to check out the Web sites of a range of personal finance product marketers, and perhaps have a brief objective grounding on a chosen topic in the personal finance arena, Moneyworld is hard to beat.

Another site worth a brief visit is Money Media. The Web address is http://www.demon.co.uk/dayco/money.html. This provides a plain English guide to the various options available in the insurance market and a particularly comprehensive tour of the market for second-hand endowment policies. This topic apart, however, the site's directory sections are less than comprehensive with only a smattering of Web links.

If you are less shy about posing their unanswered questions and initiating a more interactive discussion on the merits of different types of investment and savings products, then the Usenet *uk.finance* newsgroup offers a convenient forum. It has a reasonably consistent number of participants, a tendency broadly to stay on-topic, and an orientation towards personal finance rather than exclusively stock market investment issues.

There are also personal finance-oriented discussion groups operated by bulletin board systems such as CompuServe and CIX. Moneyweb's Ian Dickson also operates a personal finance email discussion list, although this is mainly targeted at professionals such as independent financial advisers. You can add your name to the list via the Moneyweb site.

Using newsgroups and discussion lists was discussed in Chapter 4 and so you might like to go back to the comments there to recap on the details of logging on to newsgroups and lists, and the 'netiquette' to be observed.

Harder-edged Information

As I said, one orientation of the Moneyworld site is information with a much harder edge, including comparisons of different rates of interest offered by a variety of savings institutions, and other data.

The site has, for example, details of the current 'best buys' in mortgage rates for various types of mortgage and category of borrower, together with data on the associated interest rates and the incentives and conditions underlying the loans.

In its 'rates and performance' section, similar data is available for deposit accounts with varying terms, including instant access, longer-term deposits, TESSAs, follow-on TESSAs, and similar accounts.

Information in this section also includes performance tables for life funds, pension funds, unit trusts and investment trusts, and rates for annuities, credit cards, and National Savings products. The site also gives up-to-date information on the various taxes and tax allowances relating to savings and investment.

Listing performance tables in this way takes the reader a little further forward. But the ideal is to be able to search through a spectrum of funds to determine which fits the particular investment policy and performance criteria you may have.

There are several other sites where extensive information of this type is available under one 'umbrella' and where, among the facilities on offer, is this ability to search for performance-related data and product details. The main two UK-oriented sites of this nature are Interactive Internet Investor (iii) and Trustnet, a superb searchable database of investment trusts.

Interactive Internet Investor is an umbrella site which, as well as a sizeable amount of internally provided content and access to the *Financial Times's* stable of personal finance and offshore investment magazines, also has a growing series of inbuilt links to product providers. These include Fidelity, M&G, Prolific, Standard Life and Gartmore, and organisations such as AUTIF and the AITC, respectively the trade associations for unit trust and investment trust groups.

The headings in iii's contents page include: performance; fund groups; unit trusts; investment trusts; PEPs; mortgages; offshore investment; as well as sections on advice, and directories and search engines.

The unit trust section contains links to pages provided by various leading providers including (as stated above) M&G, Fidelity, Gartmore and others. Similarly the investment trust and PEPs section contains pages sponsored by these various providers. Registration (which is free) may be required to gain access to some of these pages.

You will probably not need reminding that products put up on these pages by the various firms concerned may not represent the best value for a particular investor: the pages are, in effect, sophisticated online promotional brochures, albeit factual ones.

Elsewhere in the iii site there is data on mortgages split into sections aimed at different types of mortgage applicant, from first-time buyers through to those seeking remortgages. This page is also a sponsored one, advertising the services of London & Country Mortgages, but it does contain 'best buy' selections for each category.

The offshore section of the iii site is also sponsored. It contains news, performance data over one, three and five years for offshore funds, and some product data for sponsors' products. There are, in addition, both simple and complex guides to expatriate life and offshore investment provided by the journalists from the appropriate *FT* magazine.

The single best part of the iii site, however, is its ability to search for performance data on a wide range of funds. The statistics are courtesy of Micropal.

Getting down to really detailed data is only possible for fee-paying subscribers, but as a way of gaining a good overall view of the performance characteristics of particular funds and groups of funds, this part of the site is very useful.

Databases of unit trusts, investment trusts and PEPs can be searched separately. For instance, let's say we wish to search for the Fidelity Moneybuilder Index Fund. Entering the name of the fund in the search box produces the option to see data on the trust itself via a link to the provider's home page (if available), and information on the top 10 funds in its category. This shows the top performing fund over one, three and five years compared with the average for the category. Each one of the top 10 performers in the section can be tracked in this way.

The iii site also provides a collection of search engines on a single page. These allow the user to search in several different categories. These include: performance data; basic data on investment trusts; unit trusts; offshore funds; and PEPs; news on a specified topic; and data on independent financial advisers.

Independent financial adviser information can be interrogated to find advisers in your local area. The news searching facility scans the database of *FT* personal finance and offshore investing magazines. Typing in 'Jersey Financial Services', for instance, produced 20 hits, all of relevant articles, within a matter of seconds. 'Traded endowments' produced a further 20, and so on.

The value of this database is that it accesses a range of specialist personal finance publications published in the UK, and contains articles and content different from that contained in the searchable archives of the conventional newspaper sites referred to in Chapter 4. Reading up on an aspect of personal finance that affects you, without having to keep files of clippings on different topics just in case, is easy.

Some of the links thrown up by the searches are reserved for registered independent financial advisers, and cannot be viewed by those who are not.

This is because of the controlled circulation nature of some of the publications from which they are taken. In most searches, however, there is sufficient duplication of hits on the same topic for this not to be a problem.

TrustNet, accessed at http://www.trustnet.co.uk, is quite simply one of the best sites on the net for personal investors. A page from the site is shown in Figure 10.2. TrustNet offers comparative performance data and detailed information covering UK investment trusts and closed end offshore funds.

Basic information is available on each trust and is accessible from an easy-to-use index. It includes: the name of the management group; its address and phone number; the trust's investment objectives; its gross assets; the date of its most up-to-date net asset value (NAV) calculation; the sector in which it appears (with a link to comparative table of similar trusts); and so on.

Performance tables are available which look at all trusts (including a separate table for investment trust warrants) or separates them out by

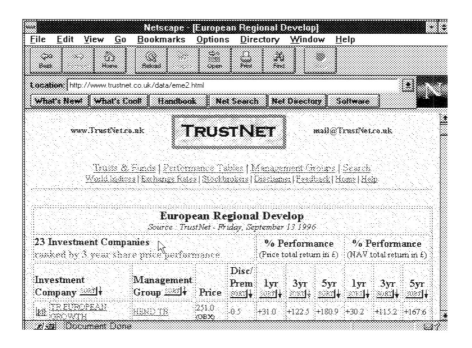

Figure 10.2   TrustNet's front page

geographical region or investment sector. The tables can analyse their constituents on the basis of the alphabetical order of fund or management group name, discount or premium to NAV, or their performance over one, three and five years.

But an attractive feature of the tables is an ability to alter the ranking criterion without leaving the table. Simply clicking on the 'sort' button above each column in the table will reorder the ranking on the basis of the descending order of the parameter in the column selected. Hence you can, for instance, look at the trusts in the sector alphabetically at first, then click to view them ranked by discount to NAV, click again to view the same trusts ranked by five year performance, and so on.

The trusts in the stable of each management group can be viewed, although not ranked. But tables are available which rank 66 world stock market indices and 37 exchange rates on the basis of their performance in local currency and sterling terms over one, three and five years.

Trustnet does not offer advice—indeed, it is precluded from doing so by City regulations—but the site is a fantastic resource for those looking for an investment trust and seeking an easy way to find out the basics. Armed with this site and a telephone to ring the manager for copies of the selected trust's annual accounts, little more is needed for successful picking of the appropriate vehicle.

Individual Product Provider Web Sites

Apart from stockbrokers, which we looked at in Chapter 6, the personal finance-related Web sites of individual product and service providers fall nicely into several distinct categories: insurance companies; banks and building societies; independent financial advisers; and specialist mortgage and property sites.

Taking insurers first, the sites differ hugely in character and are developing all the time. We'll look at some of their general characteristics.

The first is that several insurers specialising in motor and household insurance offer sites where potential customers can get quotes, either online or to be emailed out later. Some of the sites operated by the larger listed companies also give out investor information—including results announcements and an on-screen version of the company's annual report.

In addition there are several specialist insurers—examples are Applewell Insurance Services (events insurance), Aviation Direct (aircraft), and Hiscox Group (yachts, and so forth)—which have a specialist business they are keen to advertise online.

There is no shortage of links to these sites. Moneyworld arguably has the biggest selection of links, but the Wisebuy/AAA Investment Guide site also has a largish number.

Within the sites, some of the larger-scale ones have links to other related Web sites, even those of competitors. The biggest collection is currently to be found at the Guardian Assurance site, and Norwich Union also has a substantial number.

Among the really innovative are Admiral Insurance, which sponsors a site devoted to motor cover. Allied Dunbar has downloadable software that will allow the user to work out the appropriate amount of life cover. CIS, unusually for an investment organisation, includes performance data for its managed funds on the site. Norwich Union is reported to be contemplating selling policies direct via the Web. Table 10.1 gives the URLs of these sites and some brief additional comments.

Table 10.1   Insurance and fund management Web sites

Site	URL (http://www.)	Comments
Admiral Insurance	admiral-insurance.co.uk	Internet motor insurance centre; illustration, and quotes
Allied Dunbar	AlliedDunbar.co.uk	Life cover; illustrations; software
AXA	axa.co.uk	Life cover; overly heavy graphics
Churchill Insurance	churchill.co.uk	Motor and household quotes
Colonnade Insurance	colonnade.co.uk	Eye-catching graphics; motor and household quotes (not online)
Commercial Union	commercialunion.co.uk	Heavy graphics; includes investor information
Co-operative Insurance	cis.co.uk	Well designed and comprehensive; includes performance data
Direct Electronic	londonmall.co.uk/direlec	Full search of over 100 companies for quotes
General Accident	ga.co.uk	Results; news; community information; claims statistics
Guardian	gre.co.uk	Product data plus very comprehensive links (no quotes)
Intersure	intersure.co.uk	Household, motor, wedding insurance
Legal & General	legalandgeneral.co.uk	Mortgages, pensions, life; some links
Norwich Union	norwich-union.co.uk	Well laid-out site with clear graphics and good links
Quote Wizard	u-net.com/~newman/	Novel approach to getting quotes; fast and slick
Scottish Amicable	scottishamicable.com	Life, PEP, pensions, flexible life, financial advisory; good lay-out

Banking sites are equally variable, and sometimes constructed with a corporate agenda very much in mind. The sites range from the didactic (bold colours, large print, 'Janet and John' graphics) to the basic (simple factual statements with no links).

Both banks and building societies have been active launchers of Web sites. The more complex ones include information on rates for savers and borrowers, and mortgage terms. Some sites offer additional corporate facts and profiles, especially in the case of building societies planning to become listed companies in the fullness of time. Only a few of the sites, however, offer much investor-friendly information.

There are some useful innovations. An example is the online mortgage payment calculator at the Alliance & Leicester site. There are details of online banking at the Bank of Scotland site, and downloadable money management software from Barclays and from Nationwide. Nationwide also boasts what it describes as a 'jargon-buster'—in fact a glossary of the financial terminology used in its site.

Links are pretty sparse in banking sites and somewhat idiosyncratic. The links in the Abbey National site seem almost random and certainly do not have a predominantly financial theme. At the Lloyds Bank page there is a link to a site offering to foster communications between those working from home.

The basic data on these sites is shown in Table 10.2.

Other personal finance sites from product and service providers coalesce into either those relating to the independent financial adviser market or those providing property and mortgage advice.

Somewhat surprisingly, other than those grouped together in the Interactive Internet Investor site, fund management groups are conspicuous by their absence on the Web, with the exception of Fidelity, Flemings, Schroders Guinness Flight and one or two others. This may reflect the complexities of compliance with City regulations governing investor protection.

As a general rule, the sites put up by independent financial adviser firms, reflecting the 'small business' nature of many firms, are simple electronic advertisements providing contact information including email addresses, descriptions of the services provided and any particular specialism.

Some offer an interesting specialist slant. They include Allenbridge (http://www.moneyworld.co.uk/peptalk/), a PEP specialist, Fiona Price & Partners (http://www.moneyworld.co.uk/fionaprice/) which specialises in

Table 10.2   Bank and banking-related Web sites

Site	URL (http://www.)	Comments
Abbey National	abbeynational.co.uk	Managing money; issues; rates; lurid tabloid style
Alliance & Leicester	alliance-leicester.co.uk	Offers; mortgages; savings; loans; banking; online mortgage calculator
Bank of Scotland	bankofscotland.co.uk	Heavy graphics; usual banking topics plus online banking service information
Birmingham Midshires	birmingham-midshires.co.uk	Savings; mortgages; insurance; branch information; fussy graphics
Bradford and Bingley	bradford-bingley.co.uk	A 'frames' site with: history; services; what's new and rates
Chartered Institute of Banking	cib.org.uk	Comprehensive set of links to banking and bank-related Web sites
Halifix	halifax.co.uk	Incomplete 'frames' site with impossibly arty graphics
Lloyds Bank	lloydsbank.co.uk	Very limited banking information
Midland Bank	midlandbank.co.uk	Basic descriptive site with no links
Nationwide Building Society	nationwide.co.uk	Comprehensive site with many features including software and online banking
Northern Rock	nrock.co.uk	Simple site with 'Janet and John' graphics
Royal Bank of Scotland	royalbankscot.co.uk	Press releases; variety of information about the bank's activities; links to Rugby and the Edinburgh Festival; fiddly graphics
Woolwich Building Society	woolwich.co.uk	Comprehensive content but heavy graphical content on home page

financial advice for women, and GAEIA (http://www.u-net.com/~gaeia/home.htm), an independent financial adviser specialising in ethical investment which has links to a number of interesting related sites. Watersons (http://www.demon.co.uk/watersons/) is an independent financial adviser specialising in investment trusts.

Last, but not least, a site well worth a special mention is On-Line IFA (http://www.onlineifa) which offers a free financial healthcheck and substantial rebates on commissions for products purchased through the site.

This highlights an advantage of a pure Internet-based independent financial advice service. Since the firm concerned does not need to spend time meeting clients or have expensive office accommodation, substantial commission discounts are available, specially for those who need the minimum of advice selecting a product.

By the same token, a number of the independent financial advice firms with links in the Moneyworld directory offer discounts on commission, although these are normally reinvested in the product rather than re-funded in cash.

In the property and mortgage area, many sites which appear to offer countrywide property searches were either incomplete or 'under construction' at the time of writing. A number offer mortgage deals and information similar to that found on some of the building society sites.

The growth of sites offering financial products of this type has led to considerable interest in the Internet on the part of financial services regulators, and the next section looks in brief at some of the issues involved here.

Regulation

The electronic transmission and delivery of information raises a number of thorny legal issues.

Some, for instance, relate to copyright and data protection, and some to the law of contract. But from the standpoint of the financial services industry, the most pressing issue is that of ensuring that those operating Web sites, especially interactive ones, comply with existing regulations.

The financial services industry, especially that side of it dealing with 'retail' investors, is of course heavily regulated. Some would say it is over-regulated. The onus is on the product provider to make sure that the product is suitable for the customer to whom it is being sold, rather than the more normal principle of letting the buyer beware.

To date securities industry regulators have only scratched the surface, as perhaps evidenced by their general slowness to get their own Web pages up and running. But site operators can be warned. Both the Securities & Investments Board (the chief City regulator) and the Personal Investment Authority (the regulator for 'retail financial services') have begun to monitor the material displayed in personal finance Web sites for possible breaches in the code governing the advertising of financial products.

Many of the sites accordingly have heavy disclaimers, and specific 'buttons' on home pages that must be pressed to gain access to the rest of the site, supposedly to prove that the individual doing so has read and understood the disclaimer.

As is often the case, though, much of this regulation and monitoring is aimed at the wrong target. The international nature of the Internet and the World Wide Web make it perfectly simple for foreign firms, set up in tax-sheltered or low-wage domiciles, to bypass national regulatory bodies and ignore many of the regulations. At the same time they can operate with a cost base that enables a dramatic undercutting of the fees and commissions charged by the domestic players in mature markets, who have the burden of regulation and other costs to contend with.

Among the regulations that offshore operators could circumvent would be, for instance, those covering the need for the products to be marketed by properly qualified persons, the declaration of commissions, the publication of performance statistics, contract terms, and reporting requirements.

Because a Web site is essentially a passive medium, an investor sucked into an unsuitable investment by an offshore operator not adhering to UK rules has little or no redress. Some would argue that the fact that the customer entered the Web site, and while there filled in details that enabled the investment to be sold to him or her, itself implies that the contract was entered into freely and therefore that no crime was committed. Even if it were deemed that a crime had been committed, enforcement would arguably be problematic. The best that can be said is that the legal issues are cloudy.

The threat that these factors could pose to properly regulated providers of financial services may, however, turn out to be beneficial to the UK financial industry and its customers. Why? Because it may result in deregulation of the current strict regime governing the advertising of financial services products. And onshore firms operating Web sites may be able to stress more prominently the regulated nature of their businesses, and so gain a marketing edge.

Legitimate and long-established offshore investment centres such as the Channel Islands are equally concerned that the firms based there have high standards. Many financial services firms in these areas have Web sites and, though operating offshore, adhere to a strict regulatory code.

The move towards electronic marketing of financial services is one aspect of a wider trend towards electronic banking and commerce, and also raises—along with similar regulatory questions—issues related to the security of the Internet and World Wide Web links. This is, naturally, especially true where money transmission is concerned.

Electronic Banking

The idea of electronic banking is not new, but the growth in the use of personal computers and particularly the rise of the Internet and World Wide Web can take it out of its previous backwater and give it the critical mass to succeed.

In the USA, where trends in many areas are often repeated in Europe a few years later, the idea of electronic transactions linked in to personal finance software on a home PC is now taking off.

According to an article in *The Economist* in October 1995, for example, a quarter of personal banking transactions in America are now done over a phone line, mirroring similar trends in the securities industry. Persuading those who telephone instructions to their bank to simply log in on their PC is likely to be the natural starting point for banks looking to develop online.

But even in the USA there is a long way to go. It is estimated that only one customer in a thousand currently banks online. Yet the explosive growth in the acceptance of online services has led the American Banking Association to estimate that, by the end of 1997, around 40 per cent of large and medium-sized banks will offer online banking as an option. By the turn of the century, it believes this form of banking will be a $5 billion business. Some sources predict a six-fold rise in UK online banking transactions in 1997, albeit from a small base.

It should be stressed that online banking is somewhat different from the concept of digital cash. This idea, like the Mondex concept (partly owned by NatWest and Midland) now being tested in some areas of the UK, and the competing Visa 'electronic purse' (Barclays, Lloyds and others) is a different concept and somewhat beyond the scope of this book.

Currently, experiments of this nature face the challenge of replicating the convenience and simplicity of cash, debit card and credit card—while at the same not offering any significant advantages over them. Even so, if they are successful, e-cash could have profound implications for conventional currencies and exchange rates.

A related issue is the need to produce a foolproof high security electronic cash system for buying goods and services online. Which brings us back to electronic banking

Online banking is an interesting development for a number of reasons, not least because, like buying financial services over the Internet, the cheapness of the delivery mechanism means that the customer is likely to pay less for a level of service superior to the conventional branch-based bank. Citibank, a large American bank, has already scrapped charges for personal customers who bank online, and other banks are following suit. One American bank has taken this even further, actually charging customers for each visit to a physical bank branch.

More interesting still is the potential that online banking offers for the convergence of the interests of specialist software producers such as Microsoft and Intuit (the latter in particular has a powerful position in personal financial software), banks, and providers of financial services and savings and investment products.

In other words, online banking can be a route into one-stop shopping for financial services—but banks can also tap into the ready-made customer network represented by the existing installed user base of personal finance software producers.

The best example of this comes from Intuit, the makers of Quicken personal financial management software. In late 1995 it signed agreements with 21 US banks to offer PC banking using private networks and a special version of its Quicken software. This has a Netscape browser and Internet access bundled into the package. Intuit has also announced a deal to provide access to online banking for the three million users of America On-Line, the leading US Internet service provider.

The deal makes sense for Intuit because not only does it sell more software as a result, it takes a tiny commission on each transaction going over the network. It works in another sense, too, because although Quicken has an installed base of eight million in the USA, and 90 per cent of the owners of the latest version also have computers with modems, few of them have Internet access.

Banks are also attracted to the idea of online banking because of the socioeconomic profile of the typical home computer user, which is oriented towards the higher income groups and the younger end of the adult population. Here demand for banking and financial services is potentially more pronounced.

Other online banking initiatives in the USA have seen three American regional banks clubbing together to set up Security First Network Bank at http://www.sfnb.com/. The bank currently only accepts US customers, but has already attracted substantial interest. First Union, another bank, has joined forces with the telephone company MCI, while two other US banks,

BankAmerica and NationsBank, have acquired a producer of home banking software.

In the UK there have been several initiatives too. Barclays launched a pilot scheme with 2,000 customers, was overwhelmed by the response and will shortly roll out the service nationally. Bank of Scotland has long had an online banking offshoot known as HOBS (home office banking service). And Nationwide Building Society also has a PC banking facility for its FlexAccount customers. TSB operates an online banking service via CompuServe, and the Midland offshoot First Direct is expected to begin electronic banking trials soon. NatWest has a pilot project similar to the Barclays initiative.

Details of the services on offer are contained in the respective bank Web sites. All services of this type enable you to transfer funds from one account to another; set up standing orders; pay bills up to a month ahead; and check on account balances. In some cases the banks offer reduced charges for users of the service.

For the consumer, the attraction of the service lies in the added convenience of not having to visit a bank branch, and in the ease with which such a service could potentially be linked into personal finance software.

However, until comparatively recently, UK banks have generally been slow to tailor their services to standard programs. Normally accounts would be operated using proprietary software provided by the banks themselves, obliging customers to learn to use a new program and in many cases not allowing the data from the banking program to be transferred in a readable form into other software. However, Barclays is to offer online banking customers the option of using the bank's own software or a standard commercial product. Barclays has negotiated a non-exclusive arrangement for its customers to be able to operate their online accounts using Microsoft Money '97 personal financial management package, and links to suppliers such as Intuit (Quicken) may well follow. All of the UK services described above operate through private networks rather than over the Internet.

An exception to this rule is BankNet, a joint venture between MarketNet and Secure Trust, a Bradford-based licensed deposit taker. The service offers the ability to view the account live over the Web, to write electronic cheques using secure software, as well as all the usual banking services. Later phases will allow funds transfer and electronic cheque payments into banks that are not on the BankNet network.

BankNet does not charge for cheques, standing order, direct debits, transfers between accounts, ATM withdrawals, statements and monthly account maintenance. The BankNet Web site (http://mkn.co.uk/bank/) also has pointers to other sites (predominently in the USA) concerned with the development of electronic commerce and information about it.

The main problem for this service, however, is the comparative obscurity of the provider. Only when electronic cheques can be used to settle accounts with large high street banks will the service stand a chance of getting off the ground. Even then, customers will still lack the perceived security of banking with a recognised high street name.

The big issue in electronic banking is security, although arguably it is no larger an issue than it should be with telephone banking or with the normal use of credit cards. Credit card users are quite happy to present a card in the insecure environment of a public place like a restaurant or a shop, or to read their credit card number over the phone to a theatre box office. Why then should they object to digital banking over a telephone line?

Yet Internet-based banking may not really make headway until the security issues related to it can be proved to have been solved. Banking online by accessing a private network is a different matter, however, since several techniques can be used to ensure security.

One simple way is by minimising the time spent online, by using an offline 'out-tray' to record transactions and instructions to the bank. The out-tray is then emptied into the bank network in a single 'blink' of data a few seconds in duration, minimising telephone charges and making it difficult for a hacker to sniff out.

Private bank networks typically operate through several layers of password protection. Large or unusual transactions will be flagged and extra password identification demanded before they can be implemented. Similarly an alarm will be raised if an attempt is made to access the account from a computer different from the normal one used.

Internet-based banks face a different scale of challenges. According to a newspaper article, in the first six months of its operation Security First Network Bank foiled 15,000 attempts to break into its systems, and banks fear that if major frauds were perpetrated via an Internet bank, it could undermine public confidence in the banking system itself.

The issue of watertight security also troubles banking regulators, since a totally secure electronic banking link, whether over the Internet or via a private network, has regulatory implications related to tax evasion, money-laundering and other issues. For these reasons, governments tend to object to unbreakable electronic encryption in private hands.

The central point is that present banking rules and regulations (at least as they relate to 'retail' customers) are designed around face-to-face contact at bank branch level and paper records, and will soon need to be amended to take account of the digital age.

And an online banking revolution would bring casualties in its wake. The end-result of a move to online banking is likely to be large-scale redundancies of bank branch employees and greater competition for custom among the banks.

Banks should, though, end up less forbidding as a result, and customers will be able to access information on financial products without fear of embarrassment through showing their ignorance, and without invoking the unwelcome attention of cold-calling sales people.

As David Hewson put it in the *Sunday Times* (10 December 1995): 'When the world's banks are online, and you can switch accounts with a phone call or through a session on your PC, competition will be here with a vengeance . . . In five years, our personal finances will be organised around *our* choices and convenience, not those of financial institutions.'

CHAPTER 11

The Corporate Sector Online

The World Wide Web has the potential to revolutionise communications between companies, their shareholders and investors at large. Why? Because it offers the opportunity of distributing up-to-date financial and corporate information quickly and cheaply.

There are advantages on both sides: private investors need not feel inhibited, as they often do at present, about contacting companies to request basic information. From a corporate standpoint, investor relations personnel need not be burdened with fielding mundane enquiries from small investors.

But this aspect of the online revolution is linked closely to developments elsewhere on the Net. If share prices are more readily available online at low cost, if investors can access cheap sources of daily and intra-day news over the Web, if they can deal in shares and buy other financial products online, then it makes sense for companies to make financial information freely available online.

It makes sense in other ways, too. As the number of online investors grows, they may come to regard the quality of a company's Web site and the comprehensiveness or otherwise of the information presented on it as indicative of the quality of a company as an investment.

The response to this challenge has been impressive in the USA, but rather less so in the UK and elsewhere. In the spring of 1995, I conducted an informal survey by fax of the top 100 companies in the UK, to attempt to find which (if any) had a Net presence either live, imminent or in the planning stage.

The survey produced about 40 responses. Of those that did respond, fewer than a dozen were at that time either contemplating a site or had one already operating. Many companies categorically ruled out any prospect of establishing a site. A logical deduction would be that any such proposals would be thwarted by senior management ignorance of the potential for effective communication offered by a Web site.

I have not repeated the survey recently, but at the last count just over 20 of the FT-SE100 listed companies had a Web presence with at least some information of relevance to shareholders.

Another survey, conducted recently by the consultancy firm Manning Selvage & Lee, and published in 1996 as *The Corporate Cyber-Dash*, suggests that many more large companies now have Web sites in the planning stage. The survey polled over 500 multinational companies about whether or not they had a Web site operating, under construction, or planned. While in the USA 40 per cent of the companies sampled had a Web site operating, in Europe the figure was more like 30 per cent. Even this may be an exaggeration.

The survey also claimed that 20 per cent of the companies in both the USA and Europe had sites under construction, while rather more European companies than US ones, about 15 per cent of the total, had plans to do so. But the Luddites continue to hold sway. Around 30 per cent of the European companies had no plans for a site, versus 20 per cent of the USA sample.

Corporate communicators, if this survey is to be believed, are enthusiastic about using the Web and other interactive electronic media as a means of communicating with investors, financial analysts, customers, suppliers, and journalists. Where no Web sites are planned, the reason is most likely to be that a stop has been placed on the idea much higher up in the organisation.

Purposes and Issues

What makes companies shy away from the notion of a Web site? For a start, it is clearly hard to reconcile the different objectives of the various constituencies of Web users in a single site without it becoming unwieldy.

Many companies can see advantages in using the Web as a cheap means of delivering information to and interacting with customers and communicating with suppliers, particularly where such a project can prove likely to cut costs by reducing employee numbers.

The site often held up as an example here is Federal Express. Its Web site enables customers to check the progress of their parcel via the Web rather than, as was previously the case, by contacting a telephone enquiry number.

But there are companies which, for a variety of legitimate business reasons, wish to keep a low profile and not display any more information to the public than they are legally obliged to do, by listing requirements, companies legislation and the like.

Among such companies might be defence contractors and cigarette companies. It is noteworthy for example, that the UK-based BAT Industries has no Web site. The same is true of Philip Morris, an otherwise aggressive marketer and brand-builder.

There are also many corporate Web sites (especially in the UK) that simply contain consumer information and material of an educational nature. Many consumer products and financial services companies view the Web as an exciting marketing tool because of the demographic and socioeconomic profile of Internet users.

Internet users are—so the theory goes—likely to be relatively young and affluent, susceptible to new ideas and technologies, and have above average educational attainment. This makes them an ideal target group for up-market consumer products, life policies, unit trusts and so on.

Innovative consumer products Web sites are often designed to hold the interest of the consumer and to generate loyalty by offering benefits in the shape of competitions, downloadable software such as screen-savers, and other gimmicks. They generally come complete with heavy graphics and other 'bells and whistles'.

These characteristics conflict starkly with the interests of online investors, who require a speedy and efficient delivery mechanism for company information such as annual reports, results announcements, press releases, and other background information, perhaps a means of accessing a live share price on the company, and a mechanism by which an email response can easily be generated from the company to a specific question of a financial or corporate nature.

It should be possible, for instance, for a private shareholder to email a question about a results announcement to a designated contact in the investor relations department of a large company and to receive a prompt official response.

That, at least, is the theory. In practice, setting up a Web site involves any company in a host of practical business-related and legal issues which are not easily solved and which, more importantly, can be used by entrenched and traditional-minded management as an excuse for ruling out the whole idea.

These issues fall into a number of areas, which are outlined briefly below:

Domain name. The first main issue is registering a name. This is not especially difficult, but there have been cases of enterprising Internet users registering popular ones in the hope of persuading a corporation to part with some cash to buy the name from them. Is there much point having a Web address, unless you can have one that is closely identifiable with the company itself? Arguably it doesn't matter, but the issue can lead to corporate heart-searching.

Security. A more serious issue is security. As was mentioned in the previous chapter, an online bank in the USA received 15,000 attempts to penetrate its security in the first nine months of its life. Corporate managements in general—justifiably in some cases—fear that establishing a Web site which has any form of interactive content may lead to its defences being breached. In other words, that malicious hackers or those with a straightforward commercial motive may be able to enter its computer systems and browse around in sensitive areas. Though companies are becoming increasingly networked internally, it is possible to overstate the importance of this particular issue.

Cost. The establishment of a Web site can entail substantial set-up costs, especially in the area of security. Employing consultants to design and create a secure Web site insulated from the company's own internal computer system can eat up money. The issue of cost is related to the extent of in-house computer expertise. In the case of LIFFE, the Web site was established and is maintained by the minimum of personnel, but only because LIFFE is an institution with highly sophisticated technical systems and long experience of managing secure systems.

Management time. Related to the issue of cost is the fear that a Web site will lead to a rise in the volume of enquiries into the company and be a drain on management time in the departments concerned. This is nonsense. Not only does the experience of operators of large interactive sites suggest that this will not happen but also, if a site is being used either to market and generate interest in the company's products, or to promote the image of the company to investors, then email responses are something to be welcomed rather than feared.

Legal. A more potent consideration relating to corporate Web sites is the legal issue, especially if a site is dispensing information to investors. Companies need to be conscious of not disseminating any information different from that distributed officially via stock exchange and other normal investor channels, or any form of advice or information that is not in the public domain.

It is this factor which may limit the degree to which UK companies are prepared to make investor-related Web sites interactive, for instance by inviting questions by email. But it does not invalidate the idea of making more information available to ordinary investors at the same time as it is received by institutional investors and their representatives.

Offering to answer investor questions individually by email may be shaky ground, but making information available to private investors that has already been disseminated to another class of shareholders can have few adverse legal consequences. Indeed it should be applauded for potentially widening the opportunity for private shareholder involvement.

It is clear that legal and indeed any other obstacles to the creation of corporate Web sites can be overcome if sufficient will is there to make it happen. If the huge quantity of corporate Web sites set up in the USA is any guide, especially in that most litigious of countries, then corporate Web sites in Europe and the UK ought to rise sharply in number over the next few years.

The objective of the remainder of this chapter is to examine where we are now in terms of the provision of corporate Web sites in both the UK and other countries, to outline some pointers for finding them, and to measure their usefulness.

How to Find Them

One of the problems with corporate web sites is that the companies which create them—supposedly as a vehicle for effective communication with the outside world—often have a different design agenda to the one that online investors might find useful.

As one commentator put it, 'Corporations love graphics, and the bigger the better'. Web sites can easily become corporate virility symbols. Rather than creating a simple and effective site which communicates its message efficiently, companies often get side-tracked into a competition to display more sophisticated graphics than their corporate rivals. The result is that sites become a triumph of style over substance.

One reason for this may also be that company bosses and Web designers, with access to ISDN lines and other state-of-the-art communications media, often forget that the average 'hitter' of the Web site is doing so via a standard telephone line and a 28,800 bps modem. Sites are often not structured with the interests of the user in mind.

What most users want is a fast download, hard facts, easy navigation around the site (even if the images are turned off at the browser), and a site that is updated frequently.

Finding corporate Web sites has become somewhat easier than it once was, although the UK still lacks a definitive source of *listed* company Web sites. Sheila Webber's guide to Business information Sources on the Internet (http://www.dis.strath.ac.uk/business/) contains a run-down of directories from which to access information on companies, but many of the links are to directories of basic information on companies (names, addresses and telephone numbers) rather than links to corporate Web sites.

The most comprehensive guide to UK company home pages is UK-Com's 'UK Businesses on the Web' (http://www.u-net.com/ukcom/). The site (see Figure 11.1) contains around 2,000 links arranged alphabetically. However, the vast majority relate to private companies and other organisations. These include government departments, universities and other semi-official organisations. And, although comprehensive, the list is not an exhaustive one. Some major listed company Web sites are omitted. The list is, however, probably the best starting point for a UK online investor, despite not yet being searchable.

Among smaller companies with Web sites are Internet Service providers such as Demon, Pavilion and Easynet, all now listed companies, and Christies, Microfocus, Oxford Molecular, Quality Software, and Voss Net. In all, the tally of listed company sites at the time of writing was just under 50, although this number is changing rapidly as time passes. Some sites are available for subsidiaries of larger companies. Granada Television has a site, for instance, as does Logica's UK subsidiary.

In the USA, the process of identifying Web sites is considerably easier. One very good site is 'NetWorth' (http://www.networth.galt.com). It offers the opportunity to search for Web sites for the Dow Jones Industrial Average constituents, for the NASDAQ 100, for components of the

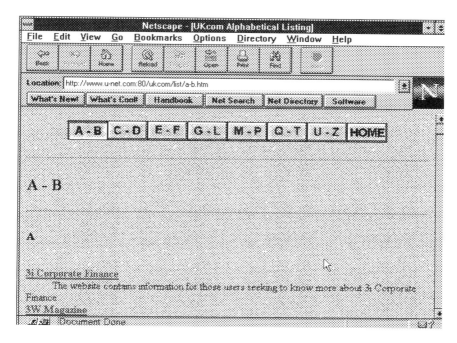

Figure 11.1 UK.com's home page

Fortune 500 list, for different sector groups, company names containing specific keywords, and so on. In all, it covers the sites of 2,000 listed companies. (See Figure 11.2.) It is also a comprehensive source of other information of use to investors.

In each case a brief description of the company is provided, together with the exchange or exchanges on which it is listed, as well as a link to the Web site.

In the case where searches for index constituents are carried out, it is interesting to see the proportion of each index's companies that have Web sites. At the time of writing I counted 23 of the DJIA's 30 constituents as having Web sites, and 67 of the NASDAQ 100. Doing the same exercise for the Standard & Poors or Fortune 500 is more time-consuming, but the obvious point is that a much higher proportion of large US listed companies have corporate Web sites than is the case in the UK.

We have seen that several US exchanges also provide links to the corporate Web sites of their listed companies, notably NASDAQ and the

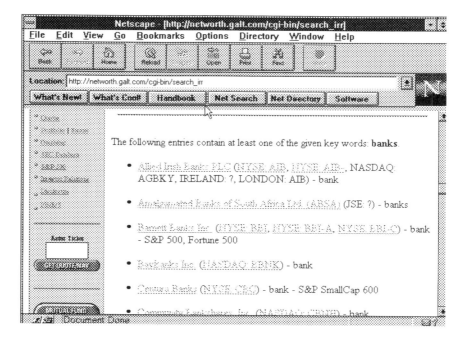

Figure 11.2   The NetWorth Web site

Chicago Stock Exchange. The latter has a useful company description which goes a little beyond the brevity of the NetWorth site, which simply records the industrial classification of the company concerned.

The Strathclyde directory also has a number of other links to corporate Web site directories in Asia, continental Europe and some other territories. Asian Business (http://asiabiz.com) has a collection of links to corporate Web sites around the Pacific Rim that is browsable by country and then by industrial sector.

Many of the Continental European resources are directories rather than guides to corporate Web sites, but Web.de (http://www.vroom.web.de) has a collection of links to corporate Web sites in Germany. The site is only available in German.

The remainder of this chapter compares a number of different Web sites in the UK and elsewhere, attempting to assess their usefulness or otherwise from the standpoint of the online investor.

The main factors considered in this comparison are outlined below:

❐ The broad thrust of the site. Whether it contains primarily customer or investor information. If it does contain primarily customer information, could this information be useful to you?

❐ The intensity of the graphics at the site. For reasons previously outlined, low graphics content is basically considered good, high graphics content bad—unless the graphics really add something to your understanding of the company.

❐ Whether an up-to-date annual report is available. This is pretty much a minimum requirement for a site to be useful. It is important, too, that the report is well laid out on the site, with clear links to different aspects of its contents.

❐ Whether press releases are available. The availability of up-to-date company-issued news releases in full is also an important aspect for online investors. If they are available, you can then rely on the company site rather than keep voluminous files of paper news releases and press clippings.

❐ Whether there is any additional useful general information on the company, such as product descriptions and prices.

❐ Whether there are any other special features available, such as video and audio clips, downloadable software, links to other sites of interest (including even perhaps those of competitors).

❐ Whether there is the facility for you to email queries on the company and its financial performance to the investor relations department or senior management at the company, and—more important—have the reasonable expectation of an intelligent response. Clearly this goes some way beyond the usual invitation present on many sites to offer comments on the construction and style of the site.

❐ Whether it is possible for you to get an up-to-date share price or stock quote from the site. Many US corporate Web sites offer this facility. Some also have a share price chart.

UK Major Company Web Sites

Table 11.1 compares the Web sites of some leading British companies, looking at the characteristics listed above.

What does the table show? First of all, the variability of the sites—not only in content, but also in design quality, user-friendliness, the heaviness

Table 11.1 UK larger company Web sites

	Barclays	British Airways	Cable & Wireless	GlaxoWellcome	Guinness	Severn-Trent Water	Tesco
URL: http://	www.barclays.co.uk	www.british-airways.com	www.cwplc.com	www.glaxowellcome.co.uk	www.guinness.ie	www.Severn-Trent.com	tesco.co.uk
Basic character	Consumer	Consumer	Corporate	Corporate/customer/scientific info	Consumer	Corporate	Consumer
Graphics content	Medium/low	Medium/high	High	Low	High	Medium	Medium/high (frames)
Regn/login required	No	No	No	No	No	Disclaimer	No
Annual report available	Yes	No	No	No	No	Yes	No
Press releases available	Yes	No	Yes	Yes	No	Yes	No
General info. on company	Yes	Yes	Yes	Yes	No	Yes	Yes
Special feature (if any)	No	Video clips	No	No	Screensavers	Price chart	Online ordering
Share quote	No	No	No	No	No	No	No
Investor email contact	No	No	No	No	No	Yes	No
Apparent frequency of updating	Daily	?	Daily/weekly	Daily	?	Weekly	Weekly
Overall rating for online investor (1 = poor, 10 = excellent)	8	2	6	6	0	10	3

of the graphics used, and the degree to which the companies invite responses from investors and potential investors.

The Barclays site is a solid offering with a considerable amount of product information, split into logical categories. Particularly good is a checkbox-style form that can be used to order further information on a comprehensive list of products.

The British Airways site is of limited use to an online investor. Although there are some detailed explanations of the group's operating environment and head office contact numbers, the basic thrust of the site is overwhelmingly consumer-oriented. The graphics are on the heavy side but the site is well-indexed and navigation around it is comparatively easy. Among the gimmicks available is a video clip of Concorde taking off. Online investors would have found an annual report and up-to-date press releases more helpful. It is also unclear how frequently the site is updated.

Cable & Wireless offers a good site that is spoilt only by rather cumbersome graphics. It focuses on corporate information. The company's UK subsidiary Mercury also has a site (at http://www.mercury.co.uk), which is more consumer-oriented although it does also contain financial information.

The C&W site does not include an annual report, but most of the useful information normally found in a report is displayed in some form at the site.

The Glaxo site is of a slightly different character. It contains a variety of information reflecting the nature of the company: there is consumer information, scientific details and investor-related data. All this is contained in a well laid-out graphics-free environment.

The overall impression of the Glaxo site is that considerable thought has gone into the content. The drawback from an online investor standpoint is that no full text of the annual report is available, although the detailed preliminary announcement is online. This criticism may simply reflect the time of year that I viewed the site. There is, however, a wealth of other information, including articles in industry newsletters relating to the company, and details of papers published by Glaxo Wellcome scientists.

Guinness, by contrast, adopts the approach of having several different sites under the broad umbrella of its beer and spirits operations. The official Irish beer site is overly arty and lacks information—criticisms sometimes made about its advertising. There are several unofficial Guinness sites.

The graphics at the Irish site are heavy and there is no information about the company that could be useful to investors. The site operated by Johnnie Walker (http://scotch.com), an offshoot of the company's United Distillers subsidiary, is more intelligible but still highly oriented towards the consumer. Guinness does, however, have plans to put its annual report and Stock Exchange announcements on a Web site in the course of 1997.

By far the best site of those surveyed in this section is that of Severn Trent. The water company's site has light graphics, a limited amount of consumer information, and an outstanding array of corporate data.

No login is necessary, but investors are required to pass a disclaimer page (a notable absence from other sites displaying investor information). There is an email contact form to request further information on the company and its activities. All corporate Web page designers interested in orienting a site towards investors would do well to look at this site, which also has a page displaying a chart of the group's share price since its privatisation in 1989. This is updated weekly.

Tesco also deserves marks for being one of the very first major UK companies to get a corporate Web page up and running, but its recently redesigned site has some drawbacks. The pages are primarily concerned with consumer information, and pages of interest to investors are hard to find. In addition the site has been configured in a 'frames' format, which also makes viewing the pages needlessly complex.

The Tesco site raises a general point about corporate Web sites. In many of them, it is often far from obvious where the information that might be of relevance to an online investor actually resides. The tendency is most likely for links containing either press information, news, or corporate information to be the ones required, but often the links are less straightforward than this. Considerable persistence is often necessary to establish whether or not the site contains the information required.

Lastly, special mention should go to a recently launched site from Railtrack (http://www.railtrack.co.uk) which is on a par with the Severn Trentone, save for the absence of an email investor relations contact address.

Smaller UK Company Web Sites

Table 11.2 shows the characteristics of a randomly selected small collection of small and medium-sized company Web sites. Here the variations in site

Table 11.2 UK smaller company Web sites

	Christies	Demon Internet	Microfocus	Oxford Molecular	Sage
URL; http://	www.christies.com	www.demon.net	www.mfltd.co.uk	www.oxmol.co.uk	www.sagesoft.co.uk
Basic character	Consumer	Consumer	Comprehensive	Corporate/scientific	Consumer/corporate
Graphics content	Light	High on home page, OK elsewhere	High on home page, OK elsewhere	Light	Medium (frames)
Regn/login required	No	No	No	No	No
Annual report available	No	No	Yes, archived	No	No
Press releases available	No	Yes	Yes	Yes	Yes
General information on company	Yes	Yes	Yes	Yes	Yes
Special feature (if any)	Image of sales	POP search engine	Online newsletter	Downloadable demos; good links	No
Share quote	No	No	No	No	No
email contact for investors	Option to ask for investment information	Yes	Yes, automailer	No	To Web editor
Apparent frequency of updating	Regular	Weekly	Weekly	Monthly?	Daily
Overall rating for online investors (1 = poor, 10 = excellent)	4	6	9	6	6

design are even more striking. There is more of an excuse for a smaller company simply to produce a consumer-related Web site than is the case, for example, for a FT-SE100 company. It is logical to expect (and it is the case) that technology-oriented companies tend to have the best sites. There are some honourable exceptions.

Christies, the world famous auctioneers, has a site that is virtually devoid of financial data but packed with detail about the company's worldwide operations. It also has an email response form phrased so as to leave open the possibility that financial information could be requested. The site has light graphics and is well indexed.

Demon Internet, a company which at the time of writing was preparing to go public, has a good site. Though it has heavy graphics and unintelligible icons on the home page, it is relatively easy to navigate around once inside the structure. Press releases and background information on the company are available, but no annual report. This may change when the company moves to a listing. A useful feature is a search engine that can be used to locate the nearest POP (point of presence) for subscribers.

The best of five sites surveyed in this section was the Microfocus one. It is comprehensive and contains both customer and investor information. Here, again, the graphics on the home page are heavy, but navigating around the site is easy once inside. The site has a comprehensive archive of results and announcements, annual reports going back several years, and comprehensive information on the company, its history, and its products and services.

A particularly interesting feature is an auto-mailer that will generate an email message whenever the site is updated. This is a useful feature for investors who wish to keep track of new developments at the company. At the time of writing, no other UK corporate Web sites visited offered this facility. With the addition of share price chart or an on-line quote, this site would rate a perfect score.

The site of Oxford Molecular is rather similar in concept to Glaxo Wellcome's, and considerable thought has gone into its design. It has light graphics and press releases are available, as well as considerable general information on the company.

The main thrust of the site is, however, related to the scientific rationale of the company, and the pages contain an extensive library of links to other related sites and topics, including Usenet newsgroups. From an investor's standpoint, the main drawback is that no annual report is available online.

Lastly, the accounting software giant Sage has a well thought-out site that is comprehensive in the angles it covers. Its format is predominantly consumer/user-oriented, but with a clearly labelled section containing press releases and other announcements. There is, however, no full text of the annual report.

With the exception of Microfocus, that all of the smaller company sites explored here fell down on this latter aspect of content should convey a message.

It is likely that this is merely an oversight rather than a lack of willingness to display what is, after all, a public document. Ambitious companies will remedy the deficiency pretty quickly.

Major US Companies Sites

How do US corporate Web sites perform on these criteria? Using the NetWorth site mentioned earlier, we can call up some details on a random selection of them. These are shown in Tables 11.3 and 11.4. A selection of Dow Jones Industrial and Fortune 500 companies are the guide for the larger end of the scale, and some constituents of the NASDAQ Top 100 used to represent the smaller end.

Larger company Web sites are compared in Table 11.3. It is clear that US companies are more attuned to the investor community than many of their British counterparts. One reason is because access to other Web facilities such as share quotes and official company filings is more advanced in the US than it is in the UK or elsewhere in Europe. All of the companies listed in Table 11.3 with the exception of American Express and Barnett Banks, have an online stock quote courtesy of one of the proprietary quote-servers. Most of the quotes are delayed 15 or 20 minutes.

Graphics on the sites range from heavy to medium, but only in the case of Amex and Coca-Cola are they irritatingly slow.

Some of the sites contain a page offering a 'bird's-eye view' of the site, which allows much easier viewing of the contents and quicker identification of the relevant links. All of the sites contain useful corporate information—although the amounts do vary.

The Amex site is a straightforward one with an annual report, press releases, background information on the company and its products and services. Unlike some of the sites, it has a facility whereby investors can email questions to an investor relations contact person. Questions on different products can be emailed via the company's email centre and routed from there to the appropriate quarter.

The Coca Cola site begins with a heavy, albeit stylish, graphic. It does not have an annual report available, but there is plenty of other financial information, including press releases and background data on the company. However, the corporate information is only a comparatively small part of the content of this large site. A special section is even devoted to the Chairman's philosophising on the meaning of business life.

The IBM site has a good mix of product and financial information. No annual report is available directly, but the last three years of quarterly press releases are available. There is also a substantial amount of relevant financial information. IBM's chairman, Lou Gerstner, has a page of his own on

Table 11.3 US major companies' Web sites

	American Express	Coca-Cola	IBM	Texaco	Merck	Nynex	Barnett Banks
URL: http://	www.american express.com	www.cocacola.com	www.ibm.com	www.texaco.com	www.merck.com	www.nynex.com	www.barnett.com
Basic character	Consumer/ corporate	Consumer	Corporate/financial	Corporate	Corporate/scientific	Corporate/ consumer	Corporate/ consumer
Graphics content	Heavy	Heavy	Medium	Medium/heavy	Medium/light	Medium	Medium
Regn/login required	No	No, but disclaimers	No	No	No	No	No
Annual report available	Yes	No	No, but quarterly back 3 years	Yes	Yes (and 10K)	Yes (downloadable in PDF)	Yes (+ SEC filings)
Press releases available	Yes	Yes	Yes	Yes	Link to SEC filings	Yes	Yes
General information on company	Yes	Yes	Yes	Yes	Yes	Yes	Yes
Special feature (if any)	No	Chairman's philosophy	Summary of AGM proceedings	Link to business news search engine	Wealth of scientific info	Searchable yellow pages	Screensavers; Florida links
Share quote	No	Yes	Yes	Yes	Yes	Yes	No
email contact for investors	Yes	Yes	Yes	No	No	No	Yes
Frequency of updating	Regular	Regular	Regular	Regular	?	Weekly	Weekly
Overall rating for online investor (1 = poor, 10 = excellent)	7	6	7	7	6	7	6

the site, and can be emailed directly. Other special features include a summary of proceedings at the company's annual general meeting, and the site does have a special email address for stockholder services.

At the Texaco site, which is primarily devoted to corporate information, there are annual reports and quarterly press releases, as well as other announcements and links to the Web sites of Texaco subsidiaries and affiliates. There is a link to an independent business-related news search engine. Overall the Texaco site has scored highly among the well-known raters of Web sites. It ranks in the top 5 per cent in the Point Survey, for example

Merck, a leading US-based international drugs group, has a site similar in concept to Glaxo Wellcome's—offering a mix of corporate and scientific information. The graphics content is low and annual reports and the equivalent SEC 1OK filings are available. Press information is confined to financial data provided via links to the SEC's EDGAR database. There is a stock quote facility, but few other press releases and only limited provision for email contact. Parts of the site are heavily research, science and medicine-oriented.

At Nynex, the New York area telephone utility, the mix is corporate and consumer information, and again the site has a 'bird's-eye view' page to enable easy navigation. Annual reports and SEC information are available, the former in downloadable PDF format. Special features include a searchable Yellow Pages.

Lastly, the Florida-based Barnett Banks pages includes a variety of corporate and customer information, as well as guides to Florida and its resources and tourism. Screen-savers and free software are available for download at the site, which also has a branch locator. Online PC-based banking is promised.

The overall impression of these sites is that the information displayed is more consistently provided than is the case with UK Web sites. At their best US sites can rival or exceed those of the companies mentioned above, but most often fall short. Though the style of each of these US sites is different, reflecting different corporate cultures, it is difficult to separate them in terms of content.

NASDAQ-listed Company Web Sites

This list of randomly chosen NASDAQ company Web sites in Table 11.4 deliberately avoids large companies such as Microsoft and Intel. These

Table 11.4   US NASDAQ company Web sites

	ADC Telecomms	Cisco Systems	McCormick	Staples Inc.	Sybase
URL; http://	www.adc.com	www.cisco.com	www.mccormick.com	www.staples.com	www.sybase.com
Basic character	Corporate/consumer	Corporate/consumer	Corporate/consumer	Consumer	Consumer/finance
Graphics content	Light	Heavy on HP, OK otherwise	Light	Light	Light
Regn/login required	No	For parts	No	No	No
Annual report available	No	Yes	Yes	via Edgar	Basic + PDF
Press releases available	Yes	Yes, archive back to 1992	Limitd number	Yes, and well indexed	Yes, and well indexed
General information on company	Yes	Yes	Yes	Yes	Yes
Special feature (if any)	Web links to business units	Two share price graphs	Spice facts	Store locator	Downloads, links to affiliates' sites
Share quote	No	Yes	No	No	Yes (+ chart)
email contact for investors	No	Yes	No	No	Yes
Frequency of updating	Weekly	Daily	?	Weekly	Daily
Overall rating for online investors (1 = poor, 10 = excellent)	5	10	6	8	10

remain NASDAQ-listed in spite of their size. The objective for Table 11.4 is to get a true comparison with Web sites in the smaller company area in the UK.

The sites are a little more variable than those of large US companies, but most still achieve a good minimum standard. Some are outstanding.

ADC Telecomms has a site with light graphics and a reasonable selection of information, although no annual report is available. There are some links to business units. Email response is exclusively product-related.

Cisco Systems, a Silicon Valley producer of Internet-related products, should have a good Web site—and it does. The graphical content on the home page is heavy. But once the site is accessed, navigating is easy and fast. A login is required for some of the more technically oriented parts of it. Annual reports are available and press releases are archived back to 1992. The archives are split into 'financial' and 'other', a useful innovation.

A share quote and two different type of share price chart are offered. There is the opportunity for investors to contact the company by email.

McCormick International is an importer and distributor of spices. It has a site devoted to corporate and financial information with light graphics. An annual report is available, but only a limited number of press releases. A special feature of the site is various 'spice facts' related to cooking with spices, and their availability. But there is no share quote and no investor-related email facility.

Staples Inc. is an office supplies retailer with stores both within the US and internationally (including some in the UK). Graphics are light and the site is primarily consumer-related. The display of press releases is farmed out to a third-party site, but the content is good and particularly well indexed. An online catalogue and ordering is available, together with a store locator. At the time of writing the company was in the process of merging with Home Depot.

Lastly, Sybase, another high-tech business, has a superb site with a wealth of information including a basic and PDF version of the annual report, well-indexed press releases, general information on the company, special features including downloadable demos of its software, a share quote and chart, and email contact addresses for investor relations people.

In a more radical departure, the site also gives access to a series of email list servers that can be used to receive either financial and corporate information or product news direct by email. Any UK companies wanting to create the ideal site would do well to have a look at this one.

Contents of the Ideal Site

The following list summarises the ideal content of corporate Web site, when seen from the standpoint of the UK online investor, taking the characteristics of the best of all the above sites as a guide.

❑ An easily-memorable URL.
❑ Light graphics, the simpler the better.
❑ A 'bird's-eye view' page, giving an overview of and links all parts of the site.
❑ Up to three years of annual reports, in both HTML and downloadable PDF format.

❏ Archived press releases back for at least the same length of time, indexed by subject area (or as a minimum, into 'financial' and 'other').

❏ A bullet point summary of the company's activities.

❏ Links to subsidiaries' and affiliates' Web sites—where present.

❏ A live share price quote, and historical share price charts.

❏ 'Something unique', downloadable software or screen-savers, or some other useful facility.

❏ A direct email contact in the company's investor relations department.

❏ An automatic email server for financial press releases and other corporate information.

❏ Links to other sites in the same industry.

With a set of data like this at a Web site, the online investor has a one-stop shop of authoritative information on which to base an investing decision. UK corporate Web designers please note.

Completing the Online Revolution

In this book I have tried to describe how, as an online investor armed with an Internet connection and a Web browser, you can level the information playing field and compete on better terms with the professionals.

The material speaks for itself and needs no reiteration here. But it will be necessary for you to try out the techniques and Web links described in the previous chapters for yourself.

Investment is an intensely personal activity. Investors vary in the way they approach it, in the information they look for, and the way they make their decisions. Only by trial and error can you decide which techniques and which Web sites will prove consistently useful to you in the ever-present search for stock market profits.

Unfortunately, the information playing field can only be levelled up to a point. Why? There are two main reasons.

The first is that the UK private investor can pay through the nose for share price data. Most exchanges charge heavily for real-time prices, but in the USA and some other markets prices delayed by 15 minutes—perfectly acceptable for most private investors—are available at a nominal cost. End-of-day prices are virtually free. US exchanges in particular have learnt that providing good-quality data at a low price to 'retail' investors generates activity, and it is high time the UK adopted this approach, too. The message is gradually getting through, but progress on this score is slow.

The second issue concerns the availability of information from companies.

Big companies want to present themselves well to professional investors. That is understandable. But it is inexcusable that they should fail to make available the same information to private investors that wish to avail themselves of it. The technology now exists to do this easily.

In the US three-quarters of the constituents of the Dow Jones index now have corporate Web sites, and among the top 100 NASDAQ companies the proportion is around two-thirds. Almost without exception these Web sites are devoted to presenting solid investor-friendly information. The best offer the facility for private investors to communicate with the company's investor relations personnel via email, and the opportunity for investors to receive emailed press releases and financial announcements.

There is no excuse for major UK companies not to pursue a similar policy. Yet at present fewer than 20 per cent of FT-SE100 companies have relevant Web sites, and many of these are poorly thought out.

Changes in technology place an obligation on exchanges and regulators to address these problems.

It is perfectly feasible for any market to make it a requirement of listing for companies to display information that is available to professional investors in a form (like a Web site) that is equally accessible to any ordinary online investor. The example of the USA demonstrates that there are few practical obstacles to this.

Addressing these two problems would, in my view, do more to popularise private share ownership than any other recent initiative. Moreover it would come at a time when individuals are increasingly being required to take charge of their own long-term savings and pension provision.

The elements of the online investor revolution are here. But they need some official encouragement. I hope that both in official circles and at the Stock Exchange there is the will to provide it.

Bibliography

Books

Gilster, Paul (1995) *The New Internet Navigator.* New York: John Wiley.

Hagstrom, Robert (1994) *The Warren Buffet Way.* New York: John Wiley.

Lynch, Peter (1992) *One Up on Wall Street.* New York: Simon & Schuster.

Lynch, Peter (1993) *Beating the Street.* New York: Simon & Schuster.

Randall, Neil (1994) *Teach Yourself the Internet.* Indianapolis: Sams Publishing.

Temple, Peter (1996) *Getting Started in Shares.* Chichester: John Wiley.

Articles and surveys

Manning, Selvage & Lee (1996). *The Corporate Cyber-Dash.*

Hewson, David (10 December 1995) 'Online banking will put an end to rip-offs'. In the Sounding Off column of the *Sunday Times.*

Tabizel, David and Rosen, Nick (January 1996) *The Internet in 1996.* Durlacher Multimedia.

Waldman, Simon (26 August 1994) 'Unfeted facet of the TV set'. *Media Week.*

List of Abbreviations

ADR	American depository receipt
AIM	alternative investment market
ARPA	Advanced Research Projects Agency
ASCII	American Standard Code for Information Interchange
BBS	bulletin board system
bps	bits per second
CCTA	Central Computer and Telecommunications Authority [UK]
CD-ROM	compact disk read only memory
CFTC	Commodity Futures Trading Commission [USA]
COI	Central Office of Information
CSV	comma separated values [used for spreadsheet data]
FAQ	frequently asked questions
FT	*Financial Times*
FTP	file transfer protocol
FTSE	Financial Times–Stock Exchange [100 Share Index] ('footsie')
HTML	HyperText Mark-up Language
HTTP	HyperText Transfer Protocol
IMRO	Investment Management Regulatory Organisation
IP	Internet Protocol
ISDN	integrated services digital network
ISP	Internet service provider (Also known as IAP–Internet access provider.)
LAN	local area network

LIFFE	London International Finance Futures and Options Exchange
Mb	megabyte
MHz	megahertz
NAV	net asset value
OHLCV	open, high, low, close and volume
OLR	offline reader
PC	personal computer
PDF	portable document file
POP	point of presence
PPP	point to point protocol
RAM	random access memory
SEC	Securities & Exchange Commission
SFA	Securities and Futures Authority
SIB	Securities and Investments Board
SLIP	serial line Internet protocol
TCP	transmission control protocol
URL	uniform resource locator
WAN	wide area network

Glossary

Archie A program that will search for files stored on *FTP* sites across the Internet.

ASCII American Standard Code for Information Interchange—format understood by all computers. An ASCII file will contain bytes of seven bits. *See also binary.*

backbone The high-capacity part of a network that links other networks.

bandwidth How much data you can send over a communications link. *See also baud.*

baud The unit of measurement for modem speeds. One-baud is one signalling element per second.

binary A format in which a file might be saved. A binary file will contain bytes of eight bits. *See also ASCII.*

bits The smallest piece of information a computer deals with. A collection of bits are a *byte.*

bits per second (bps) The standard measure of *bandwidth.*

bookmark To save the address of Web sites in your *navigator.*

Boolean operators Words such as AND, NOT and OR which you can use to help fine tune a search expression.

browser A program such as Netscape Navigator that enables your computer to download and display documents from the *World Wide Web.*

bulletin board system (BBS) A common area on the Internet where anyone can read or write messages. Private BBSs can be set up for group discussions.

buttons Small online advertisements at Web sites.

byte Seven (see *ASCII)* or eight (see *binary) bits.*

CD-ROM drive Similar to a floppy drive, but for a CD-ROM (compact disk read only memory). This is a storage device similar to a music CD that can hold a vast amount of information.

cyberspace The 'universe' of the Internet and World Wide Web.

dialog box A box on screen in which you type more information or make specific choices to enable the program to perform a particular function.

domain suffix Part of the address that specifies your computer's location, the domain suffix will show what sort of organisation the computer is used in. For example, an address that contains the suffix .ac.uk indicates that the computer is within a UK academic environment.

DOS Disk Operating System—a basic program for controlling a PC.

download To transfer data from a distant computer to your own.

email Electronic mail—a message that can be sent to any other computer connected to the Internet—provided you know the recipient's exact email address. Files and documents can be attached to email.

file transfer protocol (FTP) The computer conventions by which files are transferred across the Internet.

frequently asked questions (FAQs) A file often found in newsgroups or email lists that lists the most common questions asked by newcomers, together with their answers. If you have a question, it is good *netiquette* to check a relevant FAQ file first to see if it has already been answered.

Gopher A menu-driven facility that conveys a wide range of information.

hit A file that has been found as a result of your search using a search tool.

home page The opening page of a Web site.

host computer The computer you contact to enable you to get on the Internet.

HyperText Mark-up Language (HTML) The language used for creating documents accessible on the World Wide Web.

HyperText Transfer Protocol (HTTP) The standard for transferring HTML documents between Web servers. Web site addresses always start with the letters http.

hyperlink A file that is linked via *hypertext.*

hypertext An embedded pointer to related text. By clicking on it the user can go straight to the relevant file.

Internet A collection of computers from all parts of the world that can communicate with each other using telephone lines and modems.

jumping-off point A Web site from which to get pointers to other related sites via *hyperlinks.*

lurking Reading what is going on in a newsgroup or mailing list, but not joining in.

Lynx A simple text-based Web browser.

modem A MOdulator/DEModulator. Equipment that translates digital information into analogue information so that it can be passed down the phone lines.

navigator Another name for a *browser.*

Net Shortform for the Internet.

netiquette Generally understood rules of good behaviour while online.

Netscape The name of one of the most common navigators.

newsgroup The bulletin boards for particular topics on the Internet. They are either integral to a service provider such as CompuServe, or open to all. The largest collection of open newsgroups is operated under the auspices of *Usenet.*

offline Doing tasks while not on the phone line. For example, you can write your email messages offline, ready to send when you connect to the Internet. You can download files to read offline at your leisure, to save on phone costs.

online Doing things while you are actually connected to the Internet. For instance, you will need to be online to get updates of information.

packet switching The underlying communications methods of the Internet. A packet is a bundle of data that is transmitted across the network.

point of presence (POP) A local Internet access point set up by a service provider. By connecting to a local POP, you will be paying only local call rates when you are *online.*

protocol The way two devices on a network communicate with each other.

pull-down menu Menu headings are given along a bar at the top of the screen. When you click on one of these headings, you are given a list of further options

screen-saver A program that displays moving pictures on your screen to prevent fixed images from being branded on to the monitor. A screen-saver will start up automatically after a specified number of minutes of inaction on the screen.

search engine A tool that looks through the contents of the World Wide Web to find specified words or phrases.

server A central computer through which information (e.g. Web pages) are made available to Internet users.

service provider/access provider A commercial organisation charging users a fee (usually monthly) for using its computer to connect to the Net and send and receive email.

shell account An indirect connection to the Net offering *email, FTP* and a text-based *browser.*

smileys Small 'pictures' made up of punctuation to indicate 'emotion' in your email messages.

spamming Posting the same message to many newsgroups.

surfing 'Browsing' through files on the Internet.

TCP/IP stack A section in your computer's hard drive that generates the commands to enable connections to be made to and received from the Net.

teletext TV-based information medium such as the BBC's CEEFAX.

Telnet The Internet protocol for remote access.

ticker Scrolling real-time information (news or, for example, share prices) displayed on a small bar at the top or bottom of the computer screen.

UNIX An operating system that enables many computers to access a main computer at the same time. There are special commands for use with this system.

unzip *See zip.*

URL (uniform resource locator) The address of any resource on the Internet.

Usenet The collective name for the vast number of newsgroups or discussion groups on the Internet.

World Wide Web The generic name given to all hypertext-based documents on the Internet. These documents contain links to other documents.

zip Compress data so that it takes up less space. To read the text again, you need to unzip it. You need a special program to do this.

Useful Internet Addresses

News and email lists

The Age   http://www.theage.com.au
Australia's business newspaper on-line

Applied Derivatives Trading   http://www.adtrading.com
Free online trading guide

Bloomberg Personal   http://www.bloomberg.com
Mike Bloomberg's Web offering

Bridge Data—Knight Ridder Financial   http://www.krf.com
Financial news summaries

CNNfn   http://www.cnnfn.com
CNN online service

DejaNews   http://www.dejanews.com
Search tool for newsgroup topics

Electronic Telegraph   http://www.telegraph.co.uk
Original online paper with search facility

European Business News   http://www.ebn.co.uk
As its name implies

Financial Times   http://www.ft.com
Much improved site from the pink 'un

Globe & Mail   http://www.theglobeandmail.com
Toronto Globe & Mail business news

The Guardian   http://go2.guardian.co.uk
Quirky newspaper Web site

IBM infoMarket NewsTicker   http://infomarket.ibm.com/ht3/ticker.shtml
Scrolling news stories from wire services

Interactive Internet Investor   http://www.iii.co.uk
Periodic emails of upgrades to site

Investors Business Daily   http://ibd.ensemble.com
Good US news source online

Liszt   http://www.liszt.com
Classified email discussion lists

London Standard   http://www.standard.co.uk
Influential Business Day online

Newslink   http://www.newslink.org/
Index of online press sites

New York Times   http://nytimesfax.com
PDF version of summarised stories

PAML   http://www.neosoft.com/internet/paml
Publicly accessible email lists

Pathfinder   http://pathfinder.com/fortune
Selected articles from Fortune magazine

The Press Association   http://www.pa.press.net
General news stories

Reuters Business Alert   http://www.reuters.com
Famous newswire on the Web

Scholarly and Professional E-conferences   http://www.mailbase.ac.uk/kovaks/
    kovaks.html
Directory of email discussion lists

Times/Sunday Times   http://www.the-times.co.uk
Searchable UK heavyweights

UNS   http://www.twoten.press.net
Press releases for journalists

Wall Street Journal   http://www.wsj.com
Not much free for investors at the WSJ

Web Newsstand   http://www.web-newsstand.com
Links to press sites

Software companies

Adobe   http://www.adobe.com
For downloading Acrobat PDF reader

Autonomy Corporation   http://www.agentware.com
Details of agentware products

Microsoft   http://www.msn.com
Download various Gatesian products

Netscape   http://www.netscape.com
Browser downloads and more

PKWare Inc   http://www.pkware.com
Downloadable PKZIP software

Search engines/jumping-off points

All-in-One Search Page   http://www.albany.net/allinone/
Searches for search engines

AltaVista   http://www.altavista.digital.com
Digital's high powered engine

Business Information on the Internet   http://www.dis.strath.ac.uk/business/
Comprehensive guide from Strathclyde

Euroferret   http://www.muscat.co.uk/chd/eurotxt.htm
Euro-search tool

Excite   http://www.excite.com
General search tool

Finance OnLine   http://www.finance-online.com
Links to 2000 finance sites

Financial Information Network   http://www.finetwork.com
Index of some financial sites

FIND   http://www.find.co.uk
Newish list of finance links

Global OnLine Directory   http://www.god.co.uk
Commercial and corporate database

Global Trader   http://www.bluewave.co.uk/globaltrader
Index of some financial sites

HotBot   http://www.hotbot.com/index.html
HotWired/Berkeleys new search engine

Hot Links for Traders   http://www.io.com/%7Egibbonsb/wahoo.html
Journalist's 'Computerized Trader' site

Index of email addresses   http://www.whowhere.com
Track down that elusive email address

InfoSeek   http://www2.infoseek.com
General search tool

Internect   http://www.inect.co.uk
Index of some financial sites

Internet Sleuth   http://www.isleuth.com
Assembled search tools on various topics

Investorama   http://www.investorama.com
Comprehensive index of financial sites

Lenape Investment Corporation   http://www.enter.net/~rsauers/
The definitive list of financial Web sites

Links Dictionary   http://www.linksdic.com
Indexed links

Lycos   http://www.lycos.com
General search tool

Mauro Magnanis Finance Area   http://www.tsi.it/contrib/audies/finarea.html
Good links to a variety of finance sites

MetaCrawler   http://www.metacrawler.com
Fast multiple search engine

Mistral   http://www.mistral.co.uk
UK-based search engine

Money$earch   http://www.moneysearch.com
Links covering a range of finance sites

Moneyweb   http://www.moneyweb.co.uk
Personal finance terms explained

Moneyworld   http://www.moneyworld.co.uk
Comprehensive personal finance site

NumaWeb   http://www.numa.com
Useful collection of derivatives links

Open Text   http://index.opentext.net
General search tool

Qualisteam   http://www.qualisteam.com
Links to banks and brokers worldwide

Savvysearch   http://www.cs.colostate.edu/~dreiling/smartform.html
Heavily used meta-searcher

Silicon Investor   http://techstocks.com
Excellent site for Silicon Valley stocks

TechWeb   http://www.techweb.com
Specialist technology search tool and BBS

Traders Financial Resource Guide   http://www.libertynet.org/~beausang
Links to useful trading related sites

UK Index   http://www.ukindex.co.uk
Index of UK sites

UK Web Directory   http://www.ukdirectory.com
Index of UK sites

Waldemars List   http://apollo.netservers.com/~waldemar/list.shtm
Futures related list of sites

WebCrawler   http://www.webcrawler.com
General search tool

Website of Investment   http://www.myna.com/~invest
Extensive collection of links

Yahoo!   http://www.yahoo.com
Index and search tool

Yahoo! UK   http://www.yahoo.co.uk
UK index and search tool

Brokers on the Web

Aufhauser   http://www.aufhauser.com
US discount broker

Barclays Stockbrokers   http://www.barclays.co.uk/stock/home.htm
The big banks broking business

Cazenove   http://www.cazenove.co.uk/cazenove
Blue-blooded brokers unit trust arm

Charles Stanley   http://www.charles-stanley.co.uk
Range of services

Durlacher   http://www.durlacher.com
Options specialist, multimedia research

Electronic Share Information (ESI)   http://www.esi.co.uk
Links to three online brokers

E*Trade   http://www.etrade.com
The original cyber-broker

Fidelity   http://www.fid-inv.com
Fidelitys mutual fund site

Fidelity (UK)   http://www.fidelity.co.uk
UK execution-only broker

Infotrade   http://www.infotrade.co.uk
Private dealing and information network

Investment Brokerages Guide   http://www.cs.cmu.edu/~jdg/invest—brokers
Alphabetical Web brokers worldwide

Killik & Co.   http://www.killik.co.uk
Branches, research, market commentary

Lombard   http://www.lombard.com
US discount broker

NDB   http://pawws.com/Broker/Ndb
Stands for National Discount Brokerage

Options Direct   http://www.options-direct.co.uk
Options trading and research

Quick & Reilly   http://www.quick-reilly.com
US discount broker

Schwab   http://www.schwab.com
Sharelinks US parent

The Share Centre   http://www.share.co.uk
Discount stockbroking for the little man

Sharelink   http://www.sharelink.co.uk
Birmingham-based giant

Prices and data

Corporate Reports   http://www.corpreports.co.uk
UK company reports

Datastream   http://www.datastream.com
Markets and economic data charts/values

DBC   http://www.dbc.com
News; indices; quotes

Disclosure   http://www18.disclosure.com
Rankings of top world companies

ECU Group   http://www.ecu.co.uk
Currencies/markets/rates charted

EDGAR   http://www.sec.gov/edgarhp.htm
Online US corporate filings

FT Information   http://www.info.ft.com/companies
Company briefs and links to news

Galt Quote Server   http://quotes.galt.com
Quotes and charts on N American stocks

Hemmington Scott   http://www.hemscott.co.uk/hemscott/
Hambro Company Guide online

Hoovers Online   http://www.hoovers.com
Searchable database of brief profiles

IMF Data Dissemination   http://dsbb.imf.org
Global economic statistics links

Interquote   http://www.interquote.com
Prices site

PC Quote   http://www.pcquote.com
Quotes from site with European offshoot

PC Quote Europe   http://www.pcquote-europe.co.uk
See above

PIRC   http://www.pirc.com
Searchable consensus forecasts (US companies)

Prestel   http://www.citiservice.co.uk
UK teletext-style prices and downloads

Quote.com   http://www.quote.com
Seminal US prices services

Stockmaster (MIT)   http://www.stockmaster.com
US prices and charts from MIT

Tullett & Tokyo   http://www.tullett.co.uk
FX and derivatives data

Yardeni Economic Network   http://www.yardeni.com
PDFd data from DMG economist

Zacks   http://www.zacks.com
Searchable list of corporate information

Software

BioComp Systems   http://www.bio-comp.com/financia.htm
Neural net software

Bulletproof Software   http://bulletproof.com
Java-based price display software

Centre for Elliott Wave Analysis   http://www.iinet.com.au/~cewa/
Site for Elliott enthusiasts

Dataform   http://home.earthlink.net/~dataform/software.html
Company offering downloadable software

FinancialCAD   http://www.financialcad.com
Derivatives spreadsheet add-ins at a price

Flexsoft   http://www.flexsoft.com
Download demo of investment software

Goethe   http://www.wiwi.uni-frankfurt.de/AG/JWGI
Big German site with software links

iLanga Inc.   http://www.serv.net/ilanga/
Tradex chart software for the Mac

InvestorWEB   http://www.investorweb.com/
Warren Buffett Way spreadsheet

I-Soft   http://www.i-soft.com
Various software downloads

Liberty Research   http://www.libertyresearch.com
Demo of Investograph chart software

Market Technicians Association   http://www.mta-usa.org/~lensmith
List of chart and technical software

OptionVue   http://www.optionvue.com
Demo of pricey options software

!Options   http://pilot.msu.edu/user/steelera/index.html
Excel add-in for option pricing

Owlsoft   http://ourworld.compuserve.com/homepages/owlsoft
Company offering downloadable software

Planware   http://www.planware.ie/resource/planware
Business planning software

Quotesplus   http://www.webcom.com/~quotes
Quotesplus chart software demo

Shareware.com   http://www.shareware.com
General software downloads

Southtech   http://www.southtech.com
Easy Street software

TaxCruncher   http://www.lookup.com/homepages/55461/home.html
US orientated tax software

TCM Trading Systems   http://www2.interaccess.com/home/
Company offering downloadable software

ThinksPro   http://weber.ucsd.edu/~rtrippi/books/rtthinks.htm
Company offering downloadable software

Tierra Software   http://www.cyberspace.com/~tierra
Downloadable financial shareware

Trading Techniques   http://www.tradingtech.com
Elliott Wave related software

University of California at San Marcos   http://coyote.csusm.edu/winworld/
   diverse.html
Investment/financial software downloads

Updata Software   http://www.updata.co.uk
News and downloads

Wall Street Directory   http://www.wsdinc.com
Major investment software site

Wall Street Software   http://www.fastlane.net/homepages/wallst/wallst.html
Investment software site

Winsite   http://www.winsite.com
Windows software downloads

The World File Project   http://www.filepile.com
Large scale software site

Zanders   http://www.tip.nl/users/chrj.zanders
FX pricing add-in

Governments and regulators

Bank of England   http://www.bankofengland.co.uk
Disappointing site from UK's central bank

CCTA   http://www.open.gov.uk
Links to information on government departments

Central Office for Information   http://www.coi.gov.uk
Government information site

Commodity Futures Trading Commission   http://www.cftc.gov
US futures industry regulator

French Treasury   http://www.tresor.finances.fr/oat/
Statistics on the French bond market

IMRO   http://www.imro.co.uk
UK fund management industry regulator

Statistics Netherlands   http://www.cbs.nl
National statistics plus many global links

UK Treasury   http://www.hm-treasury.gov.uk
Excellent site from UK monetary authority

US Treasury   http://www.ustreas.gov
Background on US Treasury

Stock exchanges

AIM   http://worldserver.pipex.com/aim

American Stock Exchange   http://www.amex.com

Amsterdam Stock Exchange   http://www.financeweb.ase.nl

Athens Stock Exchange   http://www.ase.gr

Australian Stock Exchange   http://www.asx.com.au

Budapest Stock Exchange   http://www.fornax.hu

Canadian stock exchanges   http://www.telenium.ca

Chicago Stock Exchange   http://www.chicagostockex.com

Deutsche Borse   http://www.exchange.de

Geneva Stock Exchange   http://www.bourse.ch

Indonesian Stock Exchange   http://www.indoexchange.com

Johannesburg Stock Exchange   http://www.jse.co.za

Madrid Stock Exchange   http://www.bolsamadrid.es

Milan Stock Exchange   http://www.borsaitalia.

NASDAQ   http://www.nasdaq.com

New York Stock Exchange   http://www.nyse.com

NSE India   http://www.nseindia.com

OFEX   http://www.ofex.co.uk

Santiago Stock Exchange   http://www.bolsantiago.cl

SBF-Paris   http://www.bourse-de-paris.fr

Stock Exchange of Singapore   http://www.ses.com.sg

Stockholm Stock Exchange   http://www.xsse.se

Tel Aviv Stock Exchange   http://www.tase.co.il

Thailand Stock Exchange   http://www.set.or.th

Vancouver Stock Exchange   http://www.vse.ca

Zagreb Stock Exchange   http://www.zse.com.hr

Derivatives exchanges

Chicago Board Options Exchange   http://www.cboe.com

Chicago Board of Trade   http://www.cbot.com

Chicago Mercantile Exchange   http://www.cme.com

LIFFE (London)   http://www.liffe.com

MATIF (Paris)   http://www.matif.fr

New York Mercantile   http://www.nymex.com

OM Stockholm   http://www.omgroup.com

Philadelphia Stock Exchange   http://www.phlx.com

SAFEX (South Africa)   http://www.safex.co.za

SIMEX   http://www.simex.com.sg

Sydney Derivatives Exchange   http://www.sfe.com.au

Personal finance and on-line banking

AAA Investment Guide   http://www.wisebuy.co.uk
Personal finance issues in detail

Allenbridge   http://www.moneyworld.co.uk/peptalk/
PEP and tax shelter specialists on-line

BankNet   http://mkn.co.uk/bank/
Fledgling on-line UK bank

Ethical Financial   http://www.ethical-financial.co.uk
Ethical investment advice

Fiona Price & Partners   http://www.moneyworld.co.uk/fionaprice/
Female oriented IFA site

GAEIA   http://www.u-net.com/~gaeia/home.htm
Ethical investment advice

Money Media   http://www.demon.co.uk/dayco/money.html
General personal finance site

Moneyworld   http://www.moneyworld.co.uk
Rates, information, statistics, news

On-Line IFA   http://www.onlineifa.co.uk
Choose your IFA online

Security First Network   http://www.sfnb.com/
Groundbreaking Internet bank

TrustNet   http://www.trustnet.co.uk
Excellent investment trust site

Watersons   http://www.demon.co.uk/watersons
IFA site

UK insurance Web sites

Admiral Insurance   http://www.admiral-insurance.co.uk

Allied Dunbar   http://www.AlliedDunbar.co.uk

AXA Insurance   http://www.axa.co.uk

Churchill Insurance   http://www.churchill.co.uk

Colonnade Insurance   http://www.colonnade.co.uk

Commercial Union   http://www.commercialunion.co.uk/cu/

Co-operative Insurance   http://www.cis.co.uk

Direct Electronic   http://www.londonmall.co.uk/direlec

General Accident   http://www.ga.co.uk

Guardian Insurance   http://www.gre.co.uk

Intersure   http://www.intersure.co.uk

Legal & General   http://www.legalandgeneral.co.uk/lg/

Norwich Union   http://www.norwich-union.co.uk

Quote Wizard   http://www.u-net.com/~newman/

Scottish Amicable   http://www.scottishamicable.com

UK bank and building society sites

Abbey National   http://www.abbeynational.co.uk

Alliance & Leicester   http://www.alliance-leicester.co.uk

Bank of Scotland   http://www.bankofscotland.co.uk

Barclays   http://www.barclays.co.uk

Birmingham Midshires   http://www.birmingham-midshires.co.uk/bmbs/

Bradford & Bingley   http://www.bradford-bingley.co.uk

Chartered Institute of Banking   http://www.cib.org.uk

Halifax   http://www.halifax.co.uk

Lloyds Bank   http://www.lloydsbank.co.uk

Midland Bank   http://www.midlandbank.co.uk

Nationwide Building Society   http://www.nationwide.co.uk

NatWest   http://www.natwest.co.uk

Northern Rock   http://www.nrock.co.uk

Royal Bank of Scotland   http://www.royalbankscot.co.uk

Woolwich Building Society   http://www.woolwich.co.uk

Corporate Web site finders

Asian Business   http://asiabiz.com
Asian corporates on-line

Hoovers OnLine Web Sites   http://www.hoovers.com
Indexed list of corporate websites

NetWorth   http://www.networth.galt.com
The definitive index of US corporate sites

UKCom—UK Businesses on the Web   http://www.u-net.com/ukcom/
UK corporate Web site locator

Web.de   http://www.vroom.web.de
German-only site with links to corporates

Sundry corporate Web sites—UK

British Airways   http://www.british-airways.com

Cable & Wireless   http://www.cwplc.com

Christies   http://www.chrisities.com

Demon Internet   http://www.demon.net

GlaxoWellcome   http://www.glaxowellcome.co.uk

Guinness   http://www.guinness.ie

Microfocus   http://www.mfltd.co.uk

Oxford Molecular   http://www.oxmol.co.uk

Railtrack   http://www.railtrack.co.uk

Sage   http://www.sagesoft.co.uk

Severn-Trent Water   http://www.Severn-Trent.com

Tesco   http://www.tesco.co.uk

Sundry corporate Web sites—US

ADC Telecomms   http://www.adc.com

American Express   http://www.americanexpress.com

Barnett Banks   http://www.barnett.com

Cisco Systems   http://www.cisco.com

Coca-Cola   http://www.cocacola.com

IBM   http://www.ibm.com

McCormick   http://www.mccormick.com

Merck   http://www.merck.com

Nynex   http://www.nynex.com

Staples Inc.   http://www.staples.com

Sybase   http://www.sybase.com

Texaco   http://www.texaco.com

Index